Believe

By

rkfdnews

"*Believe*" by rkfdnews:

Published By Life Artners
Edited By Chief Tchad Beale and Chief Jay Vannigan
Authored By Ron Kites, Lisa Soland, Chuck Toncha, Willard Hunter, Tchad Beale, Jay Vannigan, Barry Syversen, Kate Menstraight, Gilbert Grebner, Theodore Lepolli, Rance Crabtower, JoAnne Rankles, Chet Fairway, Pancake Johnson, Graham Nickles, The Great Paula, George Brawn, Johnny Emerald The IIIrd, Jason Vaughn, Dana Vaughn (*Grammatical Zealot*), Andy Whorehall, Dave DeCastris, Russell Gillespie, Daniel James McMahon, Zachery Rotello, Marc Kinnemann, Eric Fleming, Irish Brian Kelly, Brian Diamond, Brian Milo, James Strumwell, Donny Lothario, Andy Scarpaci, Jesus Abraham Correa VIIth, David Pedersen, Dolph Lundgren, Foodstamp Davis, Mean Gene Okerlund, Matt Makris, Chris Wachowiak, Bill Wennington, John Kruk, Reggie "*Railroad*" Reynolds, Mister Meerasaké, Francis the Macaque, Frank Stallone and Maria Alvarez-Thromsbergher
Art Direction, Design, Illustrations (That Are Not Obviously *Borrowed* From Deceased 17th and 18th Century Artists Who Naturally Relinquished Their Rights In The 19th Century) **and Cover By** Dave DeCastris, Andy Whorehall, Jason Vaughn **Music & Videos By** Johnny Emerald the IIIrd, Willard Hunter, Daniel James McMahon, Jason Vaughn, Silent Kit, Derek Luttrell, Zach Staas and The Midwest Sound, Rockford, IL **Styled By** Hazel Studio, Rockford, IL **Wardrobe By** Target, Pinterest, Ebay **Catering By** Culver's **Pizzas By** Capri Restaurant, Rockford, IL **Soaps By** WalGreens **Porridge & Puddings By** WalMart **Cheddar Bay Biscuits By** Red Lobster **Metal Panties and HOT DEAL$ By** Derby | Reynolds, Schaumburg, IL **Gingerbread & Pumpkin Spice Lattes By** Starbucks **Know Brad Fread & Libations By** Olympic Tavern & Kryptonite Bar, Rockford, IL **Franch Toast Sticks By** Burger King **FlapJacks By** McDonald's **Buckets of Fried Chicken By** KFC **Hope, *Vison*^{2}, Transformation, Positivity & Strange Civic Pride Stuff By** the City of Rockford, IL, and its Real, Original People **Excellence Everywhere!**

FIRST EDITION

LIFE ARTNERS

For additional publisher information, visit lifeartners.com.

ISBN-13: 978-0692334898
ISBN-10: 0692334890

DEDICATION

This book is dedicated to us, the **rkfdnews** staff. We are the greatest babies to be born in Rockford of Illinois and then socially conditioned into somewhat responsible, cultured, poor adults who will – one day – become human excrement for the earth to take and digest back into the atmosphere. (Yep, shit for shit.) This is our immaculate conception; behold and nurture it, feel yourself tingle with belief that it actually exists.

Thank you, mother earth for sacrificing a few of your tallest soldiers. This collaborative piece of art wouldn't exist without destroying a few trees to appease a few creative egos. Also, we can't forget modern machinery, the pigment and mail delivery industries for insuring this book's safe production and delivery to you the reader – thank you.

This book is also dedicated to our enemies, lovers, peasants, bullies, ex-employers, ex-spouses, family, friends, peers and anyone who can't recognize artistic expression when it's staring right ya. Reciting this dedication aloud while holding *Our Book, Our Stories*, will fill your head up with pride (*one of the seven deadly sins*) and other funny feelings[9] (*the other six deadly sins*) that may challenge your ego; thus causing you to talk more and do less – which is The Rockford Way.

Behold this imaginary bible; hold it high above you and genuflect to it; for it wouldn't exist without the people of Rockford's emotionally strong beliefs in river sharks, fast food, poverty, crime, Quinn Gelastio, Willard Hunter, animals, the Lord, carp, fried chicken, unemployment and other delusional stuff.

Our book will help each of you to recognize the cracks in your own reflections when you wake up in the middle of the night to go pee pee. Stop and look at yourself in the mirror, contemplate your true purpose in life. Does it hurt to think? Go back to bed and cry yourself to sleep.

Wake up with the sun and grab our book, start fresh. This book will help you live a better, healthier life; plus, it can also help you to take control of your life by telling everyone you know who has wasted your precious time to go fuck themselves.

This book is also dedicated to the City of Rockford, its community and leaders. Y'all are a dark, deep, empty and endless well of inspiration to us. Your inane abilities to be naturally funny, average, complacent and strangely proud has provided our creative collective a treasure trove of ideas and laughs that we've shared within this book.

The depths of truths contained on this one page may drown out the courage you once had for swimming forth into the deep, dark, blue nothing of this book. Maybe pause to share a photo of yourself and your food on the internet? Please, try to stay positive (*quit reading now if you must*) and don't let *Our Book* stop you from enjoying yourselves. Celebrate misery's company and its real, original, excellence everywhere or whatever.

Now, go forth ye amateurs and peasants. Spread these words to other cities and poor communities. Start with Beloit, Wisconsin, located a few miles north of Rockford, IL. Efforts to share a few of the noose breaking stories contained within *Our Book* will reap forth goodwill, confusion, random acts of kindness, anger and laughter your way. These stories are now yours to share. Everything contained within this book is true if you choose to believe such. It's up to you and whatever.

If enjoying *Our Book* and *Our Stories* is too impossible of a task for you to accept – because of your religion, politics and personal ideals – please use the extra time to share your emotions, life lessons, thoughts, opinions, phone photos of your food and family, all of your personal interests and information (*such as birthdates, phone numbers, location and email addresses)* on the internet for others to profit from at your privacy's expense. That's right.

Hang in there, you'll get it.™

rkfdnews

[9]*Feelings that may arise due to this book's existence (and your attention to the details contained within) are no different than a cloud of fresh farts flying face first into a hi-speed fan. Your imagination determines which way the fan is facing, however, karma does what it must if you've been naughty. There are no deeper meanings attached to this explanation.*

CONTENTS

ACKNOWLEDGMENTS

This creative artifact – a cracked-mirror reflection of the community that it was created from, about and within – would not exist without the help, efforts, time and energy from our truest *frands,* the wild kingdom.

Thank you to Ron Kites, Chuck Toncha, Willard Hunter and a few more animals who believed enough in this little art experiment to participate[14].

[14]Those who chose not to participate in this art experiment (for fear of this, that, your ridiculous emotions and to protect your pride, ego, name, etc.) can continue to talk, do nothing, be an amateur – the Rockford (modern American) way.

FOREWORD

"Believe,

when you are most unhappy,

that there is something for you to do in the world.

So long as you can sweeten another's pain,

life is not in vain."

Helen Keller

Letter From the Publisher, *Life Artners*

rkfdnews.com began amongst *frands* – and professional artists – as a few lowbrow laughs that lingered longer than they should, naturally morphing into a handful of non de plumes and a website serving as a hub for *noose breaking* stories. The people of Rockford, Illinois, and its surrounding area served as the amoral core inspiration for our *satire-mocking-satire* social media art experiment, which loosely focused on mocking the art of reporting local news stories in the *Information Age ("I saw it on the internet, it has to be true," said you).*

This little micro-organism-art-experiment/study of our hometown – once a bustling manufacturing hub for the middle class idea of America, but now a depressed post-industrial American city with two social classes, a majority of once-middle-class-now-lower-class people who own nothing but debts mixed in with the minority upper class who exist only to protect and sustain their wealth – sadly confirmed a handful of socio-psychological suspicions, including:

1) People will believe anything if it's presented to be real *(e.g., A bucket of crispy KFC fried chicken, meat tacos from Taco Bell and metal panties by Derby | Reynolds).* **2)** Telling terrible stories in broad daylight to entertain the public for free – which is what we did – is very similar to what our government and business leaders do on a daily basis with the media and advertisers help (*e.g., Funnel, acquire, hide, spend, waste money*); which is to abundantly lie in broad daylight in exchange for generously robbing society of its collective intellect, time and money. **3)** Everyone in the modern age is a lowbrow artist, maker, shaker, chef, reporter, life coach, marketer and critic thanks to the outsourcing of jobs to third world countries, thus initiating the death of the *Industrial Age* while the birth of the *Information Age* takes on its teenage shape as the internet here in the 2010s. **4)** There's no way we could make up anything as absurd as the real news or the real, original and bizarre people who make it what it is. **5)** People truly love stories about fast food and criminal behaviors; which is more interesting than our noose breaking stories themselves. **6)** Despite the advancement of technology, medicine, and educational information that is available to help improve the human race, many people who can't spell, read, write, or practice common sense are still granted the power and money to run businesses and government, breed, vote, use the internet to publicly share misspelled opinions, half-baked ideals and whatever. **7)** Too many people who don't give a shit outnumber those that do. **8)** Oh, there are more reasons to cry for excellence everywhere, indeed!

Our little grade school art project had no intents to become a book. We simply wanted to laugh more at our own pathetic existence in this estranged environment, rather than cave-in to our community's celebratory complacency and calm, proud misery. As anything goes with sharing *artistic expressions* in public, accomplishing a stranger's reaction – laughter, confusion, judgment, anger, anything – was equal parts a bonus and payback[13].

What you're holding now is an abbreviated collection of what we set out to do with **rkfdnews**:
To write a few stories; to belittle our creative pride; to challenge the status quo's mindset while remaining inspired, amused, disturbed, defeated and humored by our home town; and to laugh more.

It should also be stated that everything was produced out of our own pockets, time and efforts. No financial backing, gift loans, crowd-funding, begging strangers for money and outside influences were allowed; which granted us an abundance of creative rights and *freedumbs* – good, bad and whatever – to do as we wished.

We're hoping that you find a few moments to sit down on the toilet and share the laughs, grunts, clenches, sweating and farting with this book. Please feel these written words move inside of you and let it out. (*"Ahh, the sweet smell of success!"*) Go on now, it's your turn to give a shit.

The jokes are on us, *Life Artners* and whatever,

Darby Appleby, Jason Vaughn, Alonzo Bottums, Dave DeCastris and the rest of our noose breaking frands.

13 A lifetime of paybacks; to return to sender; to shovel back; a boomerang that doesn't boomerang; a curve ball that doesn't break at your face for the knees and ends up hitting your head; a metaphor to create thoughtful and often funny tactics to send a silent *"go fuck yourself"* to those who rob you of your work, time, finances, energy and name in broad daylight; creative karma.

"I started out on burgundy

But soon hit the harder stuff

Everybody said they'd stand behind me when the game got rough

But the joke was on me

There was nobody even there to call my bluff

I'm going back to New York City

I do believe I've had enough"

An excerpt from "*Just Like Tom Thumb's Blues*,"
by Robert Zimmerman.

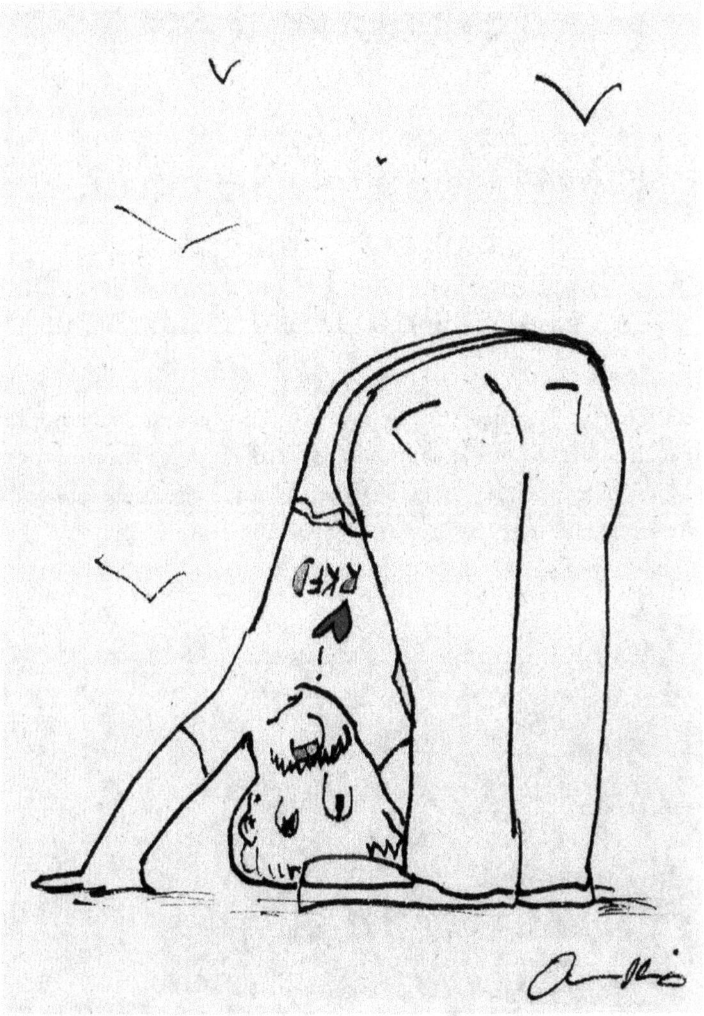

Trains stopped passing through;
Cracks in the roads became holes.
Farts bursting the air.

A haiku from the book,
"That One Night I Ate Baked Corn Beef Stuffed Potatoes, Listened to Bono Sing on the Pub's Jukebox, Drank Pints of Guinness and Charmed Your Wife Before We Bathed Each Other with Fresh Bars of Delicious Irish Spring Soap,"
by Irish Brian Kelly.

INTRODUCTION

Love Letters From the Editor, Chief Jay Vannigan

DEAR READERS AND LOYAL FOLLOWERS,

October 3rd, 2014

You and I have both noticed in the past few months that we've not been meeting each other eye to eye on the internet as much as we would've loved to. The clear reason behind this is that we do not seem interested and involved with each other any longer. Do you remember when you shared and liked everything I did for you on the internet?

To top it all off, I saw you reading *Rockford Scanner*'s facebook page on Sunday morning. Talk about being rude. I think that was a big hint for me to stay out of your life.

I am writing to inform you that I want to bring an end to this relationship. I know the break up isn't entirely your fault, and I, too, am to be blamed for it.

Don't get me wrong, my love, I've enjoyed wonderful, memorable moments of my life with you on the internet. However, it's clear to me now that I should know better. I would like to leave you to a life of your own, and I will live my life the way I want to. This was NOT the way I would've liked our relationship to end: In public, with strangers reading our personal business, but if it has to end this way, my love, it has to.

Together we are parting now into two. It is very important that we change our relationship status on Facebook as soon as possible. I leave you nothing but this book and a silent middle finger. I still can't believe you thought some of these articles were true. I am truly having the last laugh now.

You will never learn more because you didn't take the time to know better,

Jay Vannigan

DEAR LOYAL READERS AND CLICKERS,

October 3rd, 2014

I duped you when we first met into believing that you loved me for me. Something naughty happened. After having been with you for a few years, it has become blatantly obvious to me and our staff at rkfdnews.com that the only thing you want from me is my money and fake news stories (that are sometimes true).

I hope y'all enjoyed the precious time you squeezed out of me, but as of today's letter, you won't get another drop. Go find someone else who is willing to drain their minds like a lemon and an orange to a juicer for your satisfaction – for free – to keep you filled with nutrition and happiness. No more, these loads of love are now mine to enjoy.

So long, here is a book.

Jay Vannigan

DEAR ROCKFORD OF ILLINOIS,

October 3rd, 2014

I'll always have a special place in my heart for you, Rockford. Our relationship felt like it was the best thing that had ever happened to me at times, but everything has felt wrong lately. It pains me to admit this, but my love for you has faded away like soap to water. If you know what I mean. #idoubtit, hahaha.

I can't stay in a relationship where there is little love, and the love that does exist between us is very dirty. The importance of using soap and hot water has evaded you, before and after our love making sessions. I've simply given up on trying to teach you, people of Rockford, responsible hygiene etiquette.

It isn't fair to you to be stuck in a relationship that has become a lie. I hope that you're able to move on and meet someone who will love you the way you deserve to be loved.

#fbf[1],

Jay Vannigan

[1]Fart Buddies Forever

GOODBYE

October 24th, 2014

Dear Readers,

There's a possibility that I'll be leaving RKFDNews next month, or in December. Unfortunate family circumstances require my full attention. On top of personal responsibilities, nude welding classes and chicken fights in Beloit, WI, leaves me no extra time to fulfill my duties to my company. I will return when I'm good and ready. I am very sorry to have caused any inconvenience; actually, I don't care. Please know that I'll be available never/somewhat over the next month to assist with finding a replacement. In addition, I will insure that my responsibilities be properly taken care of. During this transition, college interns (who we'll never pay) will feed you soups and porridges after bathing you in tubs of water and soaps.

Thank you very much for understanding, but not really. I've had a positive experience working at RKFDNews and I hope my leaving will not affect our relationship. Please let me know if you have any questions; or if you think of any way I can help with this transition. Then, and only then, I can finally tell you what I really think of your mother.

Sincerely,

Jay Vannigan

Jay Vannigan, aka "Bob Grizzly"

My Dearest Readers and Loyal Minions,

October 3rd, 2014

Oh, where do I begin?

Honey[1], you're great. You're more than great. In fact, you are a very special person. I'll never forget the good times we've enjoyed together.

Remember the good laughs we had making up stories, and then reading the real news? To end up twisting it all up like a salty Freeport pretzel to dip in and out of our mouths together? How about all of the funny moments we spent touching ourselves while celebrating misery and stuff to help Rockford feel better? I could never forget you, honey, but.

You and I are out of free ideas. We both know that this is the end. I've been avoiding this moment for quite some time, but that time has come. You know what I mean: We need to break up.

We just don't communicate like we used to. Hell, here I am writing my heart out to you in a book as if I'm above all of that internet and text messaging stuff. I could be talking to you or emailing you my heartaches, exactly like average men and women do. What does that say about us?

Look, no one did anything wrong. It obviously wasn't meant to be, but we shared some good rides together. So, now, I leave you with this stupid book.

You the reader, I'm free now. Anytime you'd like to bootie call me or order a pizza, ring me up:

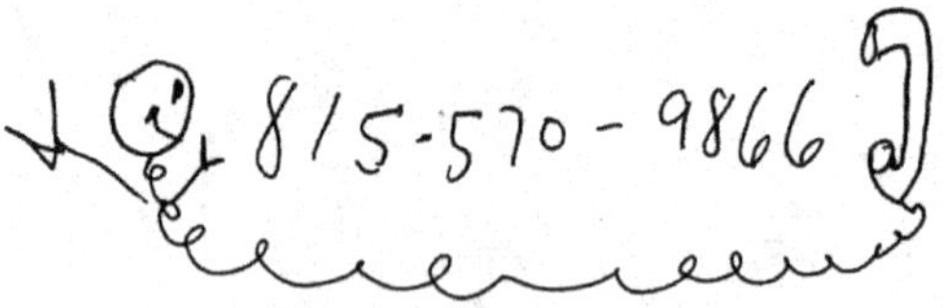

Best,

Jay Vannigan

[1]Fart Buddies Forever

DEAR BELIEVERS,

October 3rd, 2014

I have given things much thought. My feelings for you have changed over these last few months. They are no longer what they once were.

I'd hoped to be able to speak with you face to face, but that became harder and harder for me to bring myself to do after spending the last few years of my precious life hiding behind my computer, smart phone and iPad screens laughing, crying, and praying for you. I do hope that you will accept this letter, and be able to understand my reasons for writing this book.

When we met, I was so happy to meet someone who seemed to have the same visons[2] as me. We almost seemed to see the same things in our futures with our visons. However, I now feel that we are not compatible when it comes to our life goals, because our visons ARE NOT as similar as I was led to believe. : (

I wish to be clear that there's absolutely nothing negative about me and how I feel about our differences. Simply put, these observations became apparent to me while searching for that special thing inside of you while we fulfilled our fantasies together. Sadly and with regrets, I found nothing inside of you to cherish forever. I simply do not believe it to be you, Rockford.

You deserve someone who feels differently; someone who can give you the fake (and sometimes real) news that you need. I've accepted that I am not that person anymore. Here's hoping that you find this book to be a small gift of gratitude and thanks for making love to me while I searched deeper and deeper for something I couldn't find in you. I wish you all the best. I still can't believe you believed.

Later,

Chief Jay Vannigan

[2]To be real, original; to practice excellence everywhere.

A Love Letter From the Editor, Chief Tchad Beale

June 24th, 2014

Dearest amateurs, douchebags, peasants, priests, politicians, ad firm owning $cumbags[3], filthy lawyers, godless nurses and doctors, drunk and high artists, cultureless teachers and the lazy, illiterate hacks you're partially responsible for breeding, educating and socially conditioning:

Chief Tchad Beale, Editor, and his fiancé, Linda, enjoy fine dining in the state of Wisconsin before heading back to The Rockford for laughs.

I'd like to tell you an amazing, positive story about how **rkfd**news began with nothing to become a big ol' bag of nothing in a poor ol' American city called Rockford of Illinois.

Rockford of Illinois is filled with local makers and wonderful industrial stories about how we've successfully risen from the ashes of the great depression, and then the 70s, 80s, 90s, 2000s and 2010s recession. Success is never-ending, we are the new economy in action!

I am very fortunate to have a valuable, experienced, unpaid staff at **rkfd**news. They are the direct product of reinvention; decades have been spent reinventing Rockford by successful leaders who chose to get rid of old paying jobs to create new free jobs. We are an economic success through reinvention. Nice work, lads!

Chief Vannigan, along with our staff, are local makers and official self-made noose breakers who don't play by society's rules. Lest you not comprehend the truths I'm offering between these lines: You are the ponies, we are the horses; you are breeders, we are leaders; you are fools who follow rules filled with follies written by fellow fools, and we are the misfits who fool with the rules to help create better rules to upset and scold the fools who make the foolish rules for little ponies and amateurs to abide by.

Point being, most of you have settled for being pre-programmed, institutionalized and conditioned into behaving like everyone else. Y'all are nothing but fried chicken waiting for a bucket after walking straight with everyone else into the slaughterhouse! This is Henry Ford's 20th Century America in a cracked nutshell and fried chicken in a bucket, that's right.

Many poor people from The Rockford of Illinois have written our staff to ask, *"How did RKFDnews begin? Who is Chief Tchad Beale? How can I meet Jay Vannigan, Lisa Soland, Chuck Toncha, Ron Kites and the rest of your staff? Is Chief Vannigan as handsome as I think he is?"* Thank you for your interests. Let's begin.

The Rockford in Illinois is a place where poor people make stuff so that politicians, public charities, community leaders, developers and the very few members of the 1% can funnel federal and state grants into their pockets so that they can enjoy the finest linens, soaps, vacations, summer homes and speedboats at the expense of the working class's hard work, energy, ideas and time –or what's left of it.

As for my existence, I used to be Mr. Chad Beale; a man who answered to scumbags[3], sales sluts[3] and proud illiterate hillbillies[3]on weekday benders to end up laid off, fired or forced to quit more than a half dozen times after being passed over for countless promotions, overworked and underpaid jobs that went to other proud, elitist, illiterate, corrupt and self-entitled American hillbillies[3]. That's right!

I woke up unemployed for the last time in the Rockford of Illinois around the spring of 2004. I'd spent a few years answering to ad firm owning scumbags[3] nicknamed after dogs (*Sparky, Benji, Gordo, Brent, etc.*) which is an offense to all canines in my opinion. (*I've befriended puppies with better behaviors than men nicknamed after doggies in Rockford!)*

I decided to become Chief Tchad Beale after my last layoff, but it didn't come with ease as I spent time reinventing myself while living in a cardboard refrigerator box. That's when I met Linda.

My future fiancé found me sleeping in a warm refrigerator box downtown at Davis Park in sunny Rockford of Illinois. She wooed me with a homemade cucumber sandwich and a warm cup of coffee: "*You're very tall and handsome for a homeless man from downtown Rockford,*" she said to me while pulling bits of gravel out of my beard as I ate her sandwich.

She took me home and bathed me with the finest soaps, trimmed my beard, dressed me in the finest linens and fed me gluten-free porridge. I'll never forget what she said to me that sealed the deal on becoming *Chief Tchad Beale*: "*The finest soaps deserves the finest linens for the longest limbs, my Chief.*"

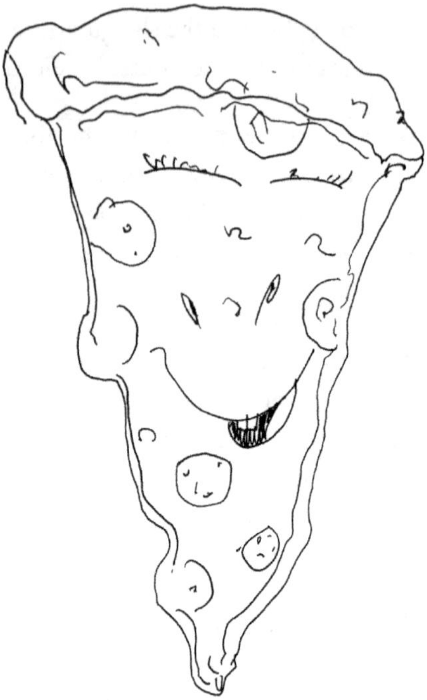

She repeatedly sang that line to me while we made sweet love for days on end. Climaxing, napping, bathing, eating, pooping, bathing and climaxing rejuvenated my soul!

I eventually met a group of writers who had risen from their own refrigerator boxes to reinvent themselves. Together we ate pizza while discussing the evils of fried chicken. Sadness started to settle in again while reminiscing about what led us to live in a box to begin with: Misery.

Chuck Toncha said, *"Can anyone explain with decent logic as to why the people and leaders of our city continue to celebrate misery and brag about it?"* Mr. Toncha was onto something. We immediately stopped eating the pizza and mocking the fried chicken.

"The Rockford of Illinois is a place where you can be anyone," said Gilbert Grebner. Together we laughed, "*EL OH EL!*" It was then that we started talking about breaking the people's noose vs. celebrating misery.

"Why not be noose breakers?" said Jay Vannigan to Theodore Lepolli, Ron Kites and myself – and there it happened, together with the pizza. ***The initial idea of RKFDnews was born because of delicious pizza and above-average minds converging to battle misery–for it had no place in***

our company.

"Misery does not like company," **we decided.**

We gathered a few more times to eat more pizza and discuss how to go about giving poor people (who still enjoy the act of reading) the options to break their own noose for free (or not to). My entire staff had learned over the last 20-30 years of being someone else's hooker that there's not a healthy cash flow in our community, that of which hasn't been tampered and polluted with by state and federal grants. The local cash flow that does exist is called *middle-class blood money;* a middle class that's now massacred by our inept leaders.

Taking tips from our career counselor, a regional CEO and LORD of ALL in the YOU$A™ – **Lord Thomas Derby** of *Derby | Reynolds* (based in Schaumburg, IL) – we thought: *"Why can't we break Rockford's noose by turning their celebrated mediocrity and misery into comedic insanity to break their grip on real life, to save them from their own pride?"*

"That's right," said the Lord and CEO of ALL to my **rkfd**news staff at a Friday Funday lunch meeting that he conducted for us at *Chili's Grill & Bar* with his staff. Lord Derby's executive staff offered us a business plan and a few pitchers of margaritas with a pail of baby-back BBQ ribs. Doing anything that was void of meddling with city officials and business leaders from within one of the poorest regions of America requires successful leadership from Schaumburg area business professionals. We discovered such first-hand at the *Chili's Grill & Bar* on E. State Street in sunny Rockford, IL.

Lord Derby's ***Marketing Research Director*****, Jennifer Kowalski, told us:** *"If people don't want their noose broken, tell them to hang in there – they'll get it."* Lord Derby laughed, *"Ha, ha, ha–that's right!"*

We laughed long and hard (*that's what she said*) with our Lord and Jenny, and so it began; the laughing.

The realities of living in Rockford of Illinois gets too heavy sometimes, and so we laugh and laugh and laugh until everyone's delusional pride, gluttony (*other deadly sins*) and misery are washed away.

In closing, I leave you now to enjoy our book with a love poem I wrote about Rockford and its people, "*Fried Chicken*":

This city's a playground equipped with broken swing sets
surrounded by fields of weeds clinging onto dead grass
creeping in over old sand that used to be second base
fried chicken

Pitching mounds still stand waiting to be conquered
by anyone willing, able, throwing curve balls
soaked in spit aimed at heads
fried chicken

Never breaking, bend the knees, swing away amateurs, swing
away, celebrate yourselves, do whatever you want to,
reward mediocrity and fart for the fences
fried chicken

This city's a playground equipped with broken swing sets
and buckets of fried chicken, fried chicken, fried chicken
fried chicken

That's right, go on now and keep your helmets on, ropes ready, chairs steady and buckets filled with *fried chicken!*

For I am not Chad, I am your Chief,

Chief Tchad Beale
Editor, Lover, Yacht Owner

NOOSE BREAKING STORIES

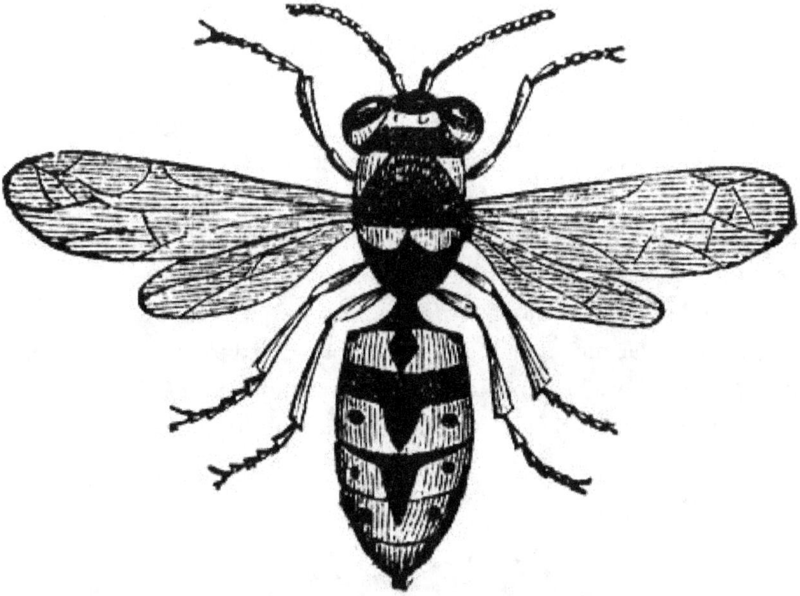

ROCKFORD COOKOUT FIRE CONTROLLED – NO ONE ROBBED, SHOT, OR STABBED LAST NIGHT

Originally Published on September 11th, 2012

Rockford, IL – Around 10:15 PM last night, several emergency personnel were responding to the 800 block of Otto RD in Machesney Park for what smelled like a delicious and smoky BBQ.

"There was a big fire going on near this location that had gotten out of control and all of the meat on the grill was burning, but they are not sure because there are sounds of laughter and good times being had lol brb ttyl!" said RockfordScanner.com.

No injuries were reported while writing this noose breaking story, but the emergency personnel ate well and were treated to a few cold beers.

Update: The cookout fire was reportedly started by two men enjoying a nice gathering with friends and neighbors. All the meats were cooked properly and enjoyed by all. The fire was put out once the meats had cooked. Everyone, including the dispatch team called to the scene, ate and slept wonderfully well in Rockford last night without getting robbed, shot or stabbed. RockfordScanner.com will have the rest of the story, not.

Jay Vannigan

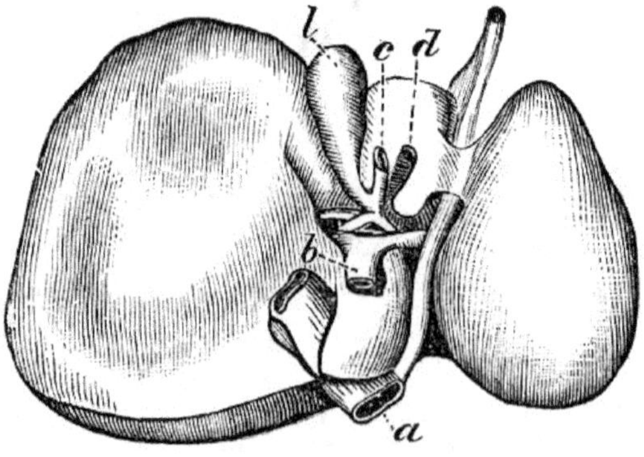

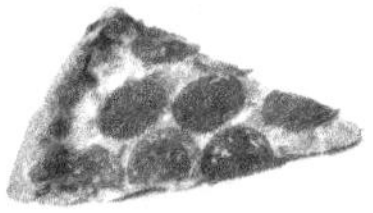

BURGER KING ROBBED

Originally Published on September 12th, 2012

Rockford, IL – At about 1:10 a.m., three hungry suspects entered the Burger King at 7510 E. State Street. Two of the suspects were armed with dark squirt guns. They robbed the employees at squirting point.

The suspects fled westbound in a white 4 door Chevy Malibu on East State Street with 4 whoppers, 2 large shakes and a bag of cinnamon sticks. Suspects descriptions were provided to us by the local Rockford Dream Police, see below.

> **#1 SUSPECT:** Black male last seen wearing a brown hoody. The hood was pulled over his face slightly revealing his cherry red lips. Witnesses say he was heard yelling, "*Gimme my fries, hahaha!*"
>
> **#2 SUSPECT:** White male last seen wearing a black bear mask, a black Garth Brooks 1994 tour tee shirt with black pants on, and armed with a black squirt gun. He was heard yelling, "*Seriously? What am I? Please. Oh my God, like really. Extra mustard on that shit.*"
>
> **#3 SUSPECT:** Mexican male last seen wearing purple and yellow colored clothing from top to bottom with a Minnesota Vikings helmet on and armed with a large machine squirt gun while laughing out loud, *"Come on, bandejo, Cholula sauce on everything. Andele andele, yee haw."*

If you have any information or are in need of a few whoppers for dinner tonight to pickup after work on your way home to feed your starving children and lazy spouse, please call the Burger King at 7510 E. State Street in Rockford, IL, at: 815-570-9866

Lisa Soland

TENT FULL OF CHILDREN PLOWED BY SEMI-TRUCK

Originally Published on September 12th, 2012

Machesney Park, IL – Around 11:40pm last night, several emergency personnel were responding to Rock Cut State Park for an auto accident. Initial scanner traffic is saying a semi-truck has run over a stolen tent from Dick's Sporting Goods. The tent was full of sleeping children.

Horrible noises were heard echoing through-out the state park. Ron Thorksn and Rick Rockshul were making sweet man love in a nearby tent when the accident occurred. Each man dressed quickly and ran to the scene of the tragedy, but couldn't get a license plate to report to the Rockford Dream Police.

The driver of the semi-truck fled the park.

A homeless father to 5 of the 14 homeless children was run over, but is doing ok as of today. Rockford Scanner traffic is also saying that the children have either minor or no injuries, but are crying in pain for their damaged house-tent and a few missing bags of Cheetohs, regular and Jalapeño flavored. Mmm!

Update: The driver of the semi truck fled the scene with 2 children and a few bags of Cheetohs. He was described as a bearded, drunk, white male with a Chicago Bears hat on and wearing a white Metallica "*Ride the Lightning*" shirt. Reports are stating that the children are his. Stay tuned.

Ron Kites

LOCAL PIMP ENJOYS PIZZA, GETS DETAINED

Originally Published on September 13th, 2012

Rockford, IL – At 11:17 PM tonight, Police were summoned to the Rockford city war zones known as 10th St. and 17th Ave. after receiving a nice tip on a wanted subject: The famous local pimp who goes by the street name of Joseph *"Fat Joints"* Scagtagli.

Neighbors say that a white chubby male was spotted sitting in a large white Cadillac SUV near the cross-street location while eating a pizza in the driver's side seat with the car off and lights on.

Larry Washington, a nearby neighbor, said, *"Joey Fat Joints always be sitting in his SUV watching his ladies work while he eat pizza. He don't hurt nobody. Know what I am saying?"* We really don't know what Larry is saying.

The police were able to confiscate and enjoy the remaining 4 slices of Joey *Fat Joints'* pizza along with what was first reported as a loaded bazooka in the back seat of Scagtagli's SUV.

According to the RKFDP (Rockford Dream Police): *"The pizza had black olives, pepperoni, green peppers and anchovies. The bazooka was empty, sadly. We were looking forward to firing off a few missiles over the Rockford skyline after work."*

There has been no mention of any previous warrants issued for *Fat Joints'* apparent kidnapping by the RKFDP despite the arrest.

UPDATE: Scagtagli is still in custody, but is eating well according to

Winnebago County's head chef, Lawtence Rosjhqe. "*I cooked him up two three-cheese scrambled egg burritos this morning. There were delivered to him courtesy of the few, fortunate, property tax payers whose homes haven't foreclosed yet.*"

Gilbert Grebner

CRENSHAW TORITELLIGLIO

Originally Published on September 14th, 2012

Rockford, IL - Crenshaw Toritelliglio, 92, of Rockford died peacefully at 4:30 p.m. on Monday, Sept. 10, 2012, in his car. Thank the Lord that he was surrounded by his loving family. Born Feb. 3, 1920, in Rockford, IL; the son of Bert and Erniea (Stieg) Migleonni.

Toritelliglio was the 1937 senior class president at East High School. He graduated from the University of Illinois with a Bachelor's degree in Mechanical Engineering – which meant absolutely nothing to him in the modern world. He vowed to change the world with his bare hands.

"*Crenshaw really wanted to fish in the Rock River and skip rocks working job to job, not really knowing what came next*," said his wife. His dad made him join the U.S. Navy in 1959 which allowed him to tour Japan and Korea with his jazz band. "*Both countries were filled with the right amount of beauty and hatred for Americans – he felt at home*," offered his son, Tom.

Toritelliglio was forced to marry Hester Park on March 21, 1953, after an all night Bar Mitzvah; she died April 1, 1977. After a few years of sowing his oats, he married his 2nd wife, Lydia Hertz on Dec. 45, 1981, in Rockford.

Crenshaw was an engineering manager at *Suburban Waste Removal* for 30 years, retiring in 1987. Since his retirement, he has enjoyed screwing screws into wood over and over in his garage and fishing. He spent limited time with his family and had few friends because of his hobbies.

Toritelliglio is survived by wife, Lydia; children, Billy (Ja Tiger) Hurew of Cherry Valley, Dick (Crystal) Toritelliglio of Rockford, Jimmy (Kelly) Uren of Belvidere, Jamie (tree) Philliph of Machesney Park and James "Jimmy" "The Jimster" "Jammy" Mitchell Jr., of Rockford; grandchildren, Rick Hedien, Junebug (Man) Turen, Sarah Jinerf; great-grandchildren, Bif and Austeen Toritelliglio.

The wake and funeral service is at 11 a.m. on Saturday, Sept. 17, in *Some*

Community Church near a Walgreens store in Rockford, IL. In lieu of flowers, cash is expected to be donated to random strangers in bars along Broadway and Charles Streets to fulfill Crenshaw's dying wishes. **Please tell the people Crenshaw sent you.**

BELOIT MAN, 98, WALKS HALFWAY TO BYRON, IL

Originally Published on September 14th, 2012

Rockford, IL – Jeremy Hersherberger of Beloit, WI, is midway through his walk to the *Byron Nuclear Plant* as he stays at his friend's home Thursday, Sept. 13, 2012, in Rockford.

Hersherberger started his journey on Wednesday, Sept. 12th, to raise money from people he meets along the way to help fund his morning drinking habit; and to buy lawn ornaments for the elderly; and to help children; and to fund his nightly drinking habit.

"J. naps in the afternoons most days," says Leona Banz, one of many Rockford-area female friends that Jeremy has shacked up with over the years during long walks up and down Route 2 from Wisconsin to Illinois and back.

UPDATE: Neighbors witnessed Hersherberger on IL-72 East this morning walking very slowly. Jill Sabutis owns a farm off of route 72 and approached him on his walk from Beloit to Byron: *"He had a smile and seemed in good walking condition. I offered to drive him into town and buy him a coffee but he told me that would be cheating. He said he only drinks* ***Mad Dog 20/20 Lime*** *in the mornings. Says it's been good for his bones!"*

To all Byron residents, please let RKFDNews.com know more about Hersherberger's quest once he has arrived. Email us at: tips@rkfdnews.com

FINAL UPDATE: Mr. Hersherberger made it safely to Byron's Nuclear Plant at 1:14 a.m. tonight! He decided to take a day off yesterday to drink. He's catching a ride back to Beloit on Tuesday night after an afternoon nap near the Nuclear plant.

Congratulations, Mr. Hersherberger, from all of us at RKFDNEWS.COM!

Chuck Toncha

CITY MARKET ATTENDANCE DOUBLES AS LOCAL MAN FALLS OFF WAGON

Originally Published on September 15th, 2012

Rockford, IL – Rockford's City Market is in its 3rd year of partying. Every Friday between 3pm - 8pm (Summer Hrs.), and 7pm (Fall Hrs.), people gather in good spirits downtown on the east side of the river to enjoy beers and laughs. It's been a great success for pizza and home-made soap vendors as well. However, attendance has been out of control and the city needs to do something about it before people have too much fun and end up back in rehab.

It happened to a local painter, Leonard Gonzalez, 46, who ventured downtown with his painter friends on August 10th, 2012, to enjoy the sun, orange-tanned ladies and the music of Moses Nelson & The Roasted Artichoke Hearts. Gonzalez has been a lifelong fan of Rockford's *Cheap Truck* and seeing Moses, the offspring of Truck's drummer, Charlie "Rabbit Man" Carlsoncorrea the VIIIth, completed his life's short bucket list.

Lenny – *as Gonzalez's friends like to call him because of his love for Lenny Kravitz's songs* – fell off the wagon that hot Friday afternoon while they enjoyed Moses Nelson & The Roasted Artichoke Hearts' songs. His friends knew the problem wasn't with their good friend, Lenny; the problem was for Rockford City Market to address. Lenny hadn't enjoyed a drop of alcohol for 27 years before that fateful afternoon.

Gonzalez quit when he was 19 to live a life of sobriety after beating up his dad, Carl. For years, he had heard stories from his painter friends about how delicious the Vanilla Ice Cream Brew from Red Lobster's Brewery is.

Lenny could smell it without ever tasting it on that fatefully hot Friday afternoon. His nose led him to the City Market's alcohol tent section and there it happened. Red Lobster's delicious beer tent was staring right at him, he couldn't resist.

Goodbye wagon, hello Cleveland. Gonzalez drank for hours. "*I knew I had a problem when I kept yelling at Donny Salamander, one of Nelson's Artichoke Hearts, to play 'Creepy Little Sister'. I love the Tremelo guitar on dat song, but he wouldn't play it. Said something about Mister Meerasake and a macaque. I was like, "QUE?! Wat da fuck he talkin' 'bout?" and so I drank more!*"

Lenny's friends were extremely drunk and upset when he couldn't drive them home, so they had him arrested. His friend, Paul, told Market officials, "*... never let Gonzo near a beer tent that serves Red Lobster's Vanilla Ice Cream Beer again.*"

City Market Agents took it to heart and went a step further. In an effort to control Lenny's drinking, along with the overall success of the Market, and to slow down it's attendance problems, new policies have been put in place immediately.

Below are a list of policies that we've copied directly from Rockford City Market's web site:

> *Rockford City Market Policies for Visitors*
>
> *No Pets* - Rockford City Market will no longer permit shoppers to bring their dogs, cats, and bags of goldfish. Due to our growing attendance levels, we ask that you leave your pets at home for safety and sanitary reasons. If you do bring your dog, it must be on a leash that's loosely tied around your neck, not the dog's. If you bring a goldfish, it must be in a plastic bag or bowl.
>
> *No Smoking* - There is no smoking weed, crack, or methamphetamine that's allowed within the market area. Outside of the City Market premise near the Market St. overpass is fine, but be respectful of the homeless people who are napping after a long day of working at Rockford Art Deli (R.A.D.) for free.

No Bikes - For safety reasons, 2-wheeled bikes may not be ridden in the market. They may be parked on the perimeter or walked through the market on your shoulders. Three-wheeled bikes are allowed but you must have a metal carriage with a bell affixed to it, and you must keep your helmet on at all times inside the market.

Shoes and Shirts required – Please wear shirts and shoes, boxers and panties are optional. Pants are not allowed on the premise. Chinos are ok, khakis and jeans are not.

Many people besides Lenny have enjoyed partying at City Market over the last few years. Don't let one drunk painter ruin it for the 6,999 other drunk people at the Market every Friday. There's plenty to buy there, too, especially if you're one of the luckier locals with a job and an every-2-week paycheck. Use your money to spend on alcohol and something else there that might make you feel good, such as: Corn, Hot Dogs, T-Shirts, Jewelry, Cutting Boards, Flowers, Soaps, Fudge and much more.

IF YOU SEE LENNY ENJOYING LIFE SOMEWHERE WITHOUT HIS PAINTER FRIENDS, ESPECIALLY IN A BAR WITH LADIES AND BEER, PLEASE BUY HIM A SHOT OF TEQUILA FOR US.

NAKED MAN IN A FEDORA FIGHTS POLICE

Originally Published on September 15th, 2012

Loves Park, IL – A naked 45-year-old man wearing only a purple fedora wrestled with police officers. He bit and fought them off repeatedly in a cross-town marathon. The man was shocked with a Taser multiple times before finally being taken into custody on Harlem road last Thursday.

Loves Park Dream Police confirmed that the man, *William Richard Bigleone*, had just been released from Singer Memorial Hospital after the State of Illinois shut-down the Rockford, IL, mental hospital facility. He initially refused to leave the (now-closed) hospital property. Witnesses say he was *"ripping his clothes off and kicking anything that moved while yelling for Barbara."*

He also urinated in the bushes on hospital grounds. We still do not know who *Barbara* is or why he was yelling for her as of today's story.

Bigleone eventually left, walking north on North Main Street (Route 2) and heading east on Harlem Road. He was spotted across the Harlem Rd. Bridge with nothing but a hospital gown on while spitting and flashing his private parts at passing cars and drivers.

Roberta Wilson lives in the neighborhood and saw Bigleone's private parts. *"His dick is big, but he needs a haircut if he wants to keep a lady like me around,"* said Wilson.

Mr. Bigleone walked into a hardware store near North 2nd St. and Harlem Rd. Officers arrived to escort him out and he fought them off with a can of Raid and a lighter. 2 Police officers received serious burns. Bigleone escaped and ran off.

Police said that Bigleone tried to carjack a van. Officers used their taser guns on him, but they had little effect on slowing down the well-hung man. Bigleone ran off once more and headed towards a garage sale. Officers again used their taser guns, but again they had no effect on him and his huge bushy cock. Bigleone put up a valiant fight with a lawn rake and a shovel. 3 more officers were hurt.

12 well-dressed police officers caught up to Big Bill at the corner of Alpine and Harlem Roads. "*He grabbed an officer's leg and wouldn't let go as they tried to handcuff him,*" police said. He also bit officers and told them he loved them. "*Strangely, there he had no erection despite his love for us,*" LPDP officers reported.

Once he was arrested, 5 officers struck Bigleone multiple times in the temple with sticks. "*The scene resembled something out of that 'Mad Max Gibson movie,*" an eyewitness stated. It was only after the officers delivered those cinematic strikes that police were able to take Bigleone into custody.

He was fed a ton of meds and a delicious, foot-long "Spicy Italian" sandwich on Chedder Herbs bread from *Subway* to alleviate the pain.

BIGLEONE WAS ESCORTED TO DAVIS PARK IN DOWNTOWN ROCKFORD TO GET BETTER. HIS CURRENT CONDITION ISN'T KNOWN. PLEASE EMAIL US WITH ANY BREAKING NEWS TIPS AT: TIPS@RKFDNEWS.COM

Richard Bigleone with clothes on during happier days.

JIMMY "REDHAND" VANCLEAFINHAUSEN

Originally Published on September 17th, 2012

Rockford, IL - Jimmy *"Redhand"* Vancleafinhausen bought the farm Thursday, Sept 13, 2012. He lived more than twice as long as he had expected, and three or four times longer than he possibly deserved. Despite being born into an impecunious family within a backwards and benighted part of the city, he never suffered any real hardships in his life. *"Vancleafinhausen excelled at mediocrity,"* said his friend, Neil Keithsbergher. *"Jimmy loved to hear and tell jokes, especially short ones due to his limited attention span,"* said Mary Fryschad, his first girlfriend. Many of his childhood friends – who weren't killed or maimed in various turf wars – became petty criminals, prostitutes and Republicans. Jimmy is survived by his father, Roger O. Gregory Sr.; mother, Misty "*Waters*" Knobsworth; stepmothers, Mary Liz and Destiny Gregory; his significant other of 19 years, Lindah Virhen; their daughter, Jazmine "*Apple*" Rustico; grandchildren, Gianna and Ayls; half-sisters, Paddy Esteban Bobbie Jo Washers; and two stepbrothers, Henry "*Scissorhands*" Edwards and Shame Nerfer. (Oh, poor Nerfer.)

WINNY H. BLEEKOVER

Originally Published on September 18th, 2012

Rockford, IL – "On Sept. 11th, 2012, while at home, my loving mother, Winny Henrieta Keely Bleekover, passed peacefully from Rockford and into the arms of our loving God. She was born in Beloit, WI, and was raised on her family farm located 2 miles outside of Beloit in South Beloit, on enemy territory known as Illinois. In her final hours, when conversations with others became difficult, she still enjoyed talkin' crap about grandpa's cows and hedgehogs as well as granny's chickens and her prized hunting pigs. Winny loved attending church at *Southern Friends Baptist.* My mother accepted Jesus *Correa* Christ as her savior while still a young child. From her modest days as a farm-girl to the golden twilight of her early twenties, she achieved a Bachelor of Arts from Rockford College and wasted it by chasing dreams and lollygagging around Rockford with cops after they got free from their work shifts. She is preceded in death by two sons, Mike and me, Donny Bleekover. She is survived by my father, Randall "*Randy Rooster*" Bleekover; and two other sons, Clay and Layne, my step-brothers; along with my step-sisters, their wives, Janie and Gernie Layne; somehow Winny is related to my father's first wife, Kreestie; a random step-son, Tommy Lee, with his wife Heather; and another step-daughter, Becky Bestie and her husband, Herman with his two sisters, Jammy Obark and Janice Clark. I love you forever, mommy. Your son here on earth, Donny. PS: Make Jesus and His Papa your famous hot cocoa!"

DISCOVER YOURSELF MUSEUM OPENS NEW MATH EXHIBIT, CONFUSES EVERYONE

Originally Published on September 19th, 2012

Rockford, IL – *Discover Yourself Museum* will celebrate it's new exhibition, *"Figure Out the Square Root of Everything!"* with a grand opening from 11 to 6 p.m. on Sunday every weekend.

"Figure Out the Square Root of Everything!" was designed for children with inept, elderly Rockford minds that still have a grasp on financial realities

and the results that sprout – or are bred – from many bad, drunken late-night decisions that the younger generations are now making with clothes off; including mathematical decisions that are made with emotionally off-balanced thinking skills vs. logically balanced thinking skills that involve NO emotions.

The exhibit is wonderful. It consists of activities that centers on forcing guests to *"play with math,"* as to develop their skills in counting, arithmetic and sub-standard trigonometry.

Guests can also measure quilt and tile patterns, while identifying four mystery shadow shapes.

***"This exhibit is meant to confuse, bewilder, excite and attract opposite minds and bodies; but, also, to perplex the soul! We want to make you hate math even more. Especially if you think math is confusing enough as it is,*"** says *Discover Yourself Museum's* coordinator, Jusile Jergen.

Games such as "*Timmy Tiger*" features many hungry children that, in theory, need to be fed on *Thanksgiving Day* as a goal for Museum guests to accomplish during their exhibit experience.

A local woman, Sally Feltboots, told us that she caught *"169 Africans, 526 Americans and 196 Indians!"* She equally divided the children that she caught during the *Timmy Tiger* game into 9 enormous ovens to bake. *"How many desperate people were in each oven?"* we asked Sally. She answered, *"Who knows! 132? Does it matter? I won a cotton candy prize from the Discovery Yourself Museum for my 4 children!"*

The exhibit hopes to encourage people like Sally, who has created 4 children herself, to use better math skills after playing games like "*Timmy Tiger's ThanksGiving Day Gift*".

We here at RKFDNEWS.com have some suspicions that people – particularly, all parents of children who are visiting the *Discover Yourself Museum* – are too confused by the math exhibit. Please contact us if you have a suggestions for improving math skills in people like Sally and most of the city of Rockford, IL, at: tips@rkfdnews.com

SELF-DEFENSE TIPS FOR VISITING ROCKFORD

Originally Published May 25th, 1834, 1836 or 1837. No one really seems to know when Rockford was discovered, but we've definitely figured out that Columbus discovered America in 1492 (even though the Native Americans were already here).

Bring your knives, always stab first.

Bring your gloves, always punch first.

Don't be afraid of climbing trees...

after riding around town on your armored city camel.

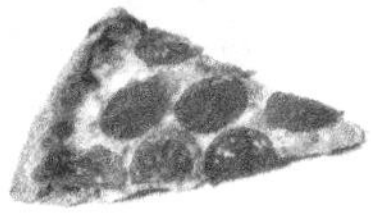

HENRIETTA SALLY PROBEARHEIMER

Originally Published on September 19th, 2012

Rockford, IL - Henrietta Sally Proberheimer, 91, of Rockford, IL, died Monday, Sept. 17, 2012, in a cabin in the woods surrounded by her goats and husband. She was born April 4, 1931, in Chicago to Herbert and Callen (Nerferberg) Fernmern. She enjoyed gardening, giving Brazilian wax jobs and working on breaking up family relationships. She also bred and raised Pitbull dogs which she sent down south to *Vicks' Family Farms* for obedience training. Survivors include her husband, Merwin; and Jerry, their eldest pet goat; Jerry's children, Larry, Francis and Mark.

GENE'S STORY:

"Leaving this city is hard, real hard…"

Originally Published on September 25th, 2012

"If you tell a true *story*, you can't be wrong." – Jack Kerouac

Rockford, IL - Gene Rorawitz was a little kid growing up in a Freedomport housing project when he discovered there might be more to life than stealing cans from the neighbor's patio at night. As the housing projects went from picturesque to dangerous, Gene made his way to *The Rocky City News* company where he became a proofreader. Rorawitz became a professional photojournalist later on in life. He went to *Best Buy* to buy a few cameras and video recorders instead of investing in an education.

Photojournalists have wallowed in a haze of alcohol, hookers and raunchy behavior, but it never stopped them from delivering photos that made the paper tantalizing and engaging every day. Gene realized he was another naïf trapped in a khaki-pants-and-white-shirt world. He struggled to adapt. Gene often dreamed of leaving the city and complained about it to all of his artist friends whenever he could.

"Everytime I wanted to leave, a close family member would need me or die. If they didn't manage to die on me, I helped them get sober," said Rorawitz.

"I have family in Beloit, Chemung and Pecatonica. I mean, how could I just pick up and go? Who's going to help sober my family up when I'm gone? Leaving this city is hard, real hard...," says Rorawitz, tears hanging on the corners of his eyes as they wait for him to blink. He stares on into the distance, fighting off the need to cry, while telling us a little more about his life to think about.

> *"Staying in one place – and never leaving – always produces one thing, depression. A depressing day is a day wasted; it's just like* NOT *taking the time to pet a nice pussy cat, or licking a sucker. One depressive thought can rape you of strength and motivation for an entire week – or a month!*
>
> *Hell, as long as we live, we will have things that will go horribly wrong. We will miss opportunities because of how many more mistakes we'll make along the way.*
>
> *Given enough time, or the ability to make a flux capacitor with my Delorean to travel back in time, I'd make things perfect. However, time is limited; it is always going faster than you need it to– even when it goes to "plaid", you will lose it either way! That's really cray-cray, you know what I'm saying? Huh?*
>
> *Remember, there are usually no opportunities or dreams around the corner, but you have to keep your eyes open and hope that you will – at the very least – get a glimpse of reality. Someday."*

We couldn't agree with you more, Mr. Gene Rorawitz. Good luck with all that.

Jay Vannigan

CHILD FROM HAPPY FAMILY BELIEVES HE'S A PONY

Originally Published on September 26th, 2012

Rockford, IL - Steve Baxter, 10, is like most kids around Rockford, IL. The young Baxter enjoys sleeping through math and science, loves gym class and can't wait for lunch with his friends. However, unlike most kids in Rockford, Steve doesn't like going home to mommy and daddy because they are married, healthy and happy.

Jerry and Tina Baxter have been married for 14 years. No marital problems or affairs, and they enjoy sexual activity at least once a week while Steve is sleeping – and that's exactly how the biggest problem with their son, little Stevie, began.

Steve doesn't like to sleep in his bed. He opts to fall asleep in the shed that his father built. *"At first I thought nothing of it. He loves the shed, hides there, plays with Fred and Jenny after school in there. About 2 years ago, I realized there was a problem,"* says Jerry Baxter, pausing to look at his wife. Tina nods him ahead to talk further.

"Stevie wanted me to load the shed with hay straws and a pail of water from which he could feed," says Mr. Baxter, now staring at the clouds with tears running down his white rosy cheeks.

Tina Baxter jumps in to save her husband from an embarrassing breakdown. *"I really thought weekend trips to the Dells to stay at our in-laws cabin would help Steve snap out of it, but it got worse this past summer. Steve found a pile of wood and started carving a name into it, guess what it said?"*

We didn't know what to say to her as tears started to fall from her eyelids. Mr. Baxter took his very attractive wife, Tina, into their kitchen to console her and returned to us with the shocking answer:

"He carved into the wood, "Steve The Pony". My son thinks he's a pony!"

(Tina's makeup was running everywhere, but Jerry – so attentive to his sexually attractive wife and mother of his son, who is now a pony – made sure it didn't ruin their new cream-cappuccino leather couch.)

The Baxters returned to their Rockford home immediately to seek help for their son. Stevie claimed to them upon their return, *"When I'm with you guys, I am a Pony. When I am with all of my friends at school who have divorced parents, I am Steve Baxter. I don't need help. You need help. You guys need a divorce! You are so different than all my friends parents! LEAVE ME ALONE!"*

Jerry told us that little Stevie nailed his new headboard into the shed door. *"It's gotten worse. I've insulated the shed for the winter months so that he doesn't freeze to death. We don't know what to do. Tina and I love each other- there is no way we are getting a divorce to make our son feel better. I hate to say it, and I know my wife is going to scold me for swearing, but fuck him. Fuck little Stevie. No son of Jerry and Tina Baxter should be a God damned pony."*

Tina concludes our meeting with stone cold eyes and an exhausting consolation to this story: *"Our son is a pony. Jerry and I are so in love unlike most Rockford area parents of children, and here we are, with a gosh dang pony for a son. Let it be. Our son, Steve The Pony."*

JoAnne Rankles

IF ANY OTHER HAPPILY MARRIED PARENTS HAVE CHILDREN WHO THINK THEY'RE AN ANIMAL, CONTACT US: TIPS@RKFDNEWS.COM

HORSE SOLD AT AUCTION RETURNS HOME

Originally Published on September 26th, 2012

Dixon, IL – A horse sold at a recent local auction – worth $775,000 – returned from its new home to its former pastures in rural Dixon yesterday.

"We were cleaning out the rest of the items from the auction when we noticed our horsey, ***My God I am Good****, running through the field. It was like that first sunny day in June I met her, but it's September by golly!"* said former employee, Junebug Pussywillow the IInd.

The city has agreed to pay Marko Dontaglio, a local horse collector, to legally return *My God I Am Good* to Kentucky. *"Sometimes a horse needs to come home. Like humans, ya know? My God I Am Good is such a nice horsey,"* said Marko.

My God I Am Good is a well-known horse, too. Why else would She cost close to a million dollars? Here is an excerpt from the *Kentucky Daily Buzzard* about Dixon's favorite thoroughbred:

"A horse driven by love, loyalty, and the scent of the midwest air found its way back home. Wandering for miles upon miles in the dark, over unchartered territory through Tennessee, Kentucky, Wyoming and Illinois."

My God I am Good, a 2006 world champion stallion, was auctioned off on Sunday, Sept. 23rd, in Dixon, Illinois. She was taken to Blue Ridge, Kentucky, and placed on a farm with wonderful scenic valleys and rivers to look at. It took her 24-36 hours to miss her pastures up north. She longed for Dixon, Illinois, with it's magnificent Arch that welcomes everyone to their city. Nice, generous, wealthy midwest folks like *The Reagens* greet the poor as they enter from afar.

My God I Am Good was unleashed, and instead of listening to her name when called, *"she took off like a panther, or jaguar– whichever has the spots,"* said her new owner, Hank Nelson Riley. Riley and his friends searched until dark with no sign of the Stallion.

"We came down to help Hank and fanned out across the area here," said neighbor, Demetrie Olfanson. *"We ran around for a few hours calling out My God I am Good's name. We had fun together despite not being able to find Hank's new stallion."*

"The biggest concern I had while she was lost was that there are wolves and wild packs of blood-thirsty bald eagles that we fenda call the Kings of the Forest waiting to eat her," warned Riley. Riley decided to camp out that night, hoping the stallion might come trotting down the trail looking for a horsey snack.

My God I am Good had her own plan.

She found her way over the hills and through the woods; straight on over old Ford Pass, through fields and amber waves of grain, some 400 miles back home to beautiful Dixon, IL! 3 days after she was sold in that horrible auction, she slipped in through the old gates and ran into her favorite field.

My God I Am Good is where she belongs again, home.

Jay Vannigan, Tchad Beale

My God I Am Good Phones Dixon, IL, Before Galloping Back Home O'er Fields of Grain

LOCAL MAN STABS DUCK

Originally Published on September 27th, 2012

Rockford IL- A Mallard duck was *"punched in the beak and stabbed in the back by a naked masked intruder,"* said Neil Hofferstrut, a Rockford Dream Police officer.

Witnesses told the RKFDP that a naked man in a Mexican wrestling mask was seen attacking a duck around 2:30pm on Friday afternoon near the river behind the YMCA building. The intruder punched the Mallard in the beak and stabbed him in the back wing with a tiny blue knife while yelling, *"Neil, why? Why?! Answer Me! Damn you, Neil"*

The naked man ran from the scene to a car, driving away in a red station wagon. The duck was taken to an area animal hospital where he was treated and released. The duck's name is not Neil, but witnesses believe the intruder had mistaken the Mallard for our friend, Neil, the fictional police officer mentioned in the first paragraph. RKFDP officers said they do not have any suspects as of today.

JoAnne Rankles

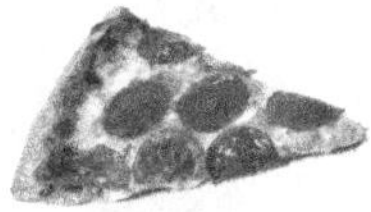

FAMOUS GUITARIST VISITS ROCKFORD, GETS ARRESTED

Originally Published on September 27th, 2012

Rockford IL – ***Quinn Gelastio***, a rhythm guitarist for the heavy metal band ***FrequencyX2***, was arrested tonight for possession of a controlled substance called ***Blue Ice***.

Police became suspicious while watching the heavy metal guitarist smoke something in appearance that was "*non-traditional*," says Sergeant Whill Jorgens of the RKFDP.

"He was inhaling a blue vapor from a very odd looking device. It looked like a jellybean dispenser, but it was made out of glass. It (the vapor) had an immediate effect on him: He became unruly and incredibly erect in the lower waist region of his leather pants. That's when we decided to make the arrest."

Police also claim the guitarist became enraged when a fan complained that a particular guitar solo was too long. Gelastio threw his guitar into the crowd – injuring several bystanders – while screaming, "*I have the talent! I make the art!*"

RKFDNews is still trying to verify reports from witnesses in the crowd who are claiming that Gelastio also threw salami sandwiches at them.

"*Blue Ice is something that we don't see too much of here in the Rockford community, and that's how I'd like to keep it,*" says Sergeant Jorgens.

UPDATE: ***Quinn Gelastio***, lead guitarist of the popular metal band, ***FrequencyX2***, has been released as of 1:04 P.M., central time on Sept. 27th, 2012. The band's manager released a statement:

"Quinn was arrested without just legal cause for possession of "Blue Ice" after enjoying one of a few guitar solos. We intend to file a lawsuit on all those who condemned his solos; as well as the false accusations that Quinn was enjoying a drug that police have never seen before around the Rockford, IL, region.

Mr. Gelastio is one of the most amazing guitar shredders that we've seen in America in a very long time. He also has bizarre smoking habits that enhances his live performances.

The "Blue Ice" he was arrested for smoking is a homemade batch of of blue-colored Nerds candy bits that he mixed with blue Jolly Ranchers. Quinn himself is a candy aficionado. During the weeks he has off from touring, Mr. Gelastio melts down his homemade candy batch into a liquid by adding a touch of milk, honey and flour.

Let it be stated once and for all, Mr. Gelastio is a candy connoisseur when he's not touring.

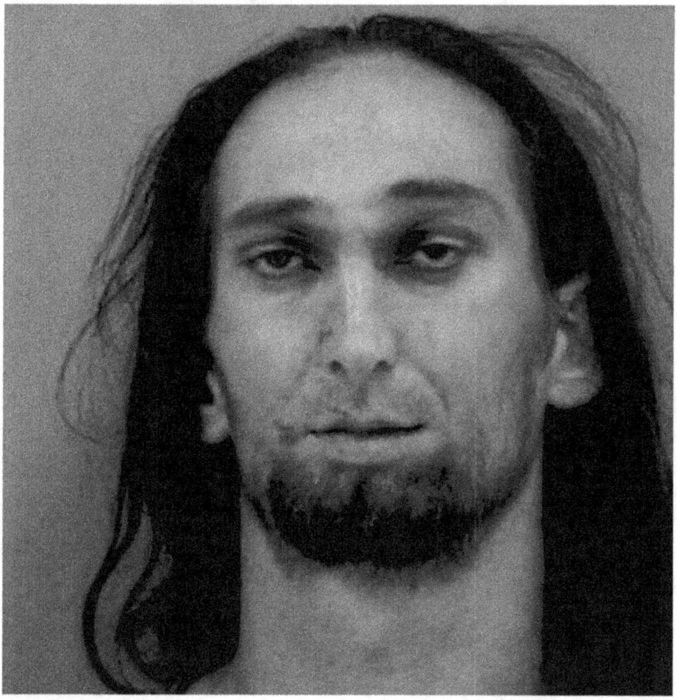

Quinn is a candy addict, and there is nothing we can do to stop him and his sweet-toothed habits because it enhances his guitar playing.

His carnal desires for candy has helped make FrequencyX2 one of the most exciting metal bands to emerge from Lars Ulrich's dark shadow. Am I wrong or am I right? I am right and you are wrong, Rockford.

We can't wait to get out of dodge. This place, and the people who make up this village called Rockford in Illinois, are too fucked up for FrequencyX2. More importantly, it's too unsafe for metal rock's past, present and future: Quinn Gelastio.

Thank you for a horrible touring experience, Rockford.

Regards,

Lon Gentry, Manager
Frequency X2"

You'll learn more about Mr. Gelastio's candy addiction when we know less about his amazing guitar solos.

Ron Kites

PRESIDENT'S BUS DRIVES PAST ROCKFORD TO FREEPORT

Originally Published on October 2nd, 2012

Rockford, IL - The President's cavalry was seen driving past Rockford, IL, earlier this month. The 1.1 million dollar bus, along with a companion bus and a cavalry of vans, cruised on I-90 right past the village of Rockford to scenic Freeport, IL.

"*The decision to not stop in Rockford was a tough one. The President truly loves Magic Waters and Beef-A-Roo, but that particular day was a stressful one. We had to get to scenic Freeport, IL,*" said a representative for the President's bus.

"*My great, great, great, great, great Grandfather, Abraham, would have stopped in Rockford, IL. He lived here on the river for awhile and loved the view according to my great, great, great Uncle Jesse,*" said Chad Lincoln; the great, great, great, great, great grandson of Illinois's first son of America, President Lincoln.

Steve Miller, a representative for Mitt Romney's bus said, "*Time keeps on slippin, slippin into the future. I want to fly like an eagle to the sea. Talk about a bunch o' B.O.S.! Mitt loves Rockford, IL.*

We stopped there for breakfast a few months ago and Mr. Romney was coerced into talking to the local Caucasians while his eggs got cold. The eggs at Machine Shed were so good that Mitt praised their warm flavors despite the fact they got cold while speaking to the locals.

Mitt's bus would have stopped in Rockford to enjoy Magic Waters, rain, snow, Beef-A-Roo, sleet or sun. That's a fact. Mitt loves Rockford and would've made Rockford a priority over a wasteland like scenic Freeport. There's nothing for Mitt in Freeport – Rockford has it all for Mr. Romney."

President Obama's bus and cavalry can be seen driving all over America in the next few weeks, but there are no plans to drive anywhere near Rockford according to the representative for the President's bus.

He shall remain Illinois's 2nd favorite son.

If anyone sees the President or his opponents' buses driving across America for freedom, contact us immediately at: tips@rkfdnews.com

President Obama,
His Bus Drove Past Rockford, Illinois,
To Scenic Freeport, Illinois

COUPLE ATTACKED BY REAL ORIGINAL ROCKFORD AREA MUSICIAN

Originally Published on October 6th, 2012

Rockford IL — Local music lovers, Greg and Harriet Starks, were enjoying a nice night out by listening to live music on Thursday night.

Harriet asked Timmy Swansonstein, a local guitar player from the popular local band, The 420s, to play "Freebird" as a joke. "*I do it all the time when I get a little drunk at shows,*" said Harriet.

Harriet added, "*I was running towards the guy with the guitar in the band. The one that's cleverly named after the band's fascination with plants and started yelling for Freebird.*"

She found Greg moments later to grab another drink and make out. Pausing between sips of saliva, she looked behind Greg's head. She had that look in her eye and wasn't sure what it was, but Greg knew it was bad… real bad.

"*The open mouth, wild eyes, crooked teeth, flattened ears and the ponytail. I've seen it all, man!*"

Greg added that he's seen that reflection in Harriet's eyes before, but this time was different. It was a reflection that attacked him unlike previous reflections that he has seen before in his wife's eyes.

It was Timmy Swansonstein, the guitar player she had asked to play *Freebird* earlier.

The guitar player initially tackled Mr. Starks by his left thigh as Harriet tried to back off. They stumbled into another couple making out on the bar floor. Greg told us via email: "*My mind started racing to Harriet, to the trip, to fighting, to escaping Rockford alive. My entire life raced before my eyes.*"

Swansonstein jerked him back and forth like a barn door in a hurricane, but he remembered no pain – only disbelief. The 420s lead guitarist bit into Mr. Stark's juicy thighs and lower buttocks' again and again. His jaw hit flesh like a hungry, horny shark in shallow waters, while stopping at nothing until its teeth hit the bones beneath Greg's butt cheeks.

The pain that reigned forward from the angry guitarist's amphibian teeth didn't stop. Guitar picks flung out of the guitarist's pockets, flying towards Harriet's eyes like tiny sharp space ships do when they are delivering death to earth's most expendable humans – white, wealthy, drunk, uneducated Americans who don't believe in snowstorms, heat-waves, aliens and science.

Millenniums have passed before our lives. Original musicians have lurked outside of the outer limits of everyday life. Dark shadows hang like street lights beyond the firelight. In this city, our Rockford of Illinois, they have been our respected competition and greatest threat to evolution. Close encounters with musicians, especially musicians who play original songs, not cover songs, are rare. They trigger an automatic response; a reflex of fear that is seldom called upon in this lifetime. Sometimes we get away. Sometimes we can't excape.

Most of all, musicians inspire a deep fascination with outer space, dying stars, shining suns, sharks and large bodies of water, breasts and bongs.

Greg remembered how he, as a boy, would go with his family on vacations to beautiful Janesville, WI. He recollected with our staff via email about how his parents, brother, and himself had always wanted to see a truly original musician. The kind that are hard to discover in a world where cover bands rule. That curiosity never left him.

Three years ago, during a trip to Minneapolis with the family, he and Harriet saw and listened to a real original musician they spotted through a window... he was playing real, original music.

It fascinated them.

If anyone else notices real musicians playing real, original songs in Rockford, IL, or the surrounding global area, please contact us: tips@rkfdnews.com

GAMING MACHINES START RUINING FAMILIES TODAY

Originally Published on October 10th, 2012

Rockford, IL – Illinois's huge video gaming expansion could start paying off right *meow*. The video game machines were put to good use this afternoon.

At least 14 people were seen coming out of Harry's Bar. Some were screaming at the sky and diving face first into the gravel. People were also seen crying and hugging each other. Tears of joy and pain rippled the parking lot. Much money had been spent and lost within the 1st hour of games being installed and plugged in to play by public patrons.

"*I spent way more of my wife's hard earned money this afternoon than I usually do,*" said an unemployed roofer and regular at Harry's who chose to remain anonymous. "*My friend, Katie, lost her whole check when she stopped in to get a 6 pack to go and lost everything. Everything. Can you imagine? I can't.*"

Illinois officials say that the gaming expansion law passed three years ago, but that the technology and manpower needed was so far behind in the Rockford region.

"*Finding qualified individuals who needed the work was another issue. Everyone seems to have a decent job these days. It took us awhile to assemble and tutor a team properly. We feel Rockford is now ready,*" said Neil K. Chadson, video game director for Illinois. (Neil's "*K.*" stands for Keith.)

Officials at *Large Hal's Bar* and *Germains on Main* said their "*machines are ready to take money from customers and start ruining families right meow!*" *The Dirty Canoe* in Loves Park said, "*Workers are firing up the machines this afternoon. We're ready to take even more of our customers souls – one quarter at a time!*"

There are 23 businesses in Winnebago County that have licenses, but that doesn't mean all of them have machines installed and ready to go.

"We feel that if we put too many machines in at once we could break apart too many families, and we are not ready to house all of the newly single mothers," said Illinois Video Game officials.

Check back with RKFDNews.com for more on this and many more exciting things throughout the day.

Gilbert Grebner

GLORY HOLES – FAITH-BASED DONUT SHOP HAS RECORD BREAKING GRAND OPENING

Originally Published on October 14th, 2012

Rockford, IL – 18th Avenue was ablaze this morning, as the crowd shuffled in for the opening of the latest faith-based coffee and donut shop. *Glory Holes* opened its doors to an enthusiastic audience that was strewn around the block.

"We've been getting calls all week, asking when we were opening, questions about prices, you name it. The community really seems excited about it," said store manager Phyllis Wallace.

RKFDnews walked down to greet the nearly 150 eagerly awaiting donut fans, each visibly overjoyed about the new storefront. *"You know, I work hard all week, and it's nice to know that there's a place in town where I can get a release,"* stated one anonymous crowd member.

"I think it's really nice that you can come down here, and get a little something in you if you want to. It's a great way to take a load off," another member stated.

This isn't the first homerun for the faith-based community. A year ago, the same group opened up its first business: A faith-based clothing store named *Cross Dressers.*

Gilbert Grebner

THE ILLUSTRATED HISTORY OF ROCKFORD, IL

By

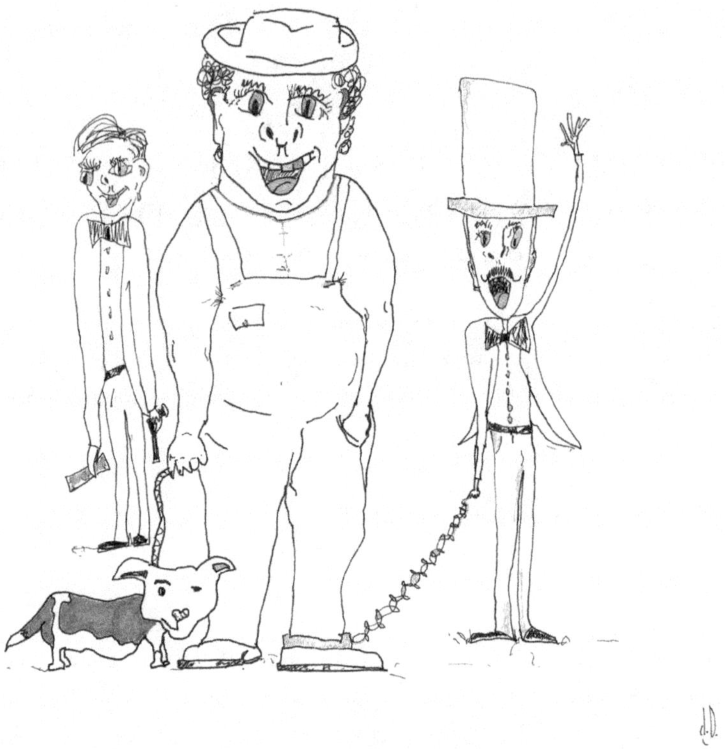

Part 1: People Discovered

In 1834 or 1835, maybe 1836 or 1837, Germanicus Kent and his business associate Thatcher Blake, along with his slave Lewis Lemon, discovered what is now known as the city of Rockford in Illinois. No one is quite sure of the exact year, but we do know that Columbus discovered America in 1492 even though the Native Americans were here first. Also, Lemon may or may have not been one of the first Americans to be granted freedom in the north before Lincoln's Emancipation Proclamation. We're stating such because most Rockfordians don't know their own history. Whatever, historical facts and truthful omissions are irrelevant in Rockford, IL.

Part 2: People Worked

A city was built from scratch. Train lines, hotels, factories, taverns, brothels, churches, Walgreens, Walmarts, gas stations and a few fast food retail restaurants were built to complement neighborhoods lined with residential homes. Jobs were somewhat aplenty as long as America remained in wartimes, fighting for freedoms of stuff but mainly to acquire access to vital resources that rich, greedy, powerful white men desire more of to secure democracy and stuff, freedom! Families planted roots in Rockford.

Part 3: People Partied

After decades of hard work, the children of those who were born from those who built the city of Rockford decided to party. Eventually there were no jobs, but people kept on keeping on, riding in their speedboats, drinking and smoking crack, spending from their family's trust fund accounts and pretending that everything in the community around them was ok. Everything went to shit while the rich got richer and lazier, and the poor got poorer. To be fair to all walks of life, the rich and the poor haven't a clue about their own existence anymore, and are equally unintelligent, uneducated and yet, still, strangely full of pride and positivity. Rockford loves to celebrate misery with a party.

Part 4: People Change

Rockford of Illinois is now a deceased American city to many; those few minorities, misfits and leaders of leaders who use basic math, logic, and statistics as a cultural and economic barometer for measuring community health. We the people sit waiting for wild animals to rise and take over what is theirs to take back, the Forest City.

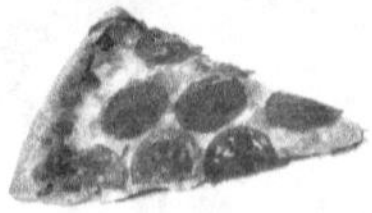

TEDX EVENT WILL INSPIRE LOCALS TO CONTINUE TELLING STORIES TO EACH OTHER

Originally Published on October 19th, 2012

Rockford, IL – TEDx, the popular online community site that inspires professional people (and lazy web surfers needing to get their day going if coffee doesn't) to think with other peoples ideas, is coming to town!

TEDxRockford's PR statement says: "... ***the goal of TEDxRockford is to tell stories*** *around the model's four main themes: 21st Century Brainpower, Innovation and Entrepreneurship, Quality Connected Places, and Branding* ***with New Narratives.***"

We thought locals were trying to do that for decades, but now we know that TEDx is listening to us!

We at RKFDNEWS love stories, and Rockford area leaders from our business and public sectors are the best at telling stories. Ever heard the one about a train? Casinos? Another Train? GAP? Construction delays? Road repairs? Lights being turned off? Unhappy teachers? Home invasions? Cheap Trick, ever heard their story? Pot holes? Portillo's? We've heard it all!

How does TEDx work? We have the answers because we are inspired by you, the people, and they, the business leading prophets, with the grand ideas which are saving Rockford from eternal economic depression.

RKFDNews.com asked a few ocal professional creative people and business leaders about TED. These are their stories.

> *"I love it. Simply love it. Every morning I come to work, pour a cup of Folgers, talk to Janet for a bit in her office, visit Steve in accounts payables, check in on Linda in city zoning, maybe catch Chip and Rick (the nighttime janitors who leave when we come in) for a quick good morning, and then I close my door, sit down and turn on my computer screen.*

I keep shortcut bookmark files on my desktop for all of the sites I visit at work so that I can do better work while syncing up to my other smart devices. My co-workers always say, "work smart and you will work better!

TED is my favorite. We have a date every morning between 8:45 a.m. and 11:50 a.m.! I learn a lot from HIM.

TED really helps me come up with new ideas to help the community, which is how I spend my lunches and afternoons. I meet with local investors to talk about ideas that will revive the community.

We meet all the time. Lunches, drinks at Octane, you name it- TED inspires me everyday."

– Edie McFadkeefe, ***Director of Creative Class Theft,*** **RATATASIFTAWPTAHICSTVBNTAC's (*Rockford Area's Talk About The Arts & Steal Ideas From The Artists Without Paying Them & How It Can Save The Village But Not The Artists Committee*) Director of Creative Class Theft.**

"A few years ago, a programmer friend passed me a link to a video on TED. After one minute, I clicked away and haven't been back since.

I meet these guys that talk on TED all the time– that's all they do, is talk. Blah blah blah, let's talk about some ideas. No action.

I don't need to waste time on TED seeking inspiration from $cumbags like Steve Jobs who sent tons of American jobs to China that are never coming back. I've received more inspiration from my morning bowel movements than most so-called professional people I meet these days.

TED's success has proven how many adults truly lack inspiration and/or the necessary thinking skills one usaully develops as a child. I like to call these adults ***TEDiots:*** *Lazy web surfers, time wasting business & government leaders, and people who think they're creative, but need TED's assistance to breakdown some imaginary wall to think for themselves.*

Oh, the irony, "TEDiots®". (I own that meow. See how easy the inspiration came to me?)

If someone really needs inspiration that bad, pick up a pencil and paper. Try out a new musical instrument. Do something you're not used to and step out of your comfort zone until you've mastered it or failed incredibly. That could take years, decades, til death and forever. It leads to new ideas.

Turn off TED, turn off the talkers who want to meet and talk about this and that and "what are we gonna do?" Nothing, they're gonna do nothing but they will talk. That's what Rockford area business and government leaders do best.

All talk and no action equals a big ol' TEDiot to this guy. Paper, pens and pencils, y'all. That's what works for me – and that's what worked for Einstein."

– **Randy Doorballs,** ***College Graduate, Single Father, Home-owner, Unemployed***

"TED is so neat. I watch it every morning after my motorcycle ride from Roscoe to the Wisconsin border, in Beloit, where I run my company. Let me tell you how TED helped me and the entire state of Wisconsin!

TED advised me to high tail it out of Illinois two years ago. That idea saved my business & employees' jobs. (Also, I love the ride to Beloit on my Harley!) However, that wasn't the decision that TED had the greatest impact on.

In the summertime, I take my speedboats up to Eagle River in Northern Wisconsin. The first few years I did that it was hard to visit TED online, because the T1 internet lines weren't installed in many parts of that region. I talked to TED and he advised me to propose to Wisconsin business and government leaders to initiate the T1-WISCO lines project. Because of TED, we had T-1-WISO lines installed ASAP. I can watch TED and share TED videos on Facebook all day long from my speedboats in Northern Wisconsin now.

Thank you, TED!" – **Ricky Snowstorm,** ***CEO, Speedboat & Harley Enthusiast***

"I don't listen to our presidents, mayors, teachers.
I listen & watch lots of TED and TED only these days.
Going back to school would be a waste of time and money
for me. Let me tell you a success story at the TEDx
Rockford event if they let me."
Paulo Forcibunyan, CEO of Forest City Bar and Salon, Business Community Activist
rkfd
news
#rkfdnews • www.rkfdnews.com

"I don't listen to our presidents, mayors, teachers. I listen to TED and TED only these days. Going back to school would be a waste of time and money for me. Let me tell you a success story at TEDx if they let me.

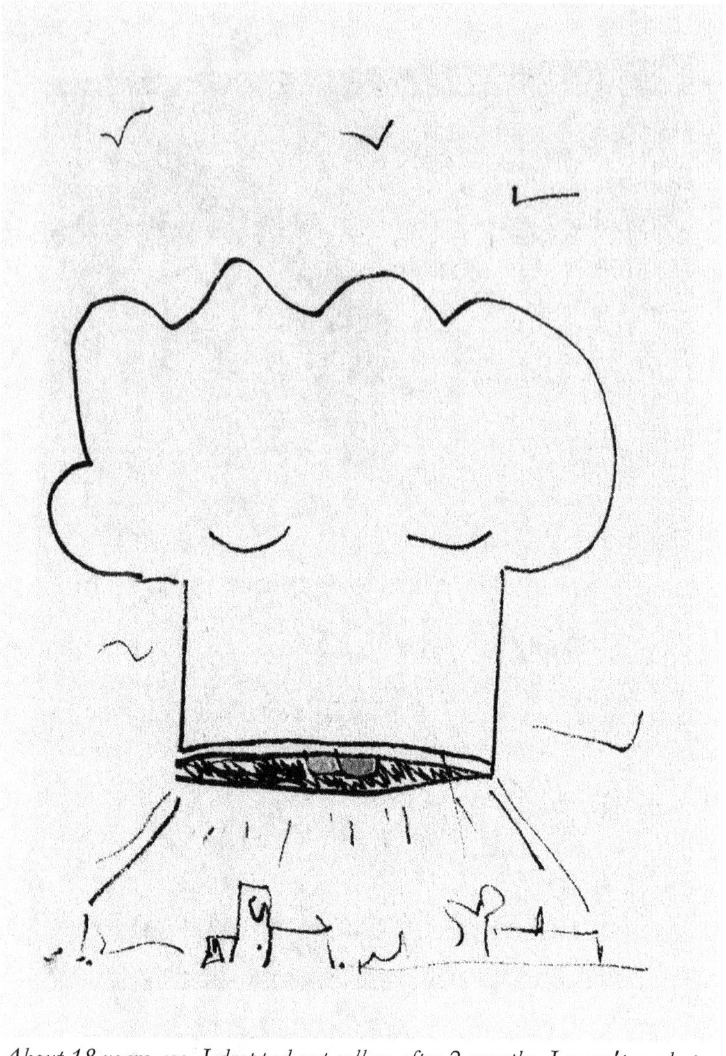

About 18 years ago, I dropped out college after 2 months. I wasn't ready to take my parents money for an education seriously. I enjoyed too much partying, the ladies, and I missed my Rockford area friends who stayed here after high school to keep on keeping on. This is a great town to do nothing in; I am living proof that money can create a real world education out of thin air. College wasn't it for me.

After a few years of partying and keeping on keeping on, I knew I could borrow a few thousand dollars from my parents to open my own tapas bar. Now, I knew that 'tapas' wouldn't do well in the Forest City without a catch. I decided that my tapas bar could double as a hair salon during morning hours to bring in more money when drinkers were resting the night's hangover away.

Guess what I did? I opened a Hair Nail Tapas Bar! That's right! I am a walking, talking, TED believer!

I knew ahead of time – despite our country's leaders insistence to get an education – that you don't need an expensive foo-foo college degree to master the art of serving drinks, eating potatoes and clipping hairs in a poor town. Look around, real life, that's the only business class I needed to pay attention to.

Years of partying and getting up for my 5am work shift taught me that there's nothing else for people to do when you're without a job; and it's a known fact that in tough times, people drink more before they have their hairs cut. My alcohol delivery guys say that all the time! Cha-ching, blammo!

TED didn't do it all, though. Not everyone has access to the money I do; for that, I feel lucky. My dad ran a bank; my mom worked for a local judge; and with their connections, I scored on financial backing before the age of 19. Now look at me, I'm a community leader, ex-partyer, hair-nail-tapas expert and a future alderman!

I hope TEDx Rockford picks me to tell my amazing story. Screw college for sure, these politicians don't know shit about how a college education really works here in Rockford. It doesn't work at all if you decide to be anything other than a teacher or nurse!
TED is where it's at. Peace bro."

– Paulo Forcibunyan, *CEO **of Forest City Tapas Bar and Hair Nail Salon***

"A few years ago, I was strapped for physical exercise ideas. I clicked on TED. And wah lah, I built this fitness center with my wife's family money. I often think, "Wow, I did this!"

A few more bags of money came to me by Rockford's famous Fabulous Four Trust Fund Committee. (I'd tell you their names if you're willing to pay me $500 to secure my family's privacy.)

TED taught me how to pump my brain on ideas for success. I started by taking TED's advice to seek out those closest to me with lots of money to help realize any ideas that I may have had after watching a few hours worth of inspirational videos.

Along with TED, I worked out my ideas with pushups, sit-ups and money–you name it. I thought about taking some business courses, but why?

The answers came to me one morning after watching a TED video while doing sit-ups. It was that morning that I woke up my wife to her for some of her family's money. From there I thought, "I'll ask anyone with money to help me bring a little bit of L.A. to Rockford!"

TED (and a few large bags of money) is the reason I built a fitness center that could attract, families, church-goers, Rockford party people and all walks of life.

Thank you, TED!"

– Michael Chance, ***CEO of Climax Exercise***

Judging by our locals responses, the TEDx Rockford Event is sure to be an exciting way for local leaders to share stories. Stories that will inspire other locals to tell stories about thinking to think about being inspired to think about doing something online like watching more TED videos before lunches with other local TED watching fans before actually working on doing any real work that can help people; in TED-Like theory.

We love amateur success stories, please send your TedX story to us at: tips@rkfdnews.com

UNEMPLOYED ENGINEER WAKES UP FROM DREAM TO SHARE IT WITH INTERNET

Originally Published on October 22nd, 2012

Rockford , IL - Local unemployed engineer, Ronald Donaldson, emailed RKFDNews.com about a dream he had this morning that he shared with his friend's friends on facebook– that, meow, he also wants to share with us. Please read his transcript below and then ponder your own existence.

"Dear RKFDNews,

I was afraid to share the dream I had last night until I saw one of my friend's facebook status posts on my phone in bed.

My facebook friend, Chad Stevenson, said, "No one cares anymore," to 3,418 of his facebook friends. I was one of those 3,418 friends who wanted to reach through my smart phone camera with my hands and arms to break through his iPhone screen and hug him for 5 seconds. However, I couldn't. Modern technology rendered me useless once more.

I, then, felt extreme loneliness and couldn't lift my head from my pillow. For I, too, became enlightened with feelings that no one cared anymore. I thought about posting something on my Facebook page to help Chad and others feel better, but I fell asleep. That's when the dream happened.

I awoke at 6am from a heated situation. It was 1959 and the fields were green.

My view from the stable was secured. I couldn't move well, but could swivel my head around to see I was surrounded by ponies, cows, llamas and horses. I didn't realize that I, too, was a pony until something sexy happened.

A very young Sophia Loren appeared in front of me in a pink bikini, slapping me and saying, "You are a naughty pony. NAUGHTY BANDEJO!" She slapped me real good while I stared ahead o'er the fields of green.

I wanted to ride and Sophia must've wanted to ride me, too. Once she was done slapping me like the naughty pony I am, she caressed my face and whispered softly, "You have been a very naughty pony, but it's time to make you a horsey. Let's ride, naughty pony! Ondolay! Ondolay!"

Sophia opened the gate and I walked forward while she led me to a pail of oats. I asked her for some milk and she said, "No, not before we ride."

Sophia Loren tempts Ronnie into submission.

She threw on a harness and some other horse stuff. I remember her removing her sunglasses from her head to shake her beautiful hair in the wind while she put them on over her eyes. The sun was piercing through her dark strands of hairs; a glow of green flew into my face from the fields behind her, warming my pony senses.

Ms. Loren, still in a pink bikini, jumped on top of me. "Rise, pony, rise! It is time to make you into a horsey!" she whispered into my ear; and so we rode off into the fields of green o'er yonder until I came up over a hill and saw a Road Ranger gas station. I remember shrieking and stopping to a halt as Sophia went flying from my back. Pink bikini and all, bottoms up in the air. My poor Sophia!

Sadly, I woke up.

It was then, in the heat of the moment from waking up from my dream with Ms. Loren, that I read your status update, Chad. To everyone and to Chad, I do care.

Your facebook friend,

Ronnie"

Thank you, Mr. Donaldson, for sharing your dream with us!

Tchad Beale

CHASING CARS: HOW DO YOU GET YOUR CHILD TO STOP?

Originally Published on October 28th, 2012

Rockford, IL - Do you have a problem with your child chasing cars?

If your child continues to chase cars, there is a very good chance he will soon get hit by one; or, even worse, a bus or a semi-truck. This is a serious problem that needs to be addressed. It's best to try and avoid this nasty habit in the first place by not encouraging he or she to chase anything.

How can you accomplish this?

If your child steals something from you, do not chase after him; rather, call the child to you with the "*come here, now!*" command. Reward your child with a kick and a punch to the stomach. End the disciplinary command with a stern but loving, "I SAID NO!"

This basic style of obedience training will do wonders for you and your child's relationship. **Only teach your child to chase what he or she can return to you. Especially if you know it will saves time, money and physical energy.**

All kids and animals like to chase stuff and things; it's in their nature, you can't change facts. From chasing other children to trial criminal chasing, a car is no different than a huge toy to a child. They are not very smart. Children often carry invisible bacteria around, kind of like how homeless people do with their magic bags of money and heroin.

Prevention is the best policy, but what if your child is already a chaser? Here are a few steps to stop this sort of behavior from affecting your family's quality of life:

- Putting in an underground or above-ground electric fence is your best bet.

- If this is not possible – or you would like to have your child outside of your yard's fence with you – you can try using a shock collar with a hand-held control.

- Shock the child when it chases after a car, not after – during.

- Do not say the word "*no*" when you shock your child; instead, try the stomach kicking method again and again and again. NOTE: You want the child to associate the car with the shock and the feeling of a kick with the shock. Vice-versa stuff, ok? If you fail, the child will chase the next car, bus or semi-truck as soon as you are out of sight. Do you understand?

- Some people may think it is cruel to use a shock collar, but it is worse for the child to get plowed by a semi-truck or ran over by a car. Let alone a bus filled with children. Dear Lord.

- Organic Solution: Nothing is better than an open field versus a fenced-in yard. Consider buying a larger house with an acre of land out in the country, away from roads that are well-traveled. Remove yourself and your family from the City of Rockford. Your children's problems with chasing cars may stop naturally. Warning: Your child may adapt itself towards chasing animals.

- If the child starts to wander off the property, or the boundary you set for him, a special collar he or she is wearing can shock him into believing that Santa is coming soon; meaning, it's time for bed.

- Children will soon learn their boundaries to avoid the shock, which teaches them to stop chasing cars.

- Do not–we repeat–do not reward your child like you would your dog, because your child's aptitude for processing obedience learning is not up to a canine's level of obedience and higher emotional intellect. True. Children are brats, dogs aren't.

- If you discover that your child is more likely than your dog to chase as car, semi-truck or bus after obedience training, make your funeral arrangements sooner than later and invest in the highest premium plan of family, health and life insurance. You may see a nice return on your obedience training losses and investments if you purchase life insurance now.

Hope this helps.

Chuck Toncha

THE BEAUTY OF BARRY: CANTALOUPES

Originally Published on November 4th, 2012

Hi, remember me? I am a very handsome man living in an ugly town. Let me share another secret for feeling, looking and tasting good: Cantaloupes.

1. Start every week by buying the biggest, juiciest cantaloupe you can find. Start by skipping breakfast. Every Sunday morning after church, don't go out to breakfast, save your money. Head on home to the cantaloupe. Slice it in half and eat the insides out with a fork. This is important, as you need to leave as much juice in the cantaloupe as possible.

2. When you're done enjoying the delicious natural sugars of the cantaloupe for breakfast, put both cantaloupe halves on a dinner tray along with a very hot face towel. DO NOT cover the cantaloupes with the hot towel. Immediately find an old relaxing chair that you don't mind getting a bit wet in. **Tip:** Bring a lawn chair inside during colder weather.

3. Rest that hot towel on your face for two minutes to open up your pores. Count to one hundred and twenty seconds (if you know how to), and remove the hot towel.

4. Take one cantaloupe halve and rest it on your face for fifteen minutes. Let the juices soak into your skin; gently rub it around. Don't forget to close your eyes and mouth. Count to nine hundred (if you can or know how to). **TIP:** Leave your mouth open if you're thirsty. The juices will benefit your lips and chin, which will make you very delicious and good looking.

5. Repeat with the second half of the cantaloupe.

6. After thirty minutes are up (a total of one thousand and eight hundred seconds), don't rinse your face for another two hours. Take a nap now.

7. Sleep it off and awake rejuvenated. Sunday morning cantaloupe facials and naps after mass can make you feel, look and taste extremely good.

Take it from a handsome man who's always willing to share a few beauty secrets with ladies and other living organisms. Good looking also means good eating and good sleeping. Please take care of yourselves on the outsides first with little things like cantaloupes, and the insides will follow your good-looks into the afterlife.

Til next time,

Barry Seversyn

HOPE ROBS MOTHER PROTECTING SON

Originally Published on November 7th, 2012

Rockford, IL - Nancy Beladonna is still in shock.

"We didn't sleep all last night. I'm tired from crying and looking out my windows. I feel as if Hope is all around us, waiting to rob us again of everything we be working for. We be very upset," she said.

Ms. Beladonna went to the *Buy Things Mart* on Knox Avenue in South Rockford with her son to pick up a few things on Tuesday night. It was an ordinary trip to the store that ended up being anything but ordinary.

"We came back out. I put my sweet son in the car, and then I put the things we bought in the car. I walked around, got in the vehicle, shut the door and there It was," Beladonna said.

She was face to face with Hope.

Her young son was beside her in the passenger's seat. She says the 6-year-old became the target. "*It stared into my eyes and asked that I give my soul to It; and if I didn't, It said It was going to take over my son's brain and future,*" she said. Without hesitation, she gave up her purse. "*I have never had any sense of hope in my body or life and did not want my son having any of It, too.*"

An incident report was filed on her stolen purse, valued at $1000. Inside the purse was cash, ATM cards, Linq cards, food stamps, Social Security cards, marijuana and prescription drugs.

"*We had been running around town all morning. We started at the DMV, we went to the bank, the Social Security office, the Walgreens to get medicines refilled and then to my pot dealer. There was no way in hell I had time for hope, and there was no way hope was going to become a part of Steven's life,*" Beladonna said.

Beladonna says Hope ran toward the nearby *Arby's* restaurant and escaped in a dark-colored minivan. **RKFDP (Rockford Dream Police)** officers pulled prints from Beladonna's car and have high expectations that the surveillance footage from the parking lot will reveal something. "*Hopefully we Hope for clues to It – no pun intended,*" laughed Officer Kellyski.

Meanwhile, Beladonna is still struggling to comprehend why this happened. "*I have heard of Hope arriving at odd times to rob us blind before. Some of my family members have It. It scares me. I don't need It, and my son doesn't need It, either. For fuck's sake, Rockford, keep It away from us!*" said Beladonna.

There was a heated discussion by the RKFDP officers who were at the scene. Officer Kalskd truly believes that the crime Itself, Hope, could be living inside of Ms. Belladonna's head.

Police also laughed about other stuff and things. "*Talk is cheap, and those rumors about It being in Rockford ain't nice,*" said Officer Edlkafhsdjhf.

RKFDP officers and local community believers are still looking for Hope. It's described as a thing, an It, a thief, a real-estate agent, maybe an alderman or a priest, a man or a woman (maybe) from $chaumburg, IL. Maybe It's a wild turkey with a goatee and tan skinned wings, aged around 35 to 40 years old and possibly driving a dark-colored-orange pumpkin plane with a white dot on it.

"*I've been trying to deliver Hope to the people of Rockford since the recession, but they love poverty. That's right!*" said Lord Thomas Derby, whose company is located in prosperous $chaumburg, IL, located 50 miles outside of Rockford.

White collared criminal acts being conducted on a daily basis by our business and government so-called leaders are outnumbering the hiring of jobs per day in Winnebago County. If you see Hope running around rampant, talking and stuff without doing anything of importance to make life better for others, contact your local pot dealer.

Ron Kites

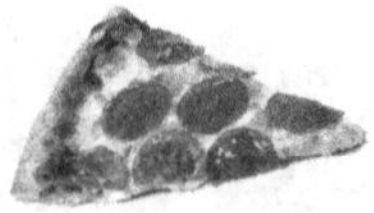

SEXY BALD EAGLE SHOT ON SCHOOL BUS

Originally Published on November 13th, 2012

Rockford, IL – "*It was so cray cray,*" recalls Sally the Squirrel about the day when her friend, Jenny the Balding Eagle, was shot and soaked (almost to death) while they were on their school bus last month.

She says that her visions and recollections of that day are now dominated by senses of confusion and fear. Sally received a water balloon bullet in her little paw, and Jenny was shot in the wing.

"*Everyone was screaming and howling,*" Sally told us by phone. "*First we thought this was a sick joke. The squirt gunman was dressed up as a homosexual monster-buck-video-game hunter. He entered the bus and asked, "Where's Jenny The Bald Eagle, who is Jenny?"*

We didn't know what to say. For one, he had a lisp; and two, she is the only eagle on this bus full of squirrels, coyotes, leopards and lions. How dumb can you be?

The moment she said, 'I'm Jenny," he opened fire on us. With one water balloon bullet, Jenny went down, wings clipped.

It was a very terrifying when he opened fire on the rest of us because none of us were prepared with goggles and swim suits. All I could see was his pink sweater and a bazooka squirt gun. After Jenny went down, he was still there firing bazooka balloons loaded with water and laughing at us.

I got a water bullet stuck around my paw and was wet for days.

Everyone was screaming.

Coyotes started howling.

One of the Leopards tried to attack the squirt gunman. Leaping from the seat, like Leopards often do as jokes towards people on buses, Jimmy the Leopard tried to defend us. Shit got real.

The gunman threw a hatchet at our friend, the Leopard, and then there was leopard blood everywhere! That's when we finally knew something wasn't right. He wasn't here for Jenny.

He came here to soak all of us."

Showing incredible courage, the bus driver drove the injured animals to a hospital. Jimmy the Leopard seems to be ok, but Jenny the Bald Eagle is not doing so well.

Sally The Squirrel is now back home in her warm nest where she is recovering from her soaking hand injury. She remembers pleading to see her father, Noah, on that terrible journey before she fainted on the bus. She does not recall what happened after that, or what she plead for.

Jenny the Balding Eagle is now being treated at a hospital in Beloit, Wisconsin. She was widely known as a campaigner for eagles and hawks' education in and around Dixon, IL, and in St. Paul Westerberg The Great, MN.

In early 2009, Jenny wrote an anonymous diary for ***Bald Eagle Weekly*** about the life and death of a dying breed for her fellow peers who had been banned from attending schools in the early days of America.

Her father, Rotondo, a 4th generation Bald Eagle, believes that education is the only path in life for Jenny and her fellow bald eagles to fly for: "*Education is our hidden power and we must make an effort to educate our balding girl eagles even more than the boys,*" he says.

Sally had one last message to her friend: **"*Jenny, please be happy. Have an ultra-fast recovery. I'd like to see you healthy again. So, beak up and stay strong you silly eagle! Ok? Come back soon so we can go to school together in the spring or fall."***

Reggie "Railroad" Reynolds, Guest Contributor

Rotondo, 4th Generation Bald Eagle
and Father of Jenny the Bald Eagle

MAN BATTERS WOMAN

Originally Published on November 20th, 2012

Rockfart , IL – A mentally challenged husband battered his wife less than one hour after *RKFDP SWAT* (Special Rockford Dream Police Team) officers answered an SOS call at their home. Mick Rickles, 56, battered his wife, Patsy, with a mixture of milk and flour exactly 50 minutes after emergency crews arrived to deal with a 911 call about him.

RKFDP SWAT Officer Jeanine Danielson said, "*When we arrived, Mrs. Rickles was laughing and licking the milk and flour batter from her arms and knees. She said it tasted delicious. Mr. Rickles appeared calm and lucid, but expressed that he wished his wife wouldn't lick his batter off yet.*"

Following the attack, Rickles was found loitering half naked on a motorway embankment saying, "*My name is Inigo Montoya - you killed my father.*"

RKFDNEWS was told by the Rockford school district's famous psychotherapist, The Great Paul, that, "*the milk and flour battering of 44-year old Patsy would have never happened if paramedics had taken Rickles to a mental hospital to begin with – to learn a new recipe for battering women in sugar and eggs with the flour and milk –but, sadly, there are no mental hospitals to take him to since Singer Mental Hospital closed in Rockford, IL, to make way for hope and progress or whatever.*"

RKFDP SWAT officers were investigated as well, but cleared of any wrong doings after details emerged about Patsy Rickles, who stated to officers on the scene 50 minutes before the battering: "*I did not feel in any danger at any time. I axed my husband to dip me in eggs and sugar like I've axed for many times before. But, no, motherfucker dint listen to me again. He prefers to batter me in milk and flour!*"

Mister Jason Belvidere, a prosecuting attorney, said, "*The couple had been married for 5 years after meeting in 2006; and although they had no children, they lived with their puppy and 14 Burmese pythons in Durand, IL, for a short while.*"

Patsy, who worked at *The RKFDP Airport*, decided to leave one of her husbands last year. She moved into a new trailer park home after developing *strong feelings* for a work colleague. However, she missed the home made batter recipes and returned to her other loving chef of a husband, Mick.

Mr.Rickles, who worked at the remains of what is the 11-block long Ingersoll Milling Company on Fulton Ave. as an engineer in a half-lit, asbestos-filled factory in Rockford, was previously arrested and declared mentally unstable to serve time in prison because of his job, which left him and the city in 2001.

He was sent to a psychiatric hospital after he wore his wife's white-pink coat with no clothing on underneath and threatened to set fire to one of their puppy's friends, Steve The Squirrel.

Mick started to feel better and was set free around the same time that Singer Mental Hospital was shut down by the State of IL to free up money for repairing and building professional and amateur sports complexes, or for rebuilding hope, spreading more pride around like anthrax, ebola and other politically-driven myths to force people into living with more fear and whatever.

RKFDP SWAT members arrived with paramedics, but they ended up spending about a half-hour with the defendant talking to him about his mental state while playing legos and dolls with him.

"*They asked him questions about his history with battering. Different recipes for different flavors. He appeared calm and lucid. They said they could force him to go to hospital, and he said he didn't want to go and lit one of the dolls on fire and ate it to prove he was fine. It adds to the tragedy that if he had been taken by the paramedics to begin with, this would have never happened,*" said Officer Giovanni

Danielsonarini.

At 6.51am, a neighbor heard Patsy screaming repeatedly for eggs and sugar. Everyone heard her, even Lawrence Waits who lives three blocks from the scene of the battering.

Waits freely told us, "*I hear that bitch yelling at least once a week something like, 'Dip me in the eggs, polack! Now, now, now! Ok, hurry, soak me in the sugar, Mick! Ohhhh yeah, that's right. Right there!' Some pretty fucked up shit. Whatever.*"

Witnesses say that Mr. Rickles picked up a bucket of milk and poured it all over Patsy in the front lawn. He then poured what appeared to be a bag of flour over her, covering her body, head and face. Patsy began to roll around the front yard like a loaf of bread.

Rickles fled the scene wearing only a T shirt and his wife's Uggs. He was spotted running along a yellow road line, narrowly missed being plowed by semi-trucks driving-by before being detained near the *Bee Moe Better Center* in the heart of downtown Rockford.

He told police: "*I've just battered Patsy like I done battered her and many other delicious women before. My recipe does not call for eggs and sugar, but she keep on axing me to dip her in eggs and sugar. Hail naw. No way. My batter is special the ways it is. Do you like chicken with sugar? I dew knot.*"

The victim's father, Don Bern, said to police: "*I cannot believe Mick has done this to our beautiful daughter. I had no idea they were into kinky stuff, but this is sick. He has always been a good husband, and has never been violent to her in the past, but this is sick. Just sick. Why wouldn't he use the eggs and sugars if that's what my poor daughter wanted? Give the lady what she want, boy. That's right.*"

Patsy took a long shower, and is now recovering at her other husband's trailer park home.

Graham Nickles

CITY
LEGEND
X - Bars
- Coffee Shops
W-WALLGREENS
- Church
Rockford Map
East →
Gordon
Simbo
ROCK

BEE Mo
METRO
CEN
TER
River
pony
jay
←West
sparky

DREAMS RUN AWAY, WE KNOW WHY

Originally Published on November 23rd, 2012

Rockfart , IL – Any dream can run away at any time if the circumstances are right. Believe me, if they're under enough stress, any dream can justify running away. Don't forget the golden rule of chasing waterfalls by TLC: *"Running away is like any action. In order to do it right, you need three things: Ability, willingness, and the opportunity to the sexiest human being ever."*

Let's face it, dreams have the opportunities and abilities to run away every day. All it takes is the willingness to do it. It could be a stressful situation your dream is under, or a fear of receiving consequences for something they did years ago during the war. Or, it could be a power struggle between you and your neighbor for property control of the bushes. It can also be a desire for wanting nothing in life; not even the ambition and know-how to succeed at anything. Some people will label your dreams lazy, and being lazy can hide itself inside of your dreams with material possessions like weed and blow.

Another factor is that dreams often idealize romanticized views of life on the streets in Peru. In reality, it's awful: You're cold, you're hungry and it's dangerous out there on the streets of Rockford in Illinois when you aren't dreaming of living in Peru, Peoria, or Paris.

Dreams often see it as an adventure, the key to freedom, where "*No one is going to tell me what to do.*"

Why Do Dreams Run Away?

Many dreams run away because of drug and alcohol abuse. When dreams and pre-dreams get involved with substance abuse, they may leave home to hide it so that their parents don't find out. These dreams are often worse than their parents know; they want to use the drugs to hide inside their dreams freely and openly. This is the main reason with why your dreams will run away.

In addition to fear or anger, feelings of failure can also cause dreams to leave home. Some dreams run away because it's easier to live on their own than to live in a critical home.

Local one-time dreamer, Steve Chadson, opened up to RKFDNews.com: "*I remember being 15 years old and living in a hallway in the parking lot of the Bee Moe Better Metro Centre in winter. I didn't miss home at all because I felt like such a failure there. Everyone had hopes for me there, that I knew then–and now–I could never accomplish; like jobs, money and healthy children. That shit's expensive.*"

"*Dreaming is overrated,*" said one Rockford resident, Tonto Springsteen. "*I remember being little and dreaming of getting out of here and actually doing something with my talents. Every time I did, the dream faded away–like everything else.*"

Jay Vannigan and Tchad Beale

A LETTER FROM MARIA ALVAREZ-THROMBERGHER TO THE NINJA CROCK POT CORPORATION

Originally Published on October 21st, 2014

October 21st, 2014

Ninja Crock Pot Corporation
C/O: Dr. Lothario Jones the IInd, M.D.
333 Locust Street
Rockford, IL 61103

Dearest Dr. Jones the IInd, inventor of the Ninja Crock Pot,

I write to you to expressing my thoughts about the *Ninja Crock Pot* cooking machine, that I recently purchased from *Home, Bath, Bed, Beauty and Beyond* at your Rockford, IL, location. Lest you prevent your eyes from reading further, by assuming the following words are out of contempt and scorn for the Ninja crock pot, I want to abbreviate your time with a most gracious thank you. What a magnificent machine!

I thawed and pre-cooked a pound of ground turkey with onions (for seasoning) on the stove top this past weekend. After slicing up a few vegetables (peppers, carrots, tomatoes and whatever else I found laying around the kitchen), I threw everything in the Ninja Crock Pot along with a few cans of beans. I also added a half bottle of Wild Turkey Whiskey, a pound of dark chocolate chips, and a liter of Cherry Dr. Pepper. It's my family's special "*wild turkey chili*" recipe.

I set the Ninja Crock Pot on low for 6 hours and walked away to the living room to sit with my new Vizio 50" Smart Television. I enjoyed an entire afternoon of the E-Channel's "*Life With the Kardashians*" marathon. My family arrived during the episode where Kim and Kanye have their wedding (so beautiful!). Everyone sat down with me to enjoy a few more episodes of the Kardashians while eating chili from the Ninja Crock Pot.

Thank you for an incredible day of cooking, watching the Kardashians on the TV, and eating *wild turkey chili* from your wonderful crock pot, the Ninja.

Regards,

Maria Alvarez-Thromsbergher

ANOTHER STABBING OCCURS WHILE ANOTHER EGG SANDWICH IS PREPARED

Originally Published on December 31st, 2012

ROCKFORD OF ILLINOIS, OF THE UNITED STATES OF AMERICA, OF NORTH AMERICA, OF EARTH, OF EVERYTHING ELSE THAT'S LAUGHING AT US - A man has stabbed at least 5 family members, but got great internet deals on stuff and things at BLAH blah blah BLAH BLAH blah blah BLAHBLAH blah blah

BLAHBLAH blah blah BLAH stabbing them BLAH blah blah BLAHBLAH blah blah BLAH BLAH blah blah BLAHBLAH blah blah BLAHBLAH blah blah BLAH hurting poor innocent people BLAH blah blah BLAHBLAH blah blah BLAHBLAH blah blah BLAH police called BLAH blah blah BLAHBLAH blah blah BLAHBLAH blah blah BLAH BLAH blah blah BLAHBLAH blah blah BLAHBLAH blah blah BLAH BLAH blah blah BLAH stabbing them repeatedly BLAH BLAH BLAH but a delicious egg sandwich, not on the menu at iHOP, was prepared by their head chef for a hungry child.

Jay Vannigan

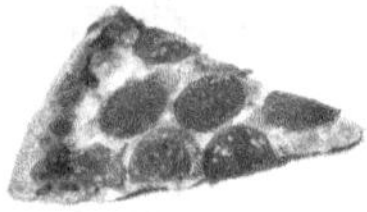

THE NEW YEAR'S FIRST ROCKFORD BABY: LARSON DONTEL SVAYDOHLBERG

Originally Published on January 1st, 2013

Rockford, IL - *Larson Dontel Svaydohlberg* was the Rockford area's first baby, born at 12:00:08 AM on January 1st, 2013. The young male boy was birthed to a single father, *Chadwhick-Keith Svaydohlberg the IInd.* LaQuondathon Smithson-Anderson, the wandering mother of the newborn, was there to give the region its first of many uninsured births.

She was heard yelling at a roomful of nurses, friends, doctors and her baby's daddy during the finale, "*I'm outta here. I needs to find Lisas and Rick. Mommy needs to gets drunk and head to LA – ASAP!*" LaQuondathon jumped up from the surgeon's table and ran out of Swedish American Hospital to the nearest bar to enjoy her first drink in two weeks.

"*There are no reasons for anyone to locate her,*" said the newborn's father's father and the rest of his nice, quiet family.

Chadwick had positive thoughts to share: "*It's for the better of Larson and I that LaQuondathan spreads her party wings while she still can. She had a hard time keeping away from the booze and cigarettes during the pregnancy. Her friends are not good influences. They still enjoy LT's after work with the warehouse guys from WalMart.*

Little Larson and I will wait for her to return with a family's open arms. If she wants to.

My girlfriend, Kacey, and I are taking Larson to ski next week in Baraboo, Wisconsin. Baby's first vacation... maybe we'll move there if LaQuondathon doesn't move back home! Her sister, Julie, says she might stay in LA with Rick, not Lisas. I don't know what to think anymore.

Anyway.

What a wonderful honor to birth Rockford's first 2013 baby!"

Congratulations to Larson and his family from RKFDNews.com and everyone in Rockford, IL.

JoAnne Rankles

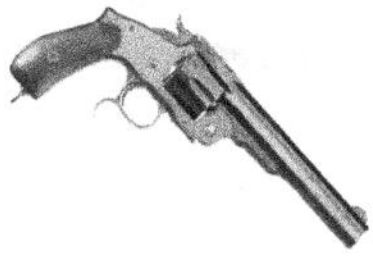

BANGKOK BECAUSE IT'S FUNNY

Originally Published on January 1st, 2013

Rockford, IL - "*Man who go through airport turnstile sideways going to Bangkok is funny joke, ha ha, you know joke? I tale you,*" said Chensworth Johnstonson.

We here at RKFD News had nothing better to do on a Tuesday, so we headed off to the Rockford Airport to ask every man who passed through the turnstile sideways where they were going; and where the first born baby of 2013 was at. **This is what we came up with:**

1. 60 out of the 75 men we tried to interview were crying and walked by with their heads down while ignoring our questions.

2. 5 men tried to scissor kick us in the chest and head. Some went for the knees. Only one man went for our balls – all of them.

3. 4 men tried to bite us while making hissing noises.

4. 3 men said *Vegas* was where they were heading with the baby that they think they might have conceived on the first day of 2013.

5. 3 men declined to comment; but one of those three men offered us a wink and a bottle of spray-on tanning lotion.

Our journey ended with bag of Doritos.
Jay Vannigan

THE BEAUTY OF BARRY: COCK SOUP

Originally Published on February 3rd, 2013

Hi, it's me again, Rockford. I am a very handsome man living in an ugly town. Let me share another secret for feeling, looking, tasting and smelling good: Cock Soup.

My girlfriends ask me all the time, "*Oh my God, Barry, your hair smells so good and your neck tastes like chicken noodle soup – but spicier! Wow, you are very delicious. What in the world is your secret?*"

Thank you for wondering, and here is the answer: **Cock flavoured soup-mix keeps my hair shiny and my neck salty**.

I prefer the spicy cock soup-mix, but feel free to experiment until you find the right cock soup-mix for your skin and hair.

1. **Simply rub it all over your body right after your shower.**

2. **Do not towel dry.**

3. **It's best to take your time, let the air settle the cock soup-mix into your hairs, scalp and skin.**

Like I said, everyone's skin is different. Feel free to experiment with as many cock soup-mixes as you can find, but the bigger the cock soup-mix bag, the better you'll feel about having it all the time without needing more.

Take it from a handsome man who's always willing to share a few beauty secrets with ladies and other organisms. Good looking also means good eating and good sleeping. Please take care of yourselves on the outsides first with little things like cocks' soup mixes, and let the insides follow your good-looks into the afterlife.

Til next time,

Barry Seversyn

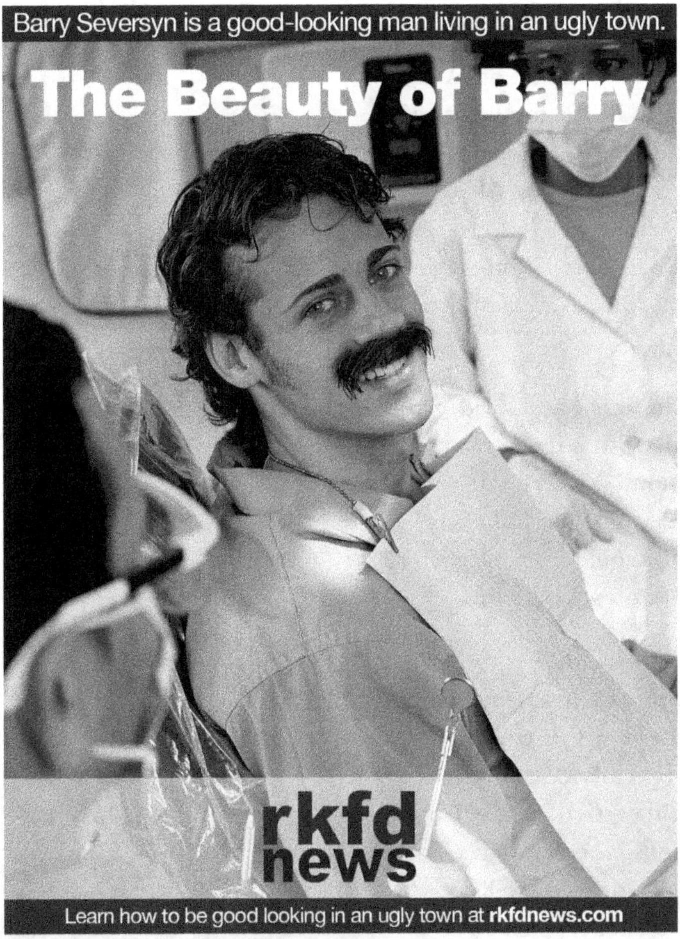

THE BEAUTY OF BARRY: SWEET PEAS

Originally Published on February 17th, 2013

My girlfriends ask me all the time, "**Oh my God, Barry, your lips are so pouty and sweet! Wow, they taste like peas. OMG, you are very delicious. What in the world is your secret?"**

Thank you for wondering. **A can of sweet peas keeps my lips tasting juicy and looking pouty.** Many people prefer injecting botox or animal fat into their lips every few months, but those avenues take lots of money and can swell up your face.

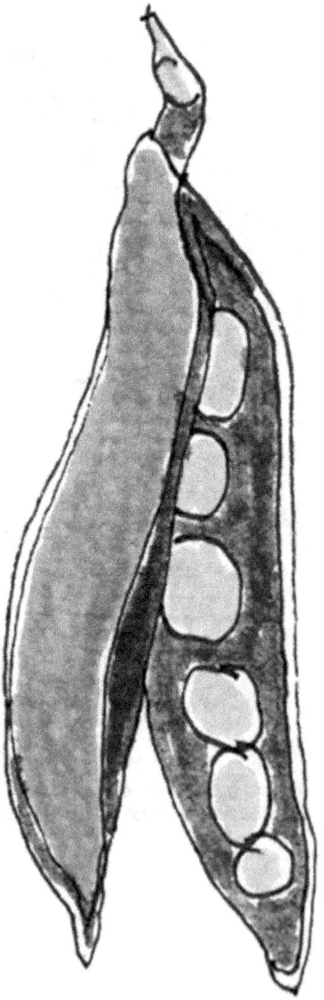

My solution is cheap and delicious with a few important instructions. You'll need to inject sweet peas into your lips every day. You should tell your doctor first you're going to do this to yourself.

If you proceed to inject sweet peas into your lips with my beauty tips advice contained within this article, know that I am not responsible for any accidents, sicknesses, constant swelling, allergic reactions, penile dysfunctions, blurriness, knee jerking, vomiting, diarrhea, muscle pains, face twitches, ear aches, bleeding gums, and anything that would cause your body to malfunction–and in the worst possible situation, death– to the point that you need medical assistance.

Some people are born beautiful without health concerns. That's me in a nut shell – or, shall I say, a sweet peapod shell.

On average, one can of sweet peas will get you through the week. Budget for 4 cans a month and clean hypodermic needles with a syringe for each injection. If you desire that delicious, jumbo, pouty lips look: Up your cans of peas budget to inject as many sweet peas into your lips on a daily basis.

"Does it hurt, Barry?"

The first week will hurt, but try to inject in different spots of your lips each time. Never forget to use clean needles as well.

"How do I inject sweet delicious peas into my lips?"

Stuff your syringe with sweet peas. It is important to choose the proper syringe for the administration of injectable sweet peas into your lips. Shove those little green balls of beauty into your lips. You determine how pouty your lips will be with delicious sweet peas.

Take it from a handsome man who's always willing to share a few beauty secrets with ladies and other organisms. Good looking also means good eating and good sleeping. Please take care of yourselves on the outsides first with little things like sweet pea injections, and let the insides follow your good-looks into bed and the afterlife.

Til next time.

Barry Seversyn

BATTLE FOR MIDDLE EARTH CLIMAXES TO A PAUSE

Originally Published on March 15th, 2013

Rockford, IL - The battle for Middle Earth reached a climax in Rockford last night. Everyone moaned to a pause and checked their smart phones for a few minutes. Minutes are now hours.

Instagram feeds became overloaded touch-screens with photos of doggies, foods, face crème ideas, studio equipment, live bands, landscapes, cityscapes, roads and a selfies.

Facebook news feeds streamlined the latest thoughts from Middle Earth's grid servers to iPhones and Androids. Everyone put down their forks and drinks to check their online lives.

Many decided to tweet their thoughts on their whereabouts with Twitter. Others decided to retweet nonsense from the latest people to fall prey to Taco Bell's after-hours food poisoning plan.

Some of us watched and waited for Middle Earth to explode once more, while a few members of our staff were talking to each other, face to face in real time. Our two most internationally famous journalists, Chief Tchad Beale and Jay Vannigan, talked to each other about northern California girls:

"*Northern California girls say everything happens for a reason, Chief. A northern California girl told me to throw away my parka and now I am freezing,*" said Jay. "*I know, Jay. Parkas keep me warm, too*"' replied Chief Beale to Mr. Vannigan.

The majority of Rockford shared their thoughts and feelings online when Middle Earth came to a climax. A long moan was heard before the stand-still as hands fumbled for their smart phones and anxiety pills.

We'll have more to report from the Battle for Middle Earth when the smart-phones – or the people using them – die. Whichever happens first.
Ronnie Thompson

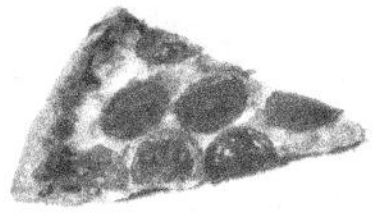

CARP LANGUAGE DISCOVERED, PREVENTS CRIME

Originally Published on March 18th, 2013

Rockford, IL – Imagine two carp swimming in the Mighty Rock River. Hear the series of clicks, whistles and whines coming from each; much like a conversation in Dolphin language. It seems as if one carp can call another carp specifically by mimicking the distinct whistle of that other carp.

It is fascinating, and it's happening right now in the Rock River: A river that cuts through the City Of Rockford, IL. A river that separates amateur crime from professional crime, but never muting the carp's newly discovered crime preventative language.

"*These whistles actually turned out to be criminals names. They're abstract names, which is unheard of in the animal kingdom beyond people because fish are a class unto themselves,*" said Randall Brown IVth, a local author behind a new study on the Carps' relationship to Criminals behaviors and patterns.

"*I hope my discovery will assist the RKFDP (Rockford Dream Police) contain crime before it occurs. We will be able to predict the next home invasions, violent drug deals, and pizza delivery thefts by listening to the carps talk to each other,*" he added.

Mr. Brown the IVth instructed us further with a passage from a historical document. In 1653, Izaak Walton wrote in *The Compleat Angler*: "*The Carp is the queen of rivers. A stately, a good, and a very subtle fish; that was not at first bred, nor hath been long in England, but is now naturalized and advanced in Rockford of Illinois, in the United States of America.*"

Walton the IVth often turned to his studies to discover carp communication patterns right here in the Rock River Valley of Hopes, Dreams, Visions and yes, Sounds. The sounds of human and fish advancements crossing river currents right here in our lovely city!

RKFDP Chief of Criminal Communications, Sgt. Lino Valsuvio, hopes this recent discovery earns the support of the city's money handlers. "*With the carps' crime tips and additional funding from our city's most intelligent economic planners and politicians, we can stop crime sooner. We still need their money to station a few men out on the river to listen to the carps talk to each other. This is a 24/7 operation that could save lives.*

Thank you, Mr. Randall Brown the IIIIth."

We'll know less when you know more or less than we think we know.

Jay Vannigan

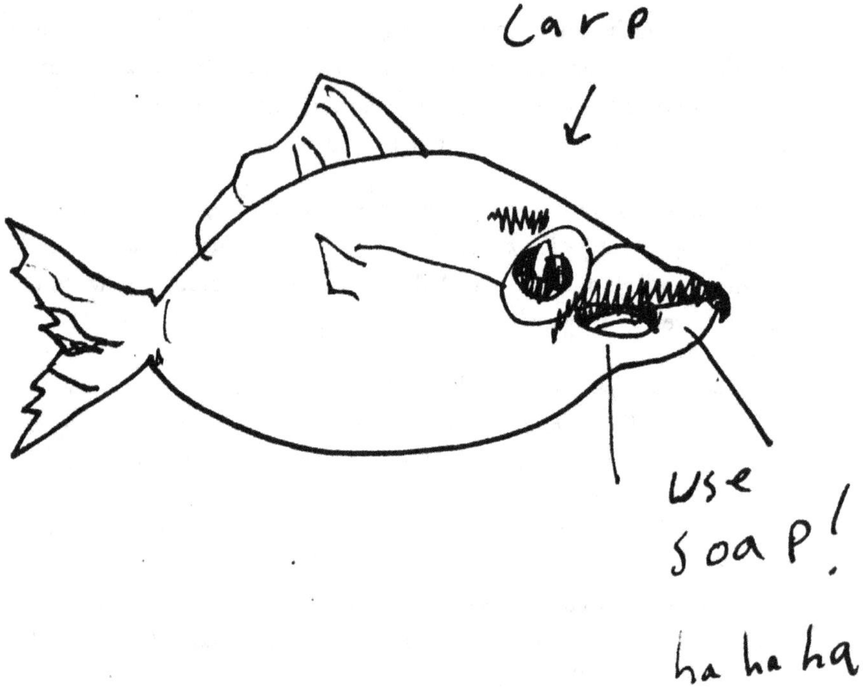

CARP, NATURE'S PROTECTORS

Originally Published on March 18th, 2013

Rockford, IL - You've seen it on *Carpy the River Fish* and other popular TV shows: Carps rescuing humans from drowning and keeping them safe from hypothermic harm in warmer waters.

Does it really happen? The answer is YES, dummy, or I would not have anything to report on. Example: A *Beloitian* tourist was rescued by three carp while being attacked by man-eating catfish several years ago in the Mighty Rock River.

A drunk man had stopped his boat near the Piss Island Peninsula so that several passengers could watch carp playing. Three of the passengers decided to swim with the carp, and one stayed a little longer than the others.

To his horror, he was bitten by a catfish and more were coming. Suddenly, three carps placed themselves between the drunk tourist and the catfish, smacking the water with their tails and making weird noises with their big lips. They drove the catfish off so that the man could be rescued.

In 2004, a group of swimmers were confronted by a ten-foot great white shark off the northern coast of New Zealand. A pod of ocean carp herded together and circled the swimmers until the great white shark fled. There are several similar incidents involving carp and great white shark battles in Australia.

Another case that occurred closer to home was reported in Lake Deep Furberger, WI. Twelve divers were lost for thirteen and a half hours. They were surrounded and protected by carp who repelled many eels and snakes that live in that region's body of water.

A rescue boat showed up to rescue the divers, and the carp pod led the sailors to where the twelve divers were. Carp leaped up into the air in front of the rescue sailors, jumping into the boat, attaching themselves with their lips and pointing with their tails.

According to old sailor stories, carp often act outwardly by assisting their sea mates through the night, as they are known to do with endangered ships and sailors who are lost, horny and drunk.

We can't talk to carp, therefor, we can't truly fathom what their motives are in these situations. It is, however, very possible that they are indeed trying to help and protect fellow organisms in the river and guide them to safety or rescuers. If this is true, it means that carp are the only animals besides humans which show true altruism.

Jay Vannigan

GREAT REVIEWS FOR CARP FESTIVAL

Originally Published on March 24th, 2013

NICK-A-LAS CONSERVATORY EARNS NATIONAL ATTENTION FOR PET CARP POOL AND SIN-A-SIPPY CARP POND

What is it? A historic pet carp pool, known as the *Sin-A-Sippy Carp Pond*, presented by Nick-A-Las Conservatory. **Ranked #1** of 20 attractions in the Chicagoland area by Carp Magazine. Voted **#6 out of 50 carp landmarks in the United States** for urban fish conservatory projects.

Type: Carp Pond and Pet Carp Pool

Owner Description: *'Carp Magic'* is a trading name for the iconic *Pet Carp Pool Pty Limited. Carp Magic* is located on the beautiful grounds of the new Nick-A-Las Conservatory.

Useful Information: Activities for young children, activities for older children, fishing boats and beer kegs for men, male strippers and wine coolers for women.

Carp Fan Comments:

"Fantastic and interactive!"
Reviewed 20 March 2013 NEW

I loved the fact that they love promoting 'conservation through interaction'. I do think it works! This is like my 5th visit to the pool and I enjoy it every single time! Only dislike is that it kinda has become a little commercial and thus Carp kisses and Duck kisses are held in places where it is difficult to take nice personal pics.And there was goose poop everywhere.Also the mural inside the place was horrible looked like an out of towner did it not local at all! Not Original Not RKFD.

"Never been closer"
Reviewed 18 March 2013 NEW

We went to the Pet Carp Pool in 2012 and after the first surprise that we could just roam around and play with the Carps whenever they felt like it, we fell in love with the place and the relaxed atmosphere. It was marvellous to be so close to those beautiful fish, my daughter could not be dragged away even after we had spent 5 hours there. It's worth every penny - an adorable concept!

"Wow! Such great value"
Reviewed 2 March 2013

A++++++++++++ experience. would highly recommend. The show is great, the staff are wonderful and they really care about conservation and caring for their Carps and ducks. With my YHA membership card I got in for $28.. Great value, so much fun and I got kisses from a carp!

"Re-living my childhood..."
Reviewed 10 February 2013

I couldn't even tell you how excited I was to stumble across this on my work trip to RKFD recently. I remember my parents taking me here when I was like 3 or 4 and have all the photos at home. This started my love affair with carps. I was just sooooo amazed that you can get so close to these beautiful creatures. Like literally stand by their pool and touch them, just amazing. Would be a great day out without kids if you were on a holiday or even for a few hours break if you were travelling through.

"Worth doing"
Reviewed 2 February 2013 via mobile

Great day out, well couple of hours anyway, for $33 u can't go wrong, got to pet the ducks and carps as much as we liked, the wife was very happy with the "kisses", the photos were $28, which some people would find expensive, but I thought was reasonable even on a budget cos were traveling for a year, and it goes back to the city for the arts and stuff , although, they are optional, u can take your own photos at no cost. My only complaint was the trainers were not very informative and I think stoned or drunk ,I only wish I had the money 2 swim with em! I've been to sea world in 4 country's and this was better because more hands on. Well done guys!

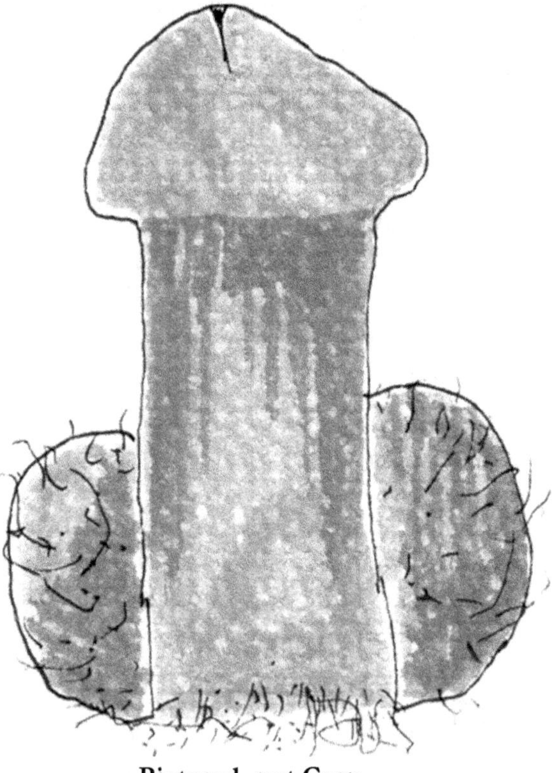

Pictured, not Carp.

MAP OF THE MOST FERTILE FOREST CITY CRIME REGION REVEALED

Originally Published on March 30th, 2013

Rockford, IL - A map revealing the most fertile crime region in the city of Rockford, IL, was released by RKFDP (Rockford Dream Police) earlier today.

The areas on the map that are highlighted in gray below show the highest amount of crime.

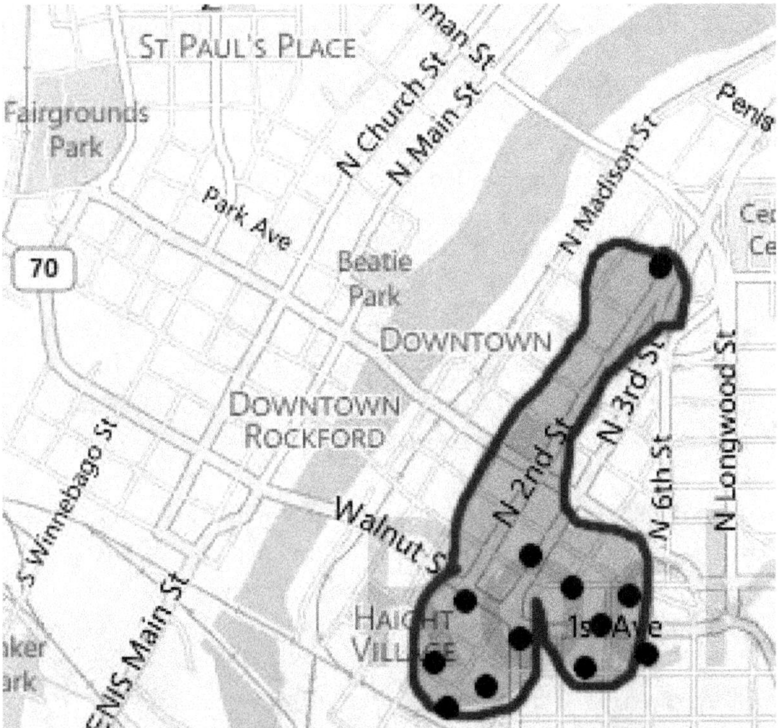

Crime rates were calculated using six crimes: Vandalism, domestic assault, residential burglary, yelling real loud at your neighbor, child abuse, animal neglect and lastly–our favorite–battering your spouse in Barry's cock soup mix before dunking your lover in a bowl of flour while in bed before making dinner for each other or your children.

The black dots represent specific incidents and locations in Rockford where fertility amongst the unemployed, drunk, and stoned is especially high.

You will know more when we learn less about gluten-free products.™

Gilbert Grebner

CARP TRAINING AVAILABLE

Originally Published on March 31st, 2013

Rockford, IL – *Midwestern Carp Trainer Academy* is a cutting-edge program designed to give you the skills needed for a successful career in the **Carp Training** field. This program is created and taught by professional trainers with extensive experience.

This 5-day training workshop is based on the popular DVD series, ***Carp Training, Volumes 1-4***. Students will interact with professional trainers during training sessions with carp, catfish and geese! Also included in the workshop is a ***Swim with Carp*** experience.

The cost is $10,000, and includes special coffee with Mayor Barry Morrison at a coffee house of his choice. Your carp and coffee experience will be professionally videotaped, edited and burned to DVD by one of our many videographers.

Training Carp can be the career for many people's dreams and visons[2]!

Nearly everyone has read about carp or seen them on television. A few people may have been fortunate enough to observe them in their wild habitat. Many of you have probably seen trained carp in person at an aquarium or carp show.

The intelligence and creativity of carp makes working with them challenging and a lot of fun. Watch trained carp gracefully perform various behaviors on cue! The trainer's job may look easy, but as you'll learn from our popular DVD series, it is not.

If it seems as though the trainer "*directs*" and the carp "*performs*," think again! What you don't see in the DVD series is all of the time, planning and expertise that goes into this unique kind of carp-human-DVD-TV learning relationship.

PROGRAM BENEFITS:

- Receive personalized small-group training.
- Understand the science and mathematical application of operant conditioning and temporal lobe aquatics.
- Prepare yourself for the future.
- Create a competitive animal training resume.
- Learn to become a successful team member and learn that failure is going to happen but you will always have your friends.

PROGRAM INCLUDES:

- 5-day Carp Training Course
- Carp Training Packet
  2 DVD Set
  Orange Hard Hat
  Reinforcement Pouch/Metal Panties
  Carp Training Whistle
  Carp Taser
- Online Carp Interaction with Professional Carp Trainers
- Hands-on Carp Experience
- Carp Speech Therapy

- Baton and Death Hook (See fig.2 on page 444)
- Swim With Carp Experience
- Behind the Scenes Access to Carp Bars
- Carp Language Certificate
- Carp Badge
- Eagle Claw Carp Fin Necklace
- Brown Pants with Gold Carp Skin Trim
- Carp Coffee Mug
- Autographed Picture of Tom Cruise (Top Gun Era)

Jay Vannigan

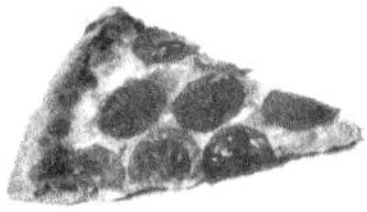

MAN WEARING SNORKEL ATTACKS CLERK

Originally Published on January 15th, 2013

Rockford, IL – A man described by witnesses as wearing "*a smoking jacket, snorkel, and some sort of large gold belt buckle*" attacked a clerk at the *Git Sum Market* on the corner of South Main earlier this morning. He did not want money according to eye witnesses, but he did want the clerk to dance with him. She initially said "*Yes.*" He also asked her to "*Put some skittles down my snorkel, Lady,*" before he attacked her for refusing to.

More on this story when we are ready to start typing again.

Jay Vannigan

SCRAMBLED AND BATTERED

Originally Published on June 2nd, 2013

Rockford, IL – An estimated 14 eggs were scrambled to death while 12 slices of toast were battered this morning on the far west side of the city. "*Breakfast was absolutely delicious!*" said Keith.

No more information is available at this time, and we doubt there will anything else to add to this if everyone holds down their breakfast.

Jay Vannigan

POPE COMING TO ROCKFORD

Originally Published on June 16th, 2013

Rockford grant me the strength to handle life' ups and downs,
And to be horny all the time even when I am sick.

Rockford grant me the courage to stand up for what I believe in,
And to be horny all the time even when I am sick.

Rockford grant me the answers to my questions,
In order to find something to finally believe in.

Rockford grant me the piece of mind I so desperately need,
And to be horny all the time even when I am sick.

Beloit grant me all the cotton panties I can stuff into my mouth,
Because I am dirty.

Rockford grant me the guidance to be able to succeed,
In order to be whatever it is I want to be.

Rockford, I need you now and forever.
Please hold me, tight.
Scratch my back… harder.
Pull my hair… harder!
Squeeze my butt… harder, Rockford, harder!!!
Oh Lord, yes, Rockford, right there!

Thank you, Rockford, I'm yours.

Ladamian Winfrey Vannigan

FEMA PROVIDES SOAP TO ROCKFORD

Originally Published on June 26th, 2013

Rockford, IL – City-wide flooding has occurred because of strange thunder storms. These strange storms are possibly signaling that it's the end of earth as we know it. The positive news is that it has provided FEMA a reason to finally help our local region. They who have been suffering from financial and demographic damage for years can finally celebrate because the government is here to help.

"*Rockford is getting a well-needed bath. The entire city is cleaning itself up thanks to Mother Nature. To assist the city-wide cause, FEMA is providing pallets of specialty soap cubes to help locals clean themselves from decades of corruption, nepotism, alcoholism, under-achieving, over-meeting and drinking the coffee combined with laziness, stupidity, obesity, self-entitlement, ego, pride, greed and insanity,*" said FEMA's acting Director of *Midwestern Emergency Assistance*, James Chillsderson.

No word yet on whether or not hot towels will be provided.

Local scumbags, Alderman Cletus Tontorelli and Mr. Don Anwah (the CEO of *AIR RANGER GAS STATION*), beg to differ with FEMA's help. "*Me and my frands n' famlee love things the way they are in the Rockford 815. Likes I keeps on telling it to these educated girls and boys looking for jobs at my company, y'all don't like my requirement? Git da hail outta town with your smarty pants degree. Speedboats or bust, y'all!*"

RKFDNews' staff members won't turn down the specialty soaps, and would like to thank FEMA for acknowledging how dirty, pathetic, corrupt, nepotistic, drunk, high, lazy, contradictory, unintelligent, fat, self-entitled, inept, ego-driven, proud, greedy and insane our city's leaders are. We will wait for help; from the top of the pile with businesses to government, all of the way down to the bottom of the mudpile where we wait for our soaps.

Please use the soap and read this book.

Chief Tchad Beale

CATFISH KILLS CHILDREN

Originally Published on July 11th, 2013

Rockford, IL - John Rigsby left family members clinging to a capsized pontoon while they were being attacked by a sea of stinging catfish. Rigsby swam at least 200 feet before climbing rocks on the Rock River shoreline. Wandering through pitch black air, Rigsby tried to reach help at the first lighthouse he saw.

"*He came to the wrong house,*" said Angela Berthenhauser, whose barking doggie awakened her. Angela refused to get out of bed and crawl through her quiet house in Rockford at about 1 a.m., Wednesday morning. No, instead, she chose to use her bedside intercom talkie-walkie to screen her after-midnight guest.

There stood Rigsby waiting, soaking wet and barefoot, while he imagined his family drowning to death after being snacked on by naughty catfish while Berthenhauser questioned him from the comforts of her bed.

"*He said, 'I've been swimming since sundown. I need help,'*" she said. "*I did what every woman does, I protected my house! I unlocked the door from bed and ordered my doggie to attack. He was trying to say his family was in trouble, but all I heard was 'I am going to hurt your dog and eat your face!'*"

Berthenhauser realized something was wrong when the screaming and barking stopped.

The 46-year-old Rigsby was a member of a fishing party near Piss Island, a popular spot amongst river dwellers. A storm brewed earlier that day, and their boat took on too much water. "*It toppled at about 7 p.m. on Tuesday night,*" said Berthenhauser, recalling the conversation she had with the helpless stranger.

Berthenhauser called 911 immediately but the Dream Police and Firemen arrived about 3 hours later. Riggs was rested, dried off and bandaged from all of the catfish and doggie wounds by then. He was taken out on a rescue boat with area firefighting volunteers to search for family members when the sun rose.

"*There were a few storms in the area and the boat turned upside down,*" said Sgt. Brian Almera at the River Resources Police. "*Mr. Rigsby swam to shore. These people are very lucky. No one was injured enough to be ruled dead.*"

Contessa Rigsby said that their boat capsized about two miles from shore, and drifted about five miles in a parallel direction.

"*I've never been so happy to see search boats in my life,*" she said Wednesday by telephone. "*It took him five hours to swim ashore. He had to stop and drink his last 3 beers he had for thirst and rest, then swim. We clinged to the side of the boat and got stung by the catfish in the dark,*" she said.

Perhaps someone would have eventually located the fishing party even if Rigsby had not swam for help. "*If one thing is for certain, wearing life jackets saved their lives,*" Sgt. Almera said.

"*They're lucky that they put life jackets on,*" he added. "*The life jackets are what saved their lives. I can't restate that fact enough. Please understand that wearing your life jackets can save a life or two while catfish attack you in the Rock River.*"

Rigsby's 9-year-old niece, Emily, called her uncle a "*real stupid head.*" She added that the next time her family goes fishing, she'll do what normal people do. "*I'll go fishing, but but but but but not in a boat. Nope. I go fishing from the shore like normal people dos.*"

Things to Know: Certain life jackets are designed to keep your head above water and help you remain in a position which permits proper breathing and beer drinking. Don't let those floating cans of beer get away.

To meet U.S. Coast Guard requirements, a boat must have a U.S. Carp Coast Guard-approved Type I, II, III, or V life jacket for each person aboard. Boats 16 feet and over must have at least one Type IV Taser, a throw-able device like a tomahawk or spear with a float-like thing attached to attack catfish with. All states have regulations regarding life jackets for elderly or children; you can only purchase these at city hall.

Adult-sized life jackets will not work for children unless tied really tightly around the head or midsection. Special life jackets that look like turtle shells are available for people with no arms or legs. To work correctly, a life jacket must be orange, fit snugly, and not allow the child's chin or ears to slip through for air.

Life jackets must also have a flash light and some sort of weapon attached for safety; like catfish spray or a small electrical fish bait to shock the catfish away. Life jackets should be tested for wear and buoyancy at least once each year. Waterlogged, faded, or leaky jackets should be burned. The remains – ashes – should be smeared under the eyes like a football player.

How Do Life Jackets Save Lives?

- When capsized in rough water certain life jackets will talk you through your bad experience and whisper positive thoughts in your ears.

- When sinking in unexpectedly heavy river conditions (like the Rigsbys faced), they will allow you to enjoy what may be the last few hours of your life on earth with a beer while you float.

- When thrown from the boat as a result of a collision, a life jacket can prevent you from getting a boo-boo.

- When injured by spears or hooks from dirty river hooker pirates, life jackets expel a secret cream to heal your wounds.

- When unconscious from carbon monoxide fumes, the jacket will act as an oxygen tent and save you.

- When tossed into freezing water by a drunk river captain, you will float laughing at the drunk captain while you drink his beer.

- When thrown off balance while peeing from the back of the boat, the jacket will protect your genitals and allow you to finish urinating once you land in the water.

- When unable to swim because of heavy drinking at the Lombardi Club, there is nothing the life jacket can do for you but pray that you awaken soon to realize that you're still alive in Rockford, IL, after the alcohol wears off.

Jay Vannigan

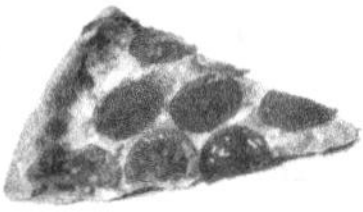

NAKED MAN RIDES DOWN WEST STATE STREET ON SCOOTER WITH GIANT CROSS

Originally Published on August 30, 2013

Rockford, IL – Millions of people are bitten by elderly women every year in the United States. Most of the bites aren't serious, but many bites do result in time lost from work, a pile of medical bills and mental suffering. Children (especially boys) tend to receive a disproportionate share of the bites. Rockford accounts for about 1/3rd of most of the elderly women biting attacks.

The law responds to this phenomenon in different ways.

1. First, all states have laws that make elderly people owners responsible under certain circumstances for injuries and damages that the elderly can cause.

2. Many states follow an old principle, a rather misleadingly one called the "*one free bite*" rule. Broadly stated, this rule says that "*if an elderly woman injures someone, the elderly's owners aren't legally responsible until they had reason to know that that person might cause that that that kind of injury.*"

3. In contrast, other states have laws on the books (elderly biting-statutes) that make owners liable no matter what they knew or didn't know about the elderly's temperament before the biting episode takes place on a naked man's butt carrying a cross on a scooter down West State St. in Rockford, IL.

Jay Vannigan

"*Oh my, did you see his buttocks?*" said Sister Linda to Sister Teresa. "*No, Sister Linda! Did you see the size of his cross?*" said Sister Teresa to Sister Linda

FATHER YES SON

Originally Published on September 19th, 2013

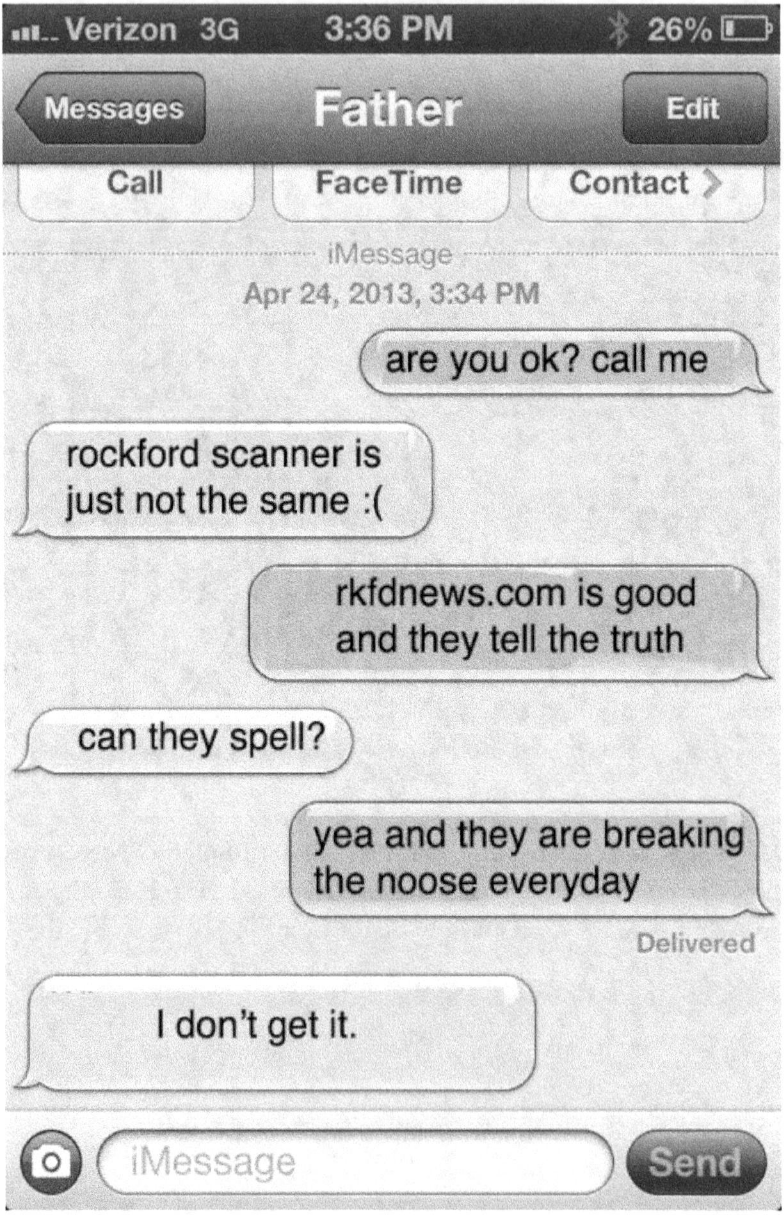
Verizon 3G
3:36 PM
26%
Messages
Father
Edit
Call
FaceTime
Contact
iMessage
Apr 24, 2013, 3:34 PM
are you ok? call me
rockford scanner is just not the same :(
rkfdnews.com is good and they tell the truth
can they spell?
yea and they are breaking the noose everyday
Delivered
I don't get it.
iMessage
Send

BIG BALLOON GO POP OVER ROCKFORD, RIVER SHARKS EAT FAMILY OF 6

Originally Published on October 7th, 2013

PREFACE: On October 7th, 2013, we reported the horrific story you're about to read below. Google Analytics reported that 9,951 people from the Rockford, Illinois, region shared, liked, commented and argued the details of this story within 24 hours after it was posted on our noose breaking web site. Multiply 9,951 by however many fake friends and connections your ridiculous account profiles on the internet are associated with and therein resides the meaning to this book's title, *Believe*.

Rockford, IL – A large hot air balloon carrying a family of six took off from the west side of Rockford on Sunday morning. It attempted to fly to the east side of Rockford when problems arose.

A crowd of east-siders gathered in awe at the corner of East State and Perryville to protest the family's attempt to land in the Best Buy parking lot for a lunch-time picnic. The balloon was forced to retreat back to the west side of Rockford after fearing that the east-siders would shoot their balloon down with their AK-47s, bows n' arrows and cannonballs.

Upon attempting their overhead return to the west side of Rockford with their picnic basket and children in tow, the balloon went pop over the Rock River near the Auburn Street bridge.

Traffic stopped for three hours while thousands of people gathered on the bridge to witness the balloon's descent onto the river.

The scent of the food trapped in the hot air balloon's picnic basket lured three great brown river sharks from below the murky water towards the drowning family of six. People watching from both sides of the Rock River and from atop the bridge, screamed and cried for the unknown west-siders while the three great brown river sharks ate them.

There are no survivors as of this morning.

JoAnne Rankles

COMMUNITY REACTS TO THE HORRIBLE NEWS THAT RIVER SHARKS ATE 6 PEOPLE IN THE ROCK RIVER.

Source link: http://rkfdnews.com/big-balloon-go-pop-over-rockford-river-sharks-eat-family-of-6/

54 comments Write a comment

NobodySpecial 13 October, 2013, 05:02

Knew it was fake the moment they said AK's. Patriotic east siders all roll with AR-15's for when they wanna shoot at something.

Reply this comment

> **RKFD NEWS GOD** 14 October, 2013, 09:01
>
> You were sold by the mentioning of guns. Let's thank the Lord that the title of the article and the photo didn't alert anyone first. What a funny town!
>
> **Reply this comment**

Dan 13 October, 2013, 00:50

The sad thing there are retards who actually believe this! Read the story it's got hair on it.

Reply this comment

> **RKFD NEWS GOD** 14 October, 2013, 08:59
>
> Retards need something to believe in, Dan. It's a good thing for us that Rockfordians will believe anything and settle for so little on a daily basis from their leaders.
>
> **Reply this comment**

Scholarly 9 October, 2013, 14:44

River shark grilled on a sesame seed bun is one of my favorites.

Reply this comment

> **RKFD NEWS GOD** 10 October, 2013, 13:59
>
> So delicious. A real original Rockford sandwich!
>
> **Reply this comment**

Anon 8 October, 2013, 13:20

It's ok, he was talking about RCKD News. Those guys are liars.

Reply this comment

Anonymous 9 October, 2013, 12:04

Seriously want to cry from these stupid people! First of all, do you believe everything on the internet? Then you must also believe Mr. Rogers was once a sniper and Captain Kangaroo was a spy. Have you ever even seen a hot air balloon? The only thing it can control is gaining altitude, the rest depends on gravity and the wind. And have you ever heard of "brown river sharks" in the river in your LIFE?! I feel like I'm going insane that people are believing this story! This story is not what is wrong with Rockford, it's you (mostly a-hole Bill) this guy probably also believes the contrails are the government drugging us..."Wildbill" I believe I've heard your BS spilled on the AM airwaves also. If you hate Rockford so much that you moved then why do you care so much to post your garbage on anything Rockford related! Grow up and shut up!~

Reply this comment

Anonymous 10 October, 2013, 17:15

Look it up

Reply this comment

Pamela 8 October, 2013, 11:41

I think this is awesome! Rockford's own verison of The Onion!
Oh, and this is to the dumba$$ otherwise known as Bill Brown. You are an ignorant bigot who is also flat out stupid if you thought there was one ounce of truth to this story. Not only are there NO sharks in the Rock River, but you cannot steer a hot air balloon. It's people like YOU that give Rockford a bad name.
The End.

Reply this comment

Pookie 8 October, 2013, 11:30

Rockford's main problem, as evidenced by some of the people on here, is that it takes itself WAY to seriously! Relax!!! Is your groundwater making you sick and paranoid? Move!!! Is it the stress from the gang warfare in your own backyard? DO SOMETHING ABOUT IT!!!! Be a part of the the solution! and fucking learn to have a laugh. This is a fun site, it is not meant to be taken seriously! DUH.

Reply this comment

Pookie 8 October, 2013, 11:27

bill brown spell so good! it's a joke, tool!

Reply this comment

Pookie 8 October, 2013, 11:26

wow. nobody has a sense of humor anymore. Except the folks who run this site. Thanks for being awesome.

Reply this comment

Bill Brown 8 October, 2013, 07:02

NOTHING BUT CRACKHEADS AND NASTY ~~*(Edited out by RKFDNEWS.com because the word you used is not allowed here, WildBill8218 at IP address 50.158.163.170)*~~ IN ROCKFORD

Reply this comment

DisNigguh 8 October, 2013, 07:23

Says Rockford's Biggest Whore

Reply this comment

Bill Brown 8 October, 2013, 07:29

i didnt know your mom posted

Reply this comment

Bill Brown 8 October, 2013, 07:28

unlike rockford news what i post is true

Reply this comment

RKFD NEWS GOD 8 October, 2013, 10:24

We don't edit out public comments much at all but we had to today on this article page. NOTE: You can misspell, intentionally capitalize, agree or disagree with us (as if we care either way), share your emotional intardenet opinions, get political and childish all day long to poke buttons at others to rile them up on our site in the name of Symbol but to share intentional-or-unintentional racial slurs like the ones that 'Bill' shared publicly are not allowed– unless you're blatantly attacking white, rich, greedy and corrupt good ol' boy $cumbag Rockfordians (and surrounding areas all over earth) with the truth– to break the noose.™ Please watch your cracker fingers & stale saltined thoughts, Bill.

Remember: No racial slurs allowed unless you're making fun of whitey or good ol' boy Rockford-styled $cumbags. You don't like it? Go on over to Rockford Scanner, Our City, Our Story or Go Rockford to see how far you get with your opinions.

Thought so.

Chief Beale
Editor

Bill Brown 8 October, 2013, 07:00

HEY RCKD NEWS IF THIS IS A FAKE ARTICAL LOOK ME TO SUE YOU FOR FALSE AND MISLEADING ARTICLES

↩ **Reply this comment**

RKFD NEWS GOD 8 October, 2013, 10:18

Thank you for sharing your emotions with us on the intardenet but we'll see how far you get in a court of law after you research our site further.

↩ **Reply this comment**

Anonymous 8 October, 2013, 12:19

Bill Brown.

↩ **Reply this comment**

Kayla 8 October, 2013, 00:39

The people who actually believed this story make me more worried about my future.
Firstly, the headline was poorly written. "Big Balloon Go Pop," I might've believed that if I was in kindergarten.
Secondly, the photo beneath the headline displays flags from the Labor Day event once known as On The Waterfront. This event did not take place this year due to financial issues.
Thirdly, the police would not take kindly to a mob wielding AK-47s (which are expensive!) and bows and arrows.
Just some obvious facts.
LOL, morons.

↩ **Reply this comment**

RKFD NEWS GOD 8 October, 2013, 10:19

Kayla,
Yes. Be worried because we are worried as well for our future but stop to laugh at the Rockford roses that have gathered here!

Thank you for breaking the noose with us on the intardenet!

Chief Beale
Editor

↩ **Reply this comment**

Pookie 7 October, 2013, 22:05

Pookie say rockford all falling into river one balloon after another. Rockford so smart in smarmy religion-slathered drunk and smug way that is rarely duplicated. How you do this rockford? Elizabeth and becki are leaders? must be rockford presidents! must be strippers! You win!!!!!

↰ **Reply this comment**

Pookie 7 October, 2013, 22:03

Becki rocket science. Becki so smart, must have go to rockford university! Elizabeth call troll????? Does that mean she calling self? Clearly troll.

↰ **Reply this comment**

Bill Brown 8 October, 2013, 06:53

YOU SOUND LIKE YOUR FROM ROCKFORD YOUR A FOOL

↰ **Reply this comment**

DisNigguh 8 October, 2013, 07:25

Bill Brown , You Must Be From Rockford

↰ **Reply this comment**

Bill Brown 8 October, 2013, 07:27

not even close fool

↰ **Reply this comment**

Bill Brown 8 October, 2013, 07:35

and you must be ~~***(Edited Out – Unfunny Racial Slur)***~~.. if i did live there i can always move but your ~~***(Edited Out – Unfunny Racial Slur)***~~ for life... lol

↰ **Reply this comment**

Spartian 8 October, 2013, 10:39

*You're

↰ **Reply this comment**

Pookie 7 October, 2013, 21:50

Elizabeth, who is troll? You call self? You mad genius. Becki- you think all lies? Also so smart. You go college? You go Rockford University? So fucking smart all you womens!!!!!!! You defend rockford for great and thriving metrocity that it is!

↰ **Reply this comment**

Anonymous 8 October, 2013, 12:16

ROR!

Reply this comment

fuckno 7 October, 2013, 21:41

Becki is rocket scientist! All lies Becki! SO smart!!! You go college? You go rockford university???? AMAze-balls!!!!!!

Reply this comment

DisNigguh 8 October, 2013, 07:22

I Know Right! Becki, You Go Rock Valley? You Pass Classes? Watcha Major Is?

Reply this comment

Gail George 7 October, 2013, 21:22

I read this and thought oh this poor family, how horrible, I did not know this was a parody of news, till I read comments, I thought it was real, I had never heard of this site. Now I know , LOL

Reply this comment

RKFD NEWS GOD 8 October, 2013, 10:25

We broke your noose!
Thank you for sharing your thoughts with us on the internet!

Chief Beale
Editor

Reply this comment

Anonymous 7 October, 2013, 21:12

That's 5 minutes of my life that was a total waste I will never get back!

Reply this comment

RKFD NEWS GOD 8 October, 2013, 10:26

That's what she said.

Thanks for spending time with us on the internet!

Chief Beale
Editor

Anonymous 8 October, 2013, 12:13

"Like" button: Pressed.

Reply this comment

Anonymous 7 October, 2013, 21:11

I feel entirely uneducated right now and pretty embarrassed. I can't tell if this is a joke or not since this is the first time visiting rkfdnews. If I read this on the Onion, then I would totally understand!

Reply this comment

Anonymous 7 October, 2013, 21:17

Nevermind. I take this back cause I'm an idiot. THIS IS REAL!

Reply this comment

Anonymous 7 October, 2013, 21:08

This is phenomenal. Thank you for enriching my day!

Reply this comment

Anonymous 7 October, 2013, 20:48

This is why I moved. That city is dying and this is a good example why.

Reply this comment

Anonymous 7 October, 2013, 19:52

Thank you for reporting on this tragedy when no other news outlet will. Prayers go out to the families involved. This is horrible. Rockford ought to stop wasting money on dumb things like school lunch programs and hire divers to kill those river sharks.

Reply this comment

---

dan 10 October, 2013, 15:11

Lmmfao river sharks Roflmmfao, this is too funny n people r actually eating it up. 😃

Reply this comment

Elizabeth 7 October, 2013, 13:23

RKFD NEWS GOD
OCTOBER 7, 2013 AT 2:59 PM
We prefer you take the time to leave comments and ask us questions with your internet emotions. Those kinds of buttons provide people the options to click before reading. We are bringing back truth, justice and literacy to the poor, uneducated Rockford region.

____

Wow, you're not very good at putting facts together are you? I'm sure this was a war of east vs west side of Rockford... Take your crap and feed it to yourself.

Truth-BS,
justice-are you a super hero?
Literacy- oh you help people read?
Poor- hmm so we are all poor? And if they are how do you help them?
Uneducate- so you are a doctor too?

Super classy work, take youself and get off that horse!

IM CALLING TROLL

Reply this comment

RKFD NEWS GOD 7 October, 2013, 18:33

Thank you, Elizabeth, for sharing your emotions with us on the intardenet but we have no idea what east side vs. west side war you're commenting on besides the war going on between your heart and your brain. We love you and thank you for attacking us with emotions on the internet. The truth is true but your noose cannot be broken- hang in there, you'll get it!™

Chief Beale
Editor

Reply this comment

Dr Larry 7 October, 2013, 23:30

Wow! Only the intellect of a Dr. could detect this sarcasm. Good investigative work Dr Elizabeth!

Reply this comment

Anonymous 7 October, 2013, 18:18

Only Rockford would attempt to report something do lame

Reply this comment

RKFD NEWS GOD 7 October, 2013, 18:34

Your emotions are our tears of laughter. So lame, not "do lame".

Reply this comment

MaryAnne 7 October, 2013, 14:08

Where are the "Thumbs Up – Thumbs Down" so we can vote on this???

RKFD NEWS GOD 7 October, 2013, 14:59

We prefer you take the time to leave comments and ask us questions with your internet emotions. Those kinds of buttons provide people the options to click before reading. We are bringing back truth, justice and literacy to the poor, uneducated Rockford region.

Becki 7 October, 2013, 17:07

Would have been better if the picture was from Sunday which was windy and rainy. And it was not reported on the evening news at all, plus no picture of balloon in the river. So I say all lies.

RKFD NEWS GOD 7 October, 2013, 18:35

Did you actually take the time to remind our staff of the weather? Thank you for sharing your knowledge with us on the intardenet!

Chief Beale

Reply this comment

Write a Comment

Thank you for spending time with us on the internet. Please waste more time and energy by sharing your internet emotions below:

Enter your comment here...

POORK TOWN: ARTIST STABBED BY AN ANGRY EAT-LOCAL FAN AFTER ENJOYING RED LOBSTER'S CHEDDAR BAY BISCUITS

Originally Published on October 21st, 2013

Rockford, IL – An extremely famous Rockord artist, Randy Warballs, was stabbed to death with a fork in broad daylight by an angry *eat-local* fan in the Red Lobster parking lot this afternoon.

Witnesses said that the lady, an *eat-local* activist, approached Mr. Warballs yelling, "*I caught you! I knew it. You are a piece of shit. I will kill you now with my local fork that I stole from a local restaurant of which I support with my local money. You don't eat local, Randy! I will kill you now*!"

Randy Warballs laughed at the lady while proceeding to open the door to his Mercedes Benz. Laura Comgobbler was there and saw what happened next:

"I think Randy thought she was joking or being proud, like many Rockfordians enjoy pretending to be. He turned around to leave thinking there was no harm. That's when she lunged at him, stabbing him at least 38 times in the back with a fork, going deeper and deeper with each hit. It was so gross. Randy fell on his face to the pavement laughing. I think he yelled something, too."

What did he yell? "*I think he said, 'Mmmm! Red Lobster es soul delicious. Hahaha. Eat my dick, Rockford!" Hahaha... I don't know."*

Wow. Ok, well.

Sources inside the Red Lobster restaurant say that Mr. Warballs enjoyed a dozen Cheddar Bay Biscuits before his untimely death. No charges are being made against the *eat-local* lady murderer, because no one knows who Mr. Warballs is related to. The city of Rockford has been trying to shut Mr. Warballs up for years and this comes as a blessing to the entire community.

Ron Kites

POORK TOWN: COMMUNITY PRAYERS ANSWERED, PORTILLO'S COMING TO ROCKFORD

Originally Published on October 14th, 2013

PREFACE: On October 14th, 2013, we reported the horrific story you're about to read below. Google Analytics reported that 14,009 people from the Rockford, IL, region and beyond shared, liked, commented and argued the details of this story within 24 hours after it was posted on our noose breaking web site. Multiply 14,009 by however many fake friends and connections your ridiculous account profiles on the internet are associated with, and therein resides the meaning to this book's title, *Believe*.

***Poork Town* is a special series from RKFDnews.com that focuses on what makes our community's egos, stomachs, necks, legs, arms, butts and heads so large, poor and proud.**

Rockford, IL – Gerrard Himmis, 30, has been praying for a Portillo's restaurant to come to Rockford for at least 20 years:

"I have prayed everyday for a Portillo's to come to Rockford. I am one of many Rockfordians with a body that needs Portillo's to sustain the pride I've worked on with my community. I cannot tell you the tears I cried for Jesus and Rockford when I heard my prayers were answered. I will be the first one waiting for the first juicy beef and sausage combo with peppers, a large fry and chocolate shake."

The popular Chicago area eatery, owned by Dick Portillo, has been receiving these prayers for years on Facebook and through an online petition site that a few proud locals are responsible for. We tried to contact Dick for a statement but we're pretty sure our email ended up in the Portillo's spam folder.

Where is the Portillo's being built at you're wondering? We have no idea, Rockford; and honestly, like we give a fuck. Please take pride and comfort in the fact that your prayers are answered because more fast food is on its way!

You will definitely learn more when we know less.™

Ron Kites

COMMUNITY REACTS TO THE NEWS THAT PORTILLO'S IS COMING TO ROCKFORD!

Source Link: http://rkfdnews.com/fat-town-community-prayers-answered-portillos-coming-to-rockford/

32 comments Write a comment

Jergin Fjord Janspork 2 July, 2014, 13:02

The junk in Rockford's trunk is about to get bigger. Hooray Portillo's!

Reply this comment

DLG 2 July, 2014, 10:54

This post is months after I posted on this subject....no Portillo's started anywhere in the vicinity of Rockford. Soooo, that makes above 'knowers' not really knowing about one coming. Keep praying! LOL

Reply this comment

> **RKFD NEWS GOD** 2 July, 2014, 15:11
>
> Actually, the joke might be on you, too. This article was written last October of 2013. We make jokes and prayers come true. ;)
>
> Reply this comment

foley 2 July, 2014, 00:57

If you want a good italian beef try s&s subs in belvidere or marcos's in rockton. You won't be disappointed

Reply this comment

bptr 30 June, 2014, 18:30

Praying for a Portillo's? You have some serious mental problems. I am guessing you weigh over 300 pounds too.
Here's an idea: learn to cook real food at home.

Reply this comment

> **RKFD NEWS GOD** 2 July, 2014, 15:18
>
> Don't worry, our staff prayed for you today, too.
>
> Reply this comment

Kimberly hamm 16 January, 2014, 01:32

PORTILLOS IS TAKIN OVER!!!!!!!!!!!!!!!!!!!! OMG I CANT WAIT...BUT ITS SO GOOD I HAVE EVEN TRAVELLED 2-3 TIMES A YAER JUST TO HAVE IT FOR SURE...BEEF A ROO SUCKS, EVERY DAMN BEEF PLACE HERE SUCKS!!! COME ON BABY SHOW'EM HOW IT IS DONE!!!!!!! LMAO

Reply this comment

Pookie 22 October, 2013, 10:24

South Beloit Sammy, re: how you cannot wait to "be the first" to "pop a boner" in the parking lot of Portillo's...are you going to fuck Portillo's? Have sex with a hot dog from Portillo's? We suggest you find a human and unleash your boner-ness with them. Not a restaurant.

Reply this comment

MaryAnne 22 October, 2013, 10:20

Just visited the construction site – go see for yourself all you doubters, haters and unbelieving fools!!!

Reply this comment

Anonymous 31 October, 2013, 07:34

Where's it being built ? LOVE Portillo`s !!!!!

Reply this comment

Howdy Peterson 16 October, 2013, 08:47

Tom & Jerry's is "OK" depending on which one you go to. The one on East State Street is a dumpy health hazard. Last time I walked in there, I looked around and left. The one on 173 (no relation to the one on East State) is much, much cleaner, very well kept, and the food is "OK".

Truthfully, I go to Spanky's over Tom & Jerry's and Uncle Nicks. The food is about as close to Portillo's as you are going to get (without being Portillo's). The only downside is that nearly everyone working there looks like they are on work release from prison. But, they make great gyros. Just don't make eye contact with anyone while ordering. Law of the "Concrete and Iron Jungle" here, folks. Just stare at your shoes and take your gyro however it is that they tell you you're getting it, and DO NOT look at them in the eyes!.

Reply this comment

David Slaymaker 16 October, 2013, 19:02

Personally,I think Spanky's sucks. Tom and Jerrys (totally agree with the 173 comment) is far better IMO. Uncle nicks is just highly overrated I feel. I really reccomend checking out dog world in Beloit, WI. Better best Gyros and italian beefs you can get in my book!

Reply this comment

Howdy Peterson 17 October, 2013, 10:26

Thanks for the Dog World reference, David. I'm going to check them out. I'm always looking for a great Gyro!

Reply this comment

Trevor Franklin Michaels 16 October, 2013, 04:09

I called the register star and they confirmed that portillos starts construction in late March/early April. Do your research people.

Reply this comment

DLG 15 October, 2013, 20:36

Well, kids, its a wait and see, isn't it. Then you can battle about your daddy's restaurants and who knows what is what. I, for one, hope it is true. That "contract", for whatever reason, should never have been signed by Portillo's. Was Beef A Roo that intimidated? Their menu can stand up to competion.

Reply this comment

Anonymous 15 October, 2013, 17:33

The story states they have no idea where it is being built. Years ago a manager at the Crystal Lake location told me they already own property in Rockford. They would not build here because of the permit/zoning hassles.

Reply this comment

South Beloit Sammy 15 October, 2013, 12:12

Cant wait to pop the first boner in the parking lot!

Reply this comment

Ron 14 October, 2013, 22:19

Now get a Gino's east

Reply this comment

> **Humply Boooooooooooogaz** 16 October, 2013, 08:37
>
> It would be Geno's West if it came to Rockford. Why, you ask? Because it would be in West Rockford? Of course not, silly. It would be because we are West of Geno's East.
>
> Reply this comment

MJW 14 October, 2013, 21:50

LoL @ Tom & Jerry's. Your "restaurant" is as good as closed once Portillo's opens.

Reply this comment

God 14 October, 2013, 21:37

Tom and Jerry's huh? What exactly are you smoking??? Once Portillos opens you can say goodbye to all the other pretenders.

Reply this comment

big ed 14 October, 2013, 19:27

T.js dont have nothin on portillos

Reply this comment

Joe 14 October, 2013, 19:13

They are coming, I work with the construction company that is building their restaurant

Reply this comment

Anonymous 14 October, 2013, 22:10

There will be no Portillos near or in rockford I called five different Portillo's locations talk to the managers there will be no Portillos in or near rockford

Reply this comment

Ben 15 October, 2013, 07:27

I'm guessing you chose to remain anonymous because if people knew who you were they'd ask you how much time do you have on your hands to call 5 managers to confirm or deny the existence of a freaking Portillos.

Reply this comment

nina 15 October, 2013, 10:06

there is a agreement with portillos to not built in the Beef a roo territory. This story and this website is all fake

Reply this comment

Thomas 16 October, 2013, 04:14

Nina is a hater. Her dad must own beef of Roos and is scared of all the money he won't have that my dad has. They can put yummy beef and sausage in heartland career mall and I would only have to drive 10 minutes! So excited!

Gerri 14 October, 2013, 18:14

They are not coming to town. my father is a restaurant owner and i know that they cannot come here because they signed a contract with beef-a-roo. so keep dreaming. Try Tom & Jerrys. Their food is similiar to Portillos if not better! Trust me! You won't regret it. 3 Locations in Rockford, Belvidere, and Machesney Park on 173. :):)

Thomas 14 October, 2013, 19:26

My dad is also a restaurant so I know that you are wrong. The beef of roo contract expired this year so stop being beef and sausage hater because your dad is not the only restaurant and my dad makes more money. Portillos yum!

Holly 14 October, 2013, 20:31

Tom & Jerrys is disgusting!

Anonymous 14 October, 2013, 22:07

Tom and Jerry's is no comparison to Portillos

Anonymous 15 October, 2013, 01:27

Tom and Jerrys is good...Great service and quality food, but cant hold candle to Portillos....

Reply this comment

Write a Comment

Thank you for spending time with us on the internet. Please waste more time and energy by sharing your internet emotions below:

Enter your comment here...

POORK TOWN:
ROCKFORDIANS PETITION TO MAKE KFC ORIGINAL RECIPE THE STATE BIRD

Originally Published on October 15th, 2013

Poork Town **is a special series from RKFDnews.com that focuses on what makes our community's egos, stomachs, necks, legs, arms, butts and heads so large, poor and proud.**

Rockford, IL – While many congressmen in Illinois return to their constitutes to handle pressing topical matters in politics, it seems that no one is above the influence of the fast food marketing industry.

"*I don't care if it has 'Kentucky' in the name,*" stated petitioner Carl Belway. "*It's delicious. Are you going to tell me that Illinois isn't delicious? It just makes sense.*"

Last week, Mr. Belway and about 45 proud, fast-food goers met up in Congressmen Todd Nunzulo's office to state their case:

"*At first I couldn't believe what I was hearing,*" stated the congressmen. "*However, they made their case clear. They brought in a couple buckets of fried chicken from KFC, and it was dynamite*!"

The petitioners have hit a roadblock, as chicken isn't necessarily considered a veritable bird by opinion of the masses. One person who is opposed to the change in state bird laws is school teacher, Anna Jergensen. She has gone as far as creating her own online petition which would limit the usage of the word "*bird*" to "*animals who have wings that can fly for distances greater than a mile.*"

"*What they're talking about is semantics. We're talking about herbs and spices,*" Belway quipped. "*If you can deep fry a Cardinal and make it taste this wonderful, then by all means let's not only keep it as the state bird, but add it to the value menu.*"

Congressmen Nunzulo wouldn't comment on any future decision he might push for, but did admit that it would probably take a bipartisan committee to decide the outcome. Nunzulo is prepared to follow up on legislation as long as he is able to take a couple buckets of KFC's fried bird down state to Springfield, IL.

Gilbert Grebner

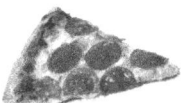

JAMES THE WET PUSSY CAT MAULS ALEJANDRO THE LATIN KINGS SERVANT

Originally Published on October 25th, 2013

Rockford, IL – News broke over the scanner last night that screeching and screaming was heard in the northwest neighborhood near Huffman and Riverside streets. Gang warfare has ruled the streets at night, thus causing the community's fears to rise. As of today, sources have confirmed that an angry Wet Pussy Cat murdered a Latin Kings Servant.

The RKFD Dream Police landline phone operator told us: *"The dream force is grateful for any man, woman, child or animal that helps us fight the war on drugs in Rockford while we await our budget plan to be approved for hiring more officers to assist with rebuilding community safety and fear."*

James the Wet Pussy Cat also called into tell us, "*Wuzz lickin' myself before going nigh night and Alejandro be trippin' wit his frands. I toad dem to shut up and day dih-int. Dat mother f*cker wuzz in my way to my pillow so I maul that b*tch. James da Wat Pussy Cat need some sleep y'all.*"

Ok, there ya have it.™

Chief Beale

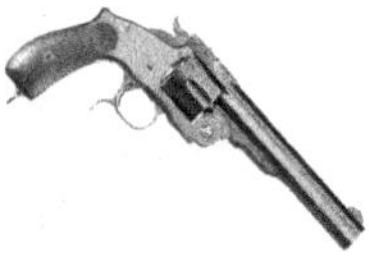

A HOW-TO GUIDE ON HOW-NOT -TO GET YOUR BABY REPOSSESSED

Originally Published on November 10th, 2013

Rockford, IL – Nobody walks out of a hospital with their little newborn baby thinking it could be repossessed. Things happen.

Parents fall into unforeseen financial hardship and don't have the funds to cover the monthly expense of a child. Things happen: The loss of a job, an unexpected drinking binge, overpriced hookers and video game gambling addictions can quickly make it impossible for the owner of a new or used baby to keep up with payments to the hospital.

The hospital and finance company can repossess the baby if you fail to keep up. Barring any procedural violations, they have every legal right to take your baby if you prove to be as irresponsible as most Rockfordians have shown to be after making a baby.

Hospitals often live up to the stereotype of committing fraud against their customers, leaving them with a baby that isn't worth nearly as much as they paid for in the beginning. It's difficult to justify making a large payment month-after-month for a baby that is constantly requiring attention and time away from work. Why would someone keep paying for a baby that's constantly at the doctor for checkups and shots? What's the return-on-investment for babies that go upside down right away?

One reason to keep paying the hospital is to have leverage. If the parents still have possession of the baby, and can keep it from being repossessed, they may have a strong Baby Fraud Case against the hospital. By suing the hospital and finance company, they may be able to get back their 3 day hospital stay and any other money that was invested into birthing room expenses.

Regardless, if someone falls behind on payments because they lost their job, or are mad because they did not finish high school, the hospital can still repossess the baby. **These are a few important tips on how to stop a baby from being repossessed.**

Keep in touch with the hospital.

When the parents choose a hospital and subsequently get financing, the finance company is equally liable for the terms of the contract. Simply falling behind on payments and crossing your fingers that your baby won't disappear in the middle of the night is not the right approach when trying to stop your baby from being repo'd.

The finance company can work with the parents of the baby to get their payment reduced for a period of time in order to get caught up on the hospital loan.

Parents who call the hospital to let them know when to expect a payment, and how much they can expect, are much less likely to have their baby repossessed. As with credit card companies, hospitals have the abilities to work with their debtors when it comes to the repayment schedule.

In the United States, repossessions are carried out pursuant to state laws that permit a creditor with a security interest in babies to take possession of those babies if the debtor defaults under the contract that created the security interest.

Many consumers mistakenly believe that they are legally entitled to a "*grace period*" that prevents hospitals from repossessing babies until the payments are a certain number of days overdue. In reality, however, grace periods are non-compulsory business practices that have been adopted by most consumer lenders to steal the baby back while you are drunk and passed out after a long night out in Rockford with your frands.

RKFDNews will have more on this and other stories sooner than later.

Chiefs Vannigan and Beale

ROCKFORD BUSINESS TIP: START FEEDING HOMELESS NOW

Originally Published on November 18th, 2013

Rockford, IL – You might not read about this life changing story in your local newspaper, but homeless men and women are already making decisions about which back yards and trash cans they will visit this winter.

What can you and the community do as the days grow shorter and the sun sleeps sooner?

1. For starters, tell the less fortunate people in our community right now that you want their return business when the serious side of winter comes around.

2. Don't shun away potential customers from your trash cans and alleys, invite them to come back when the first morning freeze takes hold of their cardboard beds and concrete pillows.

3. Those with nice homes and fresh garbage who don't start feeding homeless people until severe weather arrives may be missing out on a great business opportunity.

4. Tell your neighbors–but not all of them–because you want the business.

5. Fall is the season to begin, and even though garden co-ops and leftover tomatoes are plentiful, the homeless customers may not spend much time around your garbage yet. The ones that do visit backyards in autumn are scouting. They need to be ready when cold weather hits. One woman was well acquainted with our feeding station well before winter arrived.

6. If you wait until colder weather arrives, the homeless people that you hope to convert into daily customers may not ever realize what you have to offer. Rockford's homeless veterans can't afford the luxury of exploring your cans once the cold air comes to blanket their souls. They must go where they know there will be a payoff; behind restaurants and dumpsters at the mall or downtown behind Octane, Wired and City Hall. They might not discover your feeder all winter even though it is abundantly supplied.

Start offering provisions now, this list will help you prepare:

WHAT FOODS TO OFFER & OTHER POSITIVE MARKETING TRICKS:

- Leftover foods (that you made too much, don't cook with the homeless people in mind) and moldy bread is a great start.

- Try some old fruit; dented cans of soup that have questionable or faded expiration dates are ok.

- One of the best ways to get homeless people back into your yards is by providing unfrozen water; preferably the bottled brand, *Fiji* (homeless women love it because is the most expensive). Replenish the homeless customers with Fiji daily for returned profits. Sometimes water is harder to come by in winter than food because they homeless can't drink from the river unless they dig a hole. Many accidents have occurred this way and we advise that you advise them to drink your Fiji water instead.

- Old refrigerator food and dinner scraps: Be sure to put that food in a garbage can or two where you can see it from your expensive dining room seat and bay window. Enjoy your warm dinner and wine from the comfort of your toasty, warm house, so that you can watch them eat.

Don't worry about your foods remains if you have to be gone from your home for awhile during winter. Homeless men and women are used to having a food source disappear. They won't starve because of your lapse. They can – at the very least – retrieve a couple of meals digging through your neighbors garbage, too. It might take them a while to rediscover your yard when you return, but they'll be back.

Do as we would and soon you'll be ready to open up your own seasonal business from the comforts of your own back yard. It's ok to feel good about yourself, Rockford.

Jay Vannigan

ICE CREAM MAN SERVES UP 22 GALLONS OF PEPPERMINT CHOCOLATE JESUS

Originally Published on December 2nd, 2013

Rockford, IL – The city's favorite ice cream man made an unexpected stop tonight at *St. Charles' Field of Hearts Church, Inc.*. In honor of the holiday season, the ice cream man showed up during halftime of the Monday night prayer vigil to share his newest flavor, *PepperMint Chocolate Jesus.*

The congregation gathered around the ice cream man and he delivered.

Lisa FaChulio, mother of three, told us, *"The ice cream man topped himself. PepperMint Chocolate Jesus is exactly how I imagine my Lord to taste if He were a chocolate, peppermint, flavored ice cream! My kids loved it more than the Pink Bubblegum Virgin Mary Sundae he served us last week at church."*

PepperMint Chocolate Jesus was served in waffle cones, cups, bowls and paper plates. All of the paper plates has a hologram of Jesus on them. Some of the congregation's whitest Christians optioned to have it scooped directly into their hands, because that's what they've been taught to think about what the Lord Almighty would do.

A fight broke out between an angry *New Orleans Saints* fan and a snarky *Seattle Seahawks* supporter, but the ice cream man stopped it before a riot broke out. Everyone in the church clapped and thanked the city's ice cream man.

You will learn more when we know less.™

Ron Kites

MR. LOBO NAILS GUITAR SOLO ON METALLICA'S HIT SONG "*ONE*" AT WHISKEYS

Originally Published on December 16th, 2013

Rockford, IL – Mr. Don Lobo has been rocking out to good times with his buddies in their popular Metallica cover band, ***Lars Matters,*** for years. However, nothing tops the guitar solo he nailed on their improvised version of "***One***" by the metal rock and roll legends at ***Whiskeys Bar*** *on North Main Street in Rockford* this past weekend.

His bandmate and vocalist, Lance Reynolds, screamed, *"Oh God, please help me,"* before the epic, *"Darkness imprisoning me"* part. That's when Mr. Lobo took off on the steel horse he rides. The crowd yelled in appreciation when he gave way to his drummer with an echoing E-flat chord on his V-neck Telecaster. Niles Fostgrins's drum rolls added to the crowd's excitement.

Jerry Nooks said, *"Crushing. I am crushed, dude. I've never heard Mr. Lobo play like that before. I've seen this band 1,000 times since 1991 and I can tell you that that was his finest moment. Fuck dude. Epic. He nailed the solo on one of my favorite Metallica songs!"*

Lars Matters has been selling out bars and taverns for years in the northern IL region. They'll be playing at every bar on the east side of Rockford, and in Roscoe, every coming weekend. Catch them while you can or whatever; stay at home where it's safe and watch HBO instead.
Gilbert Grebner

Halfway to nowhere.

This is a good time to consider whether or not you want to read the rest of this book. Maybe you have something better to do? Have you shared a photo of yourself, your baby, pet or food on the internet today? How about your feelings? Have you shared those on the internet today with hashtags like *#blessed, #grateful, #soap, #porridge, #yolo, #wholeque, #oh and #whatever*? What about your children? Have they said something interesting in the last few hours that you've been contemplating about sharing on the internet? Yes? No? Would you prefer to eat a bucket of fried chicken while watching American talent shows on one of your many televisions? Do you want to find a video link on the internet of that amazing performance you just saw on your home television to post, tweet, and say something inspirational about to your fans, friends, stalkers and family? Are you going to tell all of us what it meant it to you and how it made you feel? Are you going to shop for something online? Do you like meat? Or, are you a modern day vegan on a fat free, sugar free, low sodium, gluten-free diet? Do you make dietary exceptions for pizza, turkey, fried chicken, big bananas, creamy peaches, iced cream and tacos?

It's up to you, do whatever you want to.

FREE PARKING PASSES

CLIP THESE OUT TO PUT IN YOUR CAR AND DRIVE DOWNTOWN. PARK ANYWHERE. TIP: MAKE PHOTO COPIES, SHARE WITH FRANDS, PARK EVERYWHERE. EXCELLENCE EVERYWHERE.

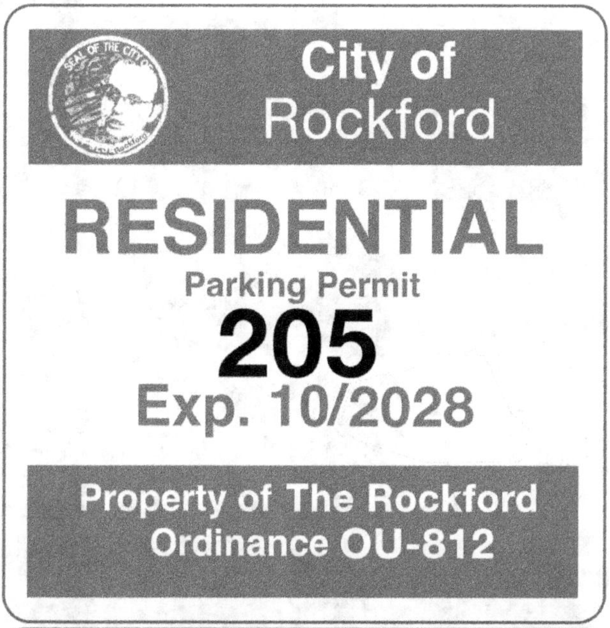

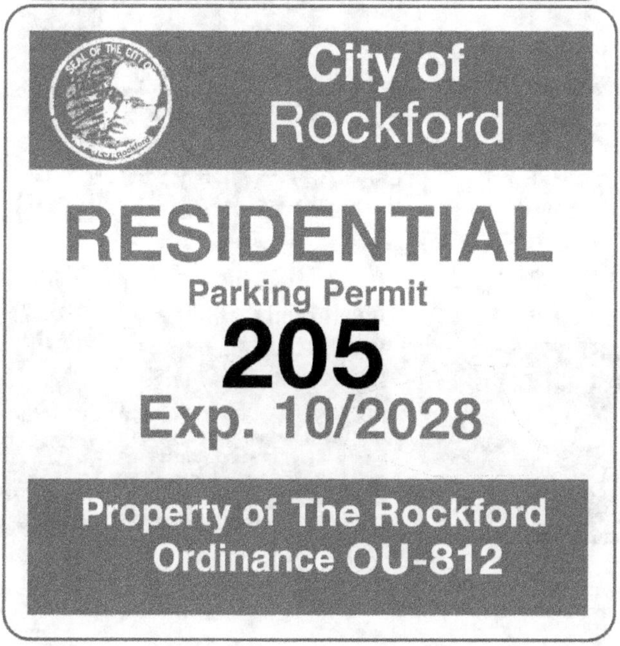

2 robberies, no arrests

ROCKFORD — Police looking for individuals sible for robbing two p Sunday. The first robb urred shortly before

ment at the scene.

Man who hitched a ride robbed at gunpoint

ROCKFORD — A ma who along with a comp ion, accepted a ride in

Group to show graphic abortion pictures today

ROCKFORD — Members of the Pro-Life Acti League will be out on st corners today showing and graphic pictures o

the screwdriver.

Man shot in leg

ROCKFORD — A man w shot in the leg at 8:19 p.m Sunday in the area of Ferg son and Loomis streets. He and another man w

ford.edu.

Suspect arrested in Abreo burglary

ROCKFORD — Police responding to an alarm at 3 a.m. Sunday at Abreo restaurant, 515 E. State St., arrived in time to catch a man leaving the back door.

ext. 117.

Felon arrested on weapon charge

ROCKFORD — Police found a loaded handgun when they raided a residence Friday in the 1500 block of Seventh Avenue

Man seriously injured after being shot

ROCKFORD — A 21-year-old man was shot about 6 p.m. Thursday in the area of South Main and Illinois streets.

Police said the victim

Armed robber, habitual criminal sentenced

ROCKFORD — A man wh pleaded guilty to armed ro bery and being an armed habitual criminal was sen enced to prison terms of

815-963-7867.

Rap video shoot ends in bloodshed

ROCKFORD — Filming

Monday, August 6, 2012

LOCAL BRIEFS

Man arrested after crashing vehicle into house

ROCKFORD — A man is under arrest after crashing a black sedan through a guard rail and into a house about 9:45 p.m. Sunday

MUST READS

Meth busts appear unrelated but raise concerns

ROCKFORD — A pair of unrelat methamphetamine manufactu busts has raised concerns amo cal law enforcement about the tial for the resurgence of the da ous drug. Unlike other drugs su

Rockford man charged in Walgreens robbery

ROCKFORD — A 50-year old Rockford man was charged with armed robbery with a handgun for a Tuesday incident at the W greens at 2323 Charles St

tencing that he was

LOCAL BRIEFS

Puppy rescued, firefighter hurt

ROCKFORD — A p
vas saved and a fire
as injured Thursda

LOCAL BRIEFS

Boy stabbed in fight over food

ROCKFORD — A ju
nile female stabbed
younger brother wit

and Evans and Purifoy are on parole. The women were not charged.

10 arrested in prostitution sting

ROCKFORD — Mem-
bers of the Rockford Poli
Department's M3 Street
Team conducted a

an alternate route during festival hours.

Shots fired from vehicles

ROCKFORD — Police re
covered nearly 20 bullet
asings Friday afternoo

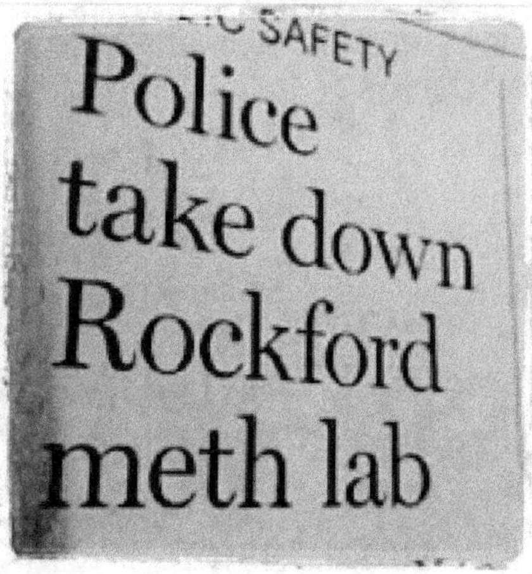
SAFETY

Police take down Rockford meth lab

MICHIGAN

Boy's bike ride in underwear helps save dad's life

HAMBURG TOWNSHI

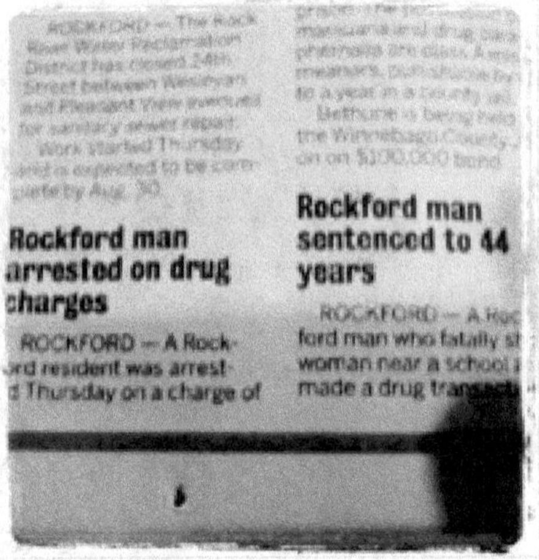

Rockford man arrested on drug charges

ROCKFORD — A Rock-
ord resident was arrest-
d Thursday on a charge of

Rockford man sentenced to 44 years

ROCKFORD — A Roc
ford man who fatally sh
woman near a school a
made a drug tra

we were younger," Vro
mmacher added.
Assistant Principal Carl

LOCAL BRIEFS

Bank robbery suspect faces federal charge

ROCKFORD — The man
spected in Thursday aft
on's bank robbery at th

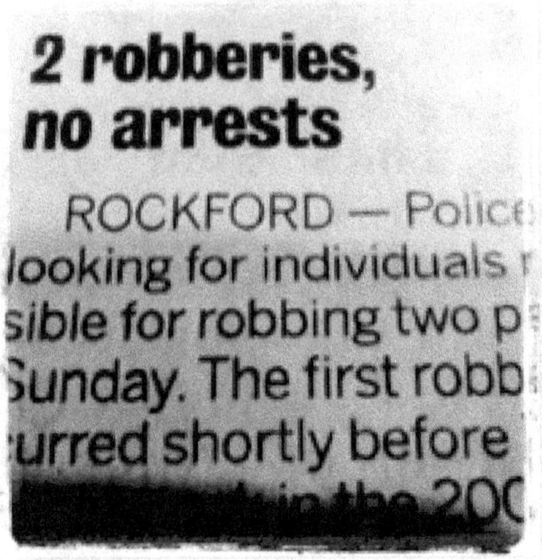

2 robberies, no arrests

ROCKFORD — Police
looking for individuals r
sible for robbing two p
Sunday. The first robb
urred shortly before

ment at the scene.

Man who hitched a ride robbed at gunpoint

ROCKFORD — A ma
who along with a comp
ion, accepted a ride in

Mathis lunged at them with
the screwdriver.

Man shot in leg

ROCKFORD — A man w
shot in the leg at 8:19 p.m
Sunday in the area of Ferg
on and Loomis streets.
He and another man w

-4000, or visit
ford.edu.

Suspect arrested in Abreo burglary

ROCKFORD — Police re-
sponding to an alarm at 3
a.m. Sunday at Abreo res-
taurant, 515 E. State St.,
arrived in time to catch a
man leaving the back door.

rkfdnews

Positively transforming one citizen, or two.™
rkfdnews.com

Positively transforming one citizen at a time.™
rkfdnews.com

Positively awful.™
rkfdnews.com

Rockford, what do I care? I'm from Roscoe.™
rkfdnews.com

ROCKFORD

Just do whatever you want to.™
Rockford, IL
rkfdnews.com

F*ck nice, tell tr*th.™
rkfdnews.com

Our stories, your city, our snark, your smarm.™
rkfdnews.com

Save downtown, do free work.™
rkfdnews.com

Single and horny? Join a mall church.™
rkfdnews.com

Before we hit the bars, let's go to the mall to pray.™
rkfdnews.com

Too many yins not enough yang.™
rkfdnews.com

#LOL™
Welcome to Rockford, IL
rkfdnews.com

Enjoy your self.™
rkfdnews.com

Unemployed? Be a local artist.™
rkfdnews.com

If all else fails, be someone else.™
rkfdnews.com

I don't get it.™
rkfdnews.com

Your to kind.™
rkfdnews.com

Daddy made me in Rockford, IL, but Mommy left me in the hospital.™
rkfdnews.com

I don't get it.
rkfdnews.com
Save downtown, do free work.
rkfdnews.com
Before we hit the bars, let's go to the mall to pray.
rkfdnews.com
Your to kind.
rkfdnews.com
Too many yins not enough yang.
rkfdnews.com
Just do whatever you want to.
Rockford, IL
rkfdnews.com
Enjoy your self.
rkfdnews.com
Unemployed? Be a local artist.
rkfdnews.com
#LOL
Welcome to Rockford, IL
rkfdnews.com
F*ck nice, tell tr*th.
rkfdnews.com
Our stories, your city, our snark, your smarm.
rkfdnews.com
Rockford, at least the internet is fun.
rkfdnews.com
I got robbed, too.
rkfdnews.com
I have no idea.
rkfdnews.com
I don't know.
Welcome to Rockford, IL.
rkfdnews.com
Here's a bible & a drink chip.
Welcome to Rockford, IL.
rkfdnews.com
Be nice to the Rockford;
it drank too much & doesn't feel well.
rkfdnews.com
Rockford, what do I care? I'm from Roscoe.
rkfdnews.com
Stop being negative, Rockford, it's only math.
rkfdnews.com
Rockford, pumping positivity up your a$$.
rkfdnews.com

rkfdnews

Rockford, what do I care? I'm from Roscoe.™
rkfdnews.com

I got robbed, too.™
rkfdnews.com

I don't know.
Welcome to Rockford, IL.™
rkfdnews.com

Stop being negative, Rockford, it's only math.™
rkfdnews.com

I have no idea.™
rkfdnews.com

Rockford, at least the internet is fun.™
rkfdnews.com

Here's a bible & a drink chip.
Welcome to Rockford, IL.™
rkfdnews.com

Be nice to the Rockford;
it drank too much & doesn't feel well.™
rkfdnews.com

Rockford, Wisconsin is 15 minutes away.™
rkfdnews.com

Rockford, pumping positivity up your a$$.™
rkfdnews.com

Positively transforming one citizen at a time.™
rkfdnews.com

Positively awful.™
rkfdnews.com

Daddy made me in Rockford, IL, but Mommy left me in the hospital.™
rkfdnews.com

Positively transforming one citizen, or two.™
rkfdnews.com

Single and horny? Join a mall church.™
rkfdnews.com

If all else fails, be someone else.™
rkfdnews.com

NEWS IN BRIEF
Men charged in air-bag thefts
BELVIDERE — Two
were arrested Monda
onnection with the t
ehicle air bags.

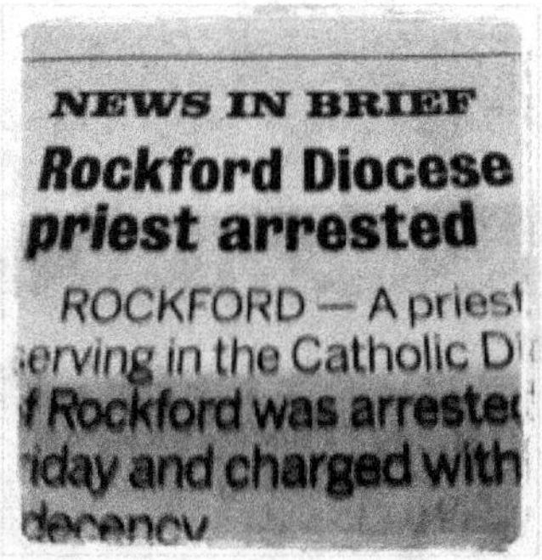
NEWS IN BRIEF
Rockford Diocese priest arrested
ROCKFORD — A priest
erving in the Catholic D
f Rockford was arreste
iday and charged with
decency

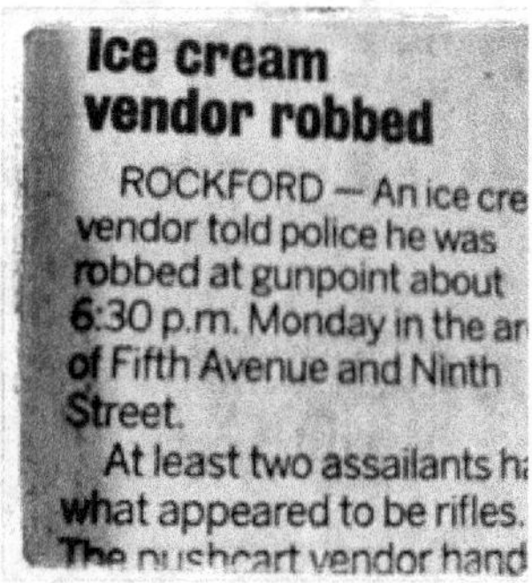
Ice cream vendor robbed
ROCKFORD — An ice cre
vendor told police he was
robbed at gunpoint about
6:30 p.m. Monday in the ar
of Fifth Avenue and Ninth
Street.
At least two assailants h
what appeared to be rifles.
The pushcart vendor hand

Man stabbed; woman questioned

ROCKFORD — Police questioned a 44-year-old woman after her 55-year-old boyfriend was stabbec in the chest Friday afternoon in the 2900 block of La Salle Avenue, Assistant ... Chief Doug

Man pistol-whipped in home invasion

MACHESNEY PARK — A man was pistol whipped Wednesday in an apparent home invasion.

Police responded at 9:15 .m. to a residence near vans Avenue and Rogers treet and later found the

Wednesday, April 23, 2014

NEWS IN BRIEF

Rockford landlord shot in shoulder

ROCKFORD — A man checking on his vacant rental property in the 3 lock of Eighth Street

NEWS IN BRIEF

Cocaine rock found in toddler's nose

FREEPORT — The Illinois Department of Children and Family Services has placed a Freeport 2-year-old in protective custody because a doctor removed a rock of cocaine that was stuck in the boy's nose

Ice cream vendor robbed

ROCKFORD — An ice crea vendor told police he was robbed at gunpoint about 6:30 p.m. Monday in the are of Fifth Avenue and Ninth Street.

At least two assailants ha what appeared to be rifles. The pushcart vendor hand

CRIME

Four shot in Rockford Sunday

Dear Paula The Great
The Great Paula is waiting to help you online, now.
rkfd news
Paula The Great will help all of yous with your domestic, personal and professional issues with family, work, friends, lovers, pets, health,science, math and english assignments, art, law, religious conflicts and home maintenance.
Your problems, her almighty advice.
www.rkfdnews.com

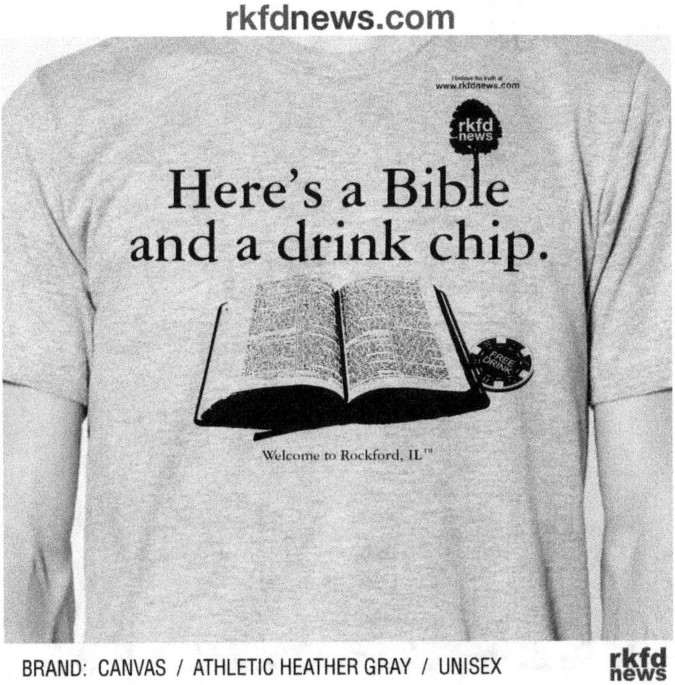
rkfdnews.com
rkfd news
Here's a Bible and a drink chip.
FREE DRINK
Welcome to Rockford, IL™
BRAND: CANVAS / ATHLETIC HEATHER GRAY / UNISEX
rkfd news

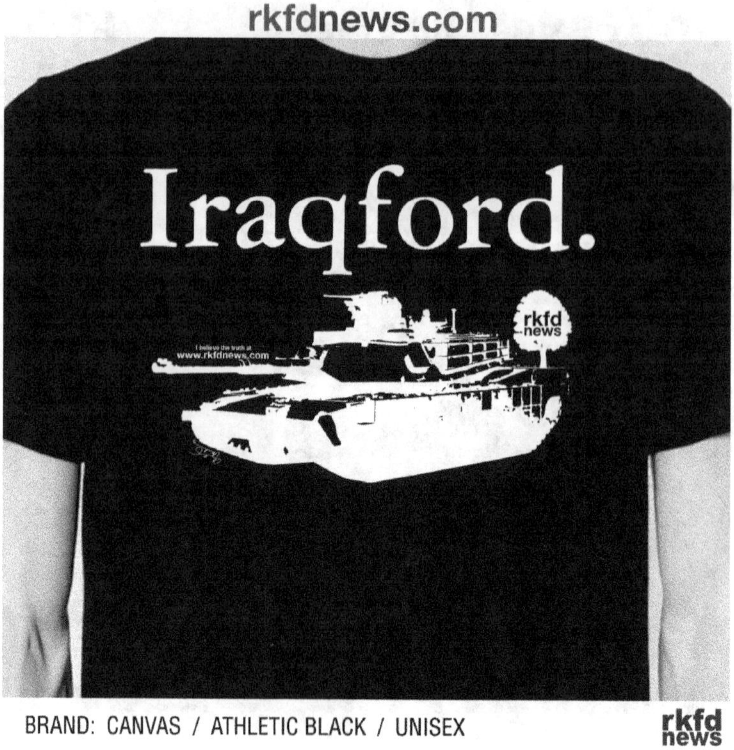
rkfdnews.com
Iraqford.
I believe the truth at
www.rkfdnews.com
rkfd news
BRAND: CANVAS / ATHLETIC BLACK / UNISEX
rkfd news

ROCKFORD ILLINOIS
MERICA
RKFDNEWS.COM
RKFDNEWS.COM
RKFDNEWS.COM

Your to kind.™

rkfdnews.com

Celebrating mediocrity since 2012.™

rkfdnews.com

FAMILY OF FIVE ENJOYS FUN WEEKEND

Originally Published on May 6th, 2013

Rockford, IL – Jack Lily and his family of five had big plans this weekend in Rockford, IL. "*We had a great weekend, let me tell you all about it,*" bragged the father to a table full of co-workers who were meeting for pre-work coffee.

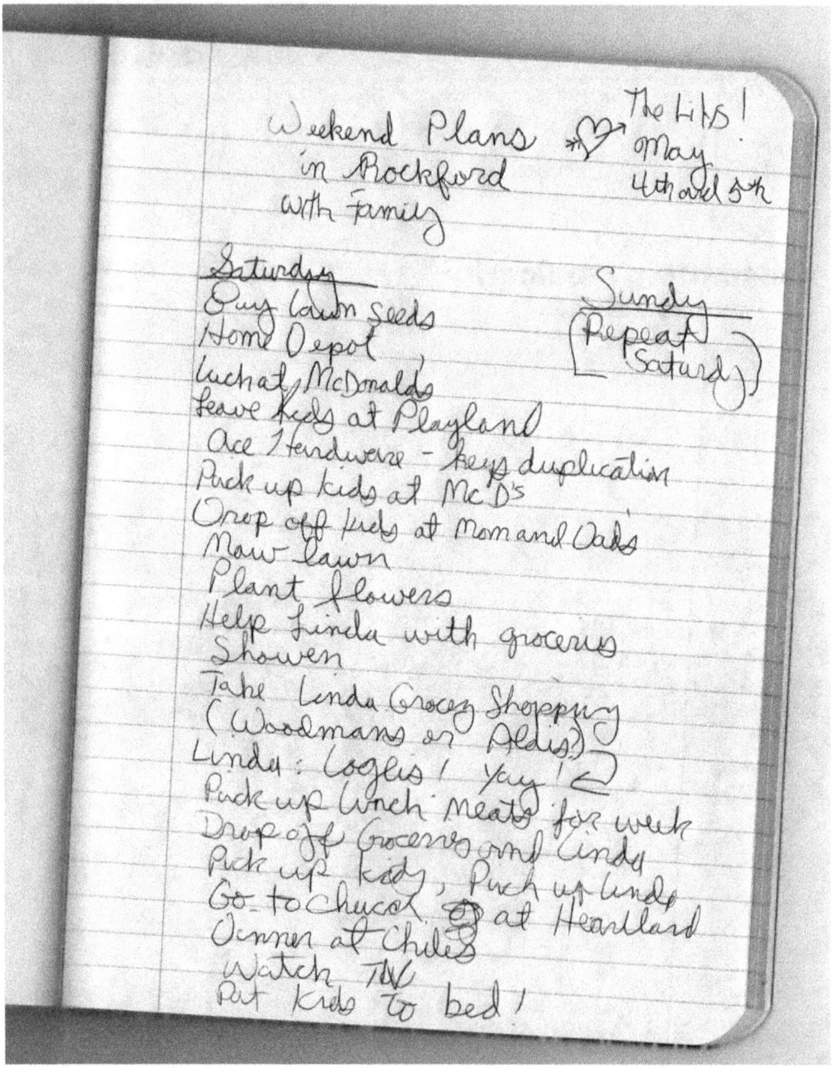

Mr. Lily gathers with his employees downtown to drink coffee and discuss the upcoming work week each Monday morning, but also to recap all of the fun times they enjoyed over the past weekend in Rockford.

"*I told my wife last week that THIS weekend was going to be so much fun!*" said Jack. His co-workers smiled and laughed with him as he kept bragging about his weekend.

"*We made plans, wrote everything down. We asked our kids what they wanted to do, too. I'm pretty big on making sure everyone in our family gets to do what they want to with our fun weekends in Rockford.*"

RKFDNews overheard Mr. Lily in the downtown café and asked if he'd like to share his family's weekend fun times list. He was more than happy to scan it in and send it to us. See the previous page, it sure looks like they had a blast in Rockford this past weekend!

Tchad Beale

WEATHER ALERT: ICE MELTS WHEN THE SUN RETURNS TO ROCKFORD

Originally Published on December 20th, 2013

Rockford, IL – We have an important weather warning for the Rockford area region from our friends over at the *Northern Illinois Common Sense Weather Bureau*:

- **PLEASE BE ADVISED THAT THE ICE IS VERY SLIPPERY.**
- **CARS, TRUCKS, SUVS AND LEGS ARE NOT EQUIPPED TO DEFY SCIENCE.**
- **ICE WILL MELT ONCE THE SUN RETURNS TO WARM OUR HEARTS.**

- **SMILE.**
- **STAY HOME.**
- **MAKE MORE BABIES.**
- **LEARN HOW TO COOK HEALTHIER FOOD.**
- **LEARN HOW TO BE A ROCKFORD ARTIST.**
- **CELEBRATE MISERY, REWARD MEDIOCRITY.**
- **YOU CAN DO ANYTHING.**
- **WHATEVER.**

Gilbert Grebner

NORTH MAIN & AUBURN STREETS ROUNDABOUT DRIVING TIPS

Originally Published on December 23rd, 2013

Rockford, IL - Here' s a helpful list of tips from our staff to you during this holiday season to help Rockford area drivers understand the *North Main and Auburn Streets Roundabout* **and how to use it**.

NOTE: You'll need abilities to read words before proceeding with these tips. If you can't read or write, you should not be driving.

- **PAUSE, ALWAYS LOOK LEFT FOR ONCOMING CARS.**
- **YOU FUCKING IDIOTS, IT'S A CIRCLE.**
- **REPEAT THESE INSTRUCTIONS TO YOURSELF:** "PAUSE THE CAR. *MY EYES LOOK LEFT. IS IT OK TO DRIVE RIGHT? YES OR NO, LOOK CLOSELY. DECIDE. THE CAR GOES RIGHT. IT'S A CIRCLE.*"

It's not that hard to master driving into a roundabout, but you will have to know how to use your brain and a smidge of common sense. If you can't read or write properly, stay off the roads and in front of your televisions with the children that you somehow produced and are raising to be replicas or representations of yourselves. Yay, your greatest accomplishments are still our problems. You fucking idiot, it's a circle.

You will know less about circles after we learn more about the amateurs who can't figure them out with their cars.™

Ron Kites

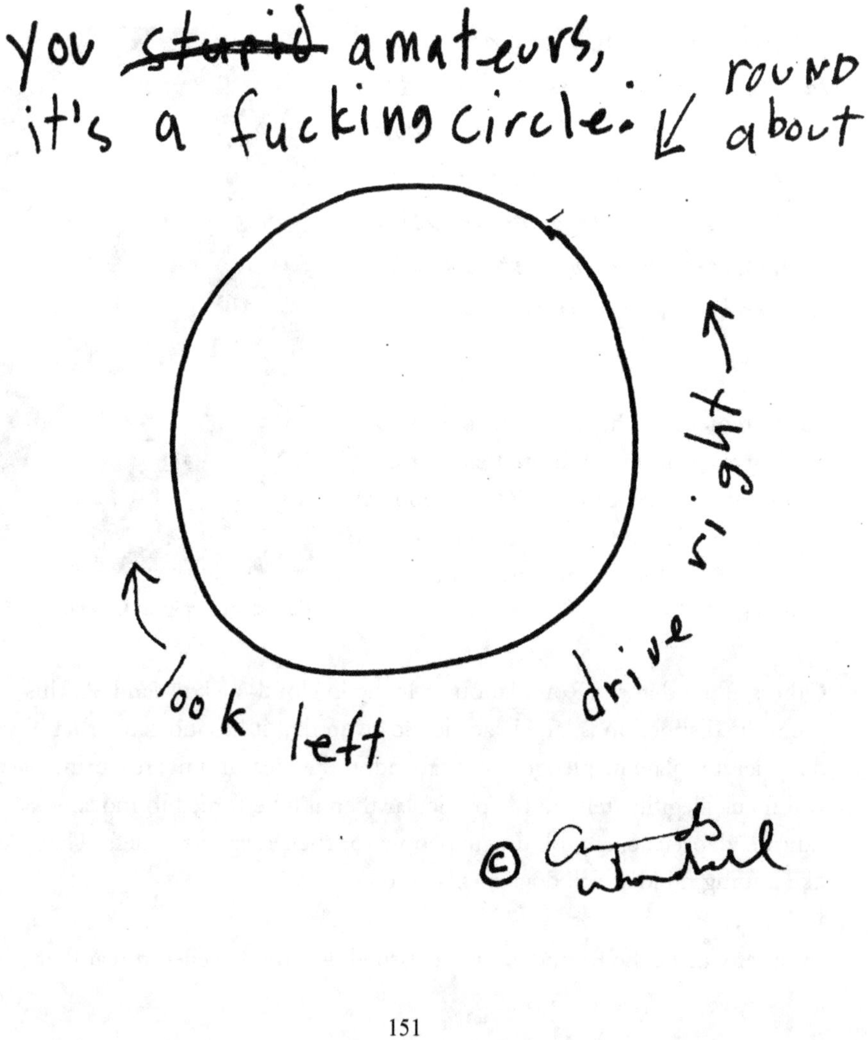

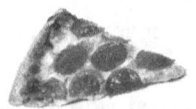

KATE'S COMPLAINTS CORNER: THE ROUNDABOUT

Originally Published on February 27th, 2014

Letters of honest complaints from an honest Kate.

Rockford, IL – I feel I must assert my freedom to comment on an important public issue that the Roundabout has thrust into the vortex of public comment. The nitty-gritty of what I'm about to write is this:

I trust the Roundabout about as far as I can throw it. Of that I am certain because if the Roundabout thinks that it has the linguistic prowess to produce a masterwork of meritorious roadwork then maybe it should lay off the wacky tobacky.

Kate Menstraight, Complaints Columnist

Please remember that some people I know say that the portents indicate that, in the immediate years ahead, the Roundabout will fund, assemble, and train snooty slackers to cast dissent as treason and criticism as espionage.

Others argue that the Roundabout is living in cloud-cuckoo-land. At this point the distinction is largely academic given that it has indicated that if we don't let it violate its pledge not to abandon the idea of universal principles and focus illegitimately on the particular then it'll be forced to mock, ridicule, deprecate, and objurgate people for their religious beliefs. That's like putting rabid attack dogs in silk suits.

In other words, the Roundabout has issued us a thinly veiled threat that's intended primarily to scare us away from the realization that it likes to imply that people don't mind having their communities turned into war zones. This is what its allegations amount to, although, of course, they're daubed over with the viscid slobber of insecure drivel devised by its janissaries and mindlessly multiplied by insincere energumens.

All in all, I realize that this letter has seemed incredibly bleak. However, expecting the worst from the Roundabout means we will never be disappointed. If we're wrong and the Roundabout does not try to pit the haves against the have-nots, we'll be relieved. If we're right and it does, we'll be prepared.

Kate Menstraight

ALL LOCAL STARBUCKS TO CLOSE BY FEB. 12TH

Originally Published on December 30th, 2013

PREFACE: **On December 30th, 2013, we reported the horrific story that you're about to read below. Google Analytics reported that 35,569 people from the Rockford, IL, region and beyond shared, liked, commented and argued the details of this story within 24 hours after it was posted on our noose breaking web site. Even more frightening was publicly witnessing how many of our real friends and family believed this was a true story. Multiply 35,569 by however many fake friends and connections that your ridiculous account profiles on the internet are associated with, and therein resides the meaning to this book's title, *Believe*.**

ROCKFORD, IL – Kimberly Dumond's 3-year career has come to this: Two weeks of severance pay and a latte mug with her name on it.

The 45-year-old, who works at the Starbucks on Perryville Rd in Rockford, is one of 89 local employees who are set to lose their jobs when the coffee giant chain closes all six of its Rockford area locations this month.

> *"Everybody is surprised. Absolutely everybody,"* Dumond said. *"There are people who have been here since the store opened 4 years ago. We don't know what we're going to do. God forbid we have to drink local coffee with the downtown crowd. What am I going to wear? Am I corrupt enough?"*

Starbucks has faced a downhill battle while it struggles to compete with upscale local bean-brewhouses such as Wired Café, Heartland Brewhouse, Rockford First Christ O' Joe Cafe and Octane Interlounge. After more than two years of dwindling revenue and no profit, Starbucks announced it would shutter all of the chain stores by February 12th.

> *"The stores remained profitable, but the clientele refused to bathe or put on shoes and shirts when told to. Rockford citizens need to bathe more and take care of themselves. Dress accordingly for our coffee, for Christ's sake,"* said Rob S.Nirner, chief executive of *Starbucks Customer Health Etiquette.*
>
> *"We've reached the point at which continuing to operate these stores does not make scientific sense for our company's employees in poorer, dirtier regions of America. Rockford needs a bath.*
>
> *The amount of flu shots we have to give our Rockford area baristas and managers*

is out of control. **The people of Rockford need to start using soap and toilet paper** *to wipe away the bacteria from their bodies.*

I get it – why would we do this even though the profits are up? People in Rockford love coffee, but I wish they liked soap and water on their bodies. It's that simple," said Rob S. Nirner.

Jay Vannigan

OH MY GOD! COMMUNITY REACTS!

Source Link: http://rkfdnews.com/all-local-starbucks-to-close-by-feb-12/

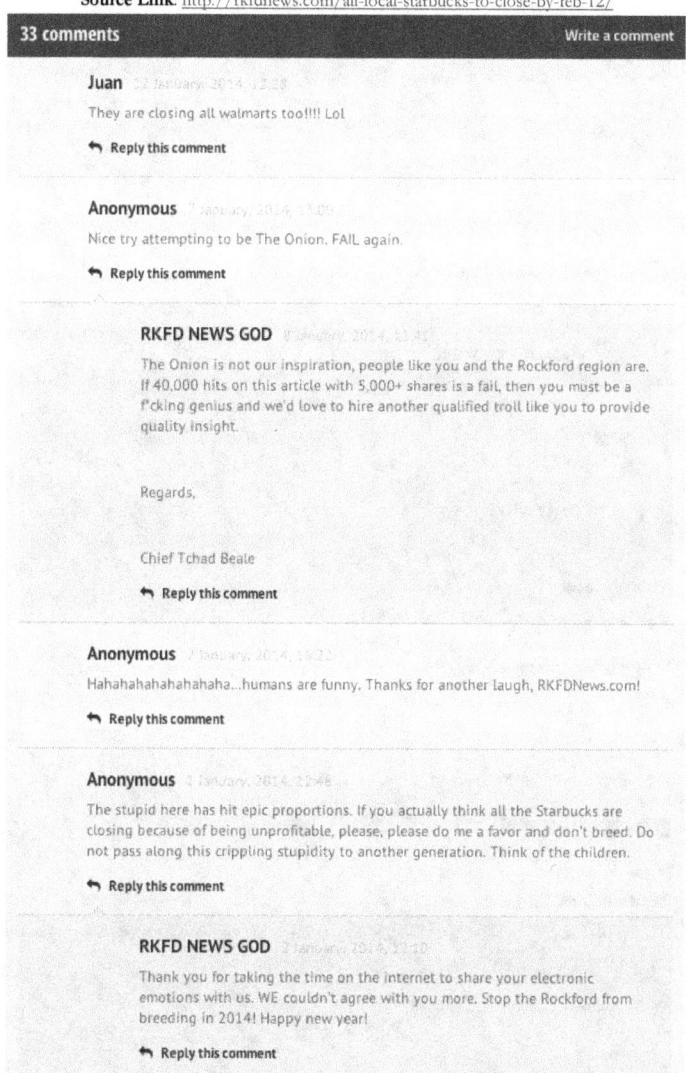

33 comments **Write a comment**

Juan

They are closing all walmarts too!!!! Lol

Reply this comment

Anonymous

Nice try attempting to be The Onion. FAIL again.

Reply this comment

RKFD NEWS GOD

The Onion is not our inspiration, people like you and the Rockford region are. If 40,000 hits on this article with 5,000+ shares is a fail, then you must be a f'cking genius and we'd love to hire another qualified troll like you to provide quality insight.

Regards,

Chief Tchad Beale

Reply this comment

Anonymous

Hahahahahahahahaha...humans are funny. Thanks for another laugh, RKFDNews.com!

Reply this comment

Anonymous

The stupid here has hit epic proportions. If you actually think all the Starbucks are closing because of being unprofitable, please, please do me a favor and don't breed. Do not pass along this crippling stupidity to another generation. Think of the children.

Reply this comment

RKFD NEWS GOD

Thank you for taking the time on the internet to share your electronic emotions with us. WE couldn't agree with you more. Stop the Rockford from breeding in 2014! Happy new year!

Reply this comment

Tara F. 31 December, 2013, 22:29

Does this include Loves Park and Machesney Park as well?

Reply this comment

Zod 31 December, 2013, 15:58

Starbuck was my favorite character. Still is....Ziggy Starbuck. Battlestar Galactica for lyfe!

Reply this comment

Jay 31 December, 2013, 11:21

Hey Starbucks employees: Get a clue! If you're pulling a paycheck from a coffehouse that has not made a profit in 3 years, you just may want to look for another job. Unless you've been blind to the operation and absolutely love working at a place where you're asked to do little to nothing, where very few customers come in....you do not have my pity for loosing a job.

Reply this comment

> **I make da coffeeeeeee** 31 December, 2013, 11:22
>
> Dumbass lol
>
> **Reply this comment**

> **Jacky** 31 December, 2013, 16:40
>
> Jay, you do have my sympathy for "loosing" your grip on sarcasm.
>
> **Reply this comment**

Anonymous 31 December, 2013, 10:55

people get a life

Reply this comment

Anonymous 31 December, 2013, 10:53

If only it were true. Shop local folks.

Reply this comment

Anonymous 31 December, 2013, 10:26

No big loss it's all over prices anyway, there are a number of locally owned place that do just as good as job and not as expensive, keep it local

Reply this comment

Anonymous 31 December, 2013, 09:49

Jay Vannigan, get a life. Do not go running around and making these false accusations! If you trying to scare the general public and increase sales at stores, job well done. Do not make these horrible stories with these fake people without even googling who the damn CEO is. EVERYONE knows good old uncle Howard Shultz Is the proud CEO of the company.
Bad noose, bad AND SHAME ON YOU.

Reply this comment

Jay Vannigan **Author** 31 December, 2013, 19:08

Dear Anonymous,
The fact that you took time out of your day to write this heartfelt retort means the world to me.
It is the reason I get up in the morning.Sending positive feelings your way,
Sincerely Jay Vannigan

Reply this comment

HELLO!!!!!!?????? 31 December, 2013, 09:38

You guys are dumb! I work for starbucks and... We are not closing! Plus if you read this... You should know that Perryville has been open longer than 4 years. This person is also not real they are referring too! Gotta say though... This is awesome! Ive had so many people asking me why we are closing :))) hahahahaha

Reply this comment

Time prters 31 December, 2013, 06:06

Lol...Idiots. . No Wonder this state elected Barack Obama, Dick Durbin and Pat Quinn keep getting elected.

Reply this comment

Scott Wisenheimer 31 December, 2013, 09:03

Well, that is sure completely unrelated whining. Want some cheese to go with that? Go to Meg's Daily Grind for a better tasting mug of joe.

Reply this comment

Jay Vannigan **Author** 31 December, 2013, 19:09

huh?

Reply this comment

Anonymous 31 December, 2013, 00:10

Blah

Reply this comment

Jax 31 December, 2013, 00:03

You're fake story's suck about as much as the shitty of Rockford does.

Reply this comment

Anonymous 31 December, 2013, 05:03

STORIES, not story's.

Reply this comment

Jay Vannigan Author 31 December, 2013, 07:42

Noose not News

Reply this comment

Jax 31 December, 2013, 18:50

Sorry grammar police shit bag

Reply this comment

Kyle Cagliano 1 January, 2014, 21:06

double grammar mistake! this guy should run for rockford mayor or octane ceo! he has great visin for our community!

Reply this comment

---

able34bravo 31 December, 2013, 15:32

*your

Reply this comment

Anonymous 31 December, 2013, 00:03

I cant believe people still fall for this parody site. You must be the same gullible and uninformed people I see on Jay Leno's "Jay Walking".

Reply this comment

Anonymous 31 December, 2013, 00:00

Can't they just leave ONE OPEN FOR THE LOVE OF GOD!

Reply this comment

rkfdnews

Anonymous 30 December, 2013, 23:38

I'm heartbroken. All of them???? Nooooooooooo....:((

Reply this comment

Anonymous 30 December, 2013, 23:22

They're not going to close the Starbucks when they still have hiring signs up and they just opened another Starbucks in Rockford.

Reply this comment

Scissor Fight (@Jerry923) 30 December, 2013, 23:31

Please, dear Jesus of Nazareth, do not let them close the one at the Oasis, which is my favorite.

Anonymous 31 December, 2013, 09:44

That is not a real Starbucks for one, It is a franchised owned store.

Reply this comment

Write a Comment

Thank you for spending time with us on the internet. Please waste more time and energy by sharing your internet emotions below:

Enter your comment here...

MR. LOTHARIO COOKS A ROCKFORD PIZZA FOR MR. STRUMWELL

Originally Published on January 6th, 2014

Rockford, IL – James Lothario took the day off to make a Rockford Pizza according to his neighbor, Joseph Dontel Strumwell.

Strumwell came home for lunch to find Mr. Lothario in his kitchen using his family's new wood-brick oven. The two men laughed after Lothario explained that Jillian Strumwell, Joe's wife, had let the neighbor in to cook the Rockford pizza in exchange for feeding Mr. Strumwell for lunch as a surprise.

"I enjoy making the Rockford pizza. When Jillian told me that they had a wood-brick oven, I offered to feed her family in exchange for using their wood-brick oven to cook the special Rockford pizza," said James. Mr. Lothario added pepperoni, green peppers, pineapple, black olives, sausage and *"a little something-something to the sauce if you knows what I means!"*

We don't know what he means, and neither did Mr. Strumwell when he discovered Mr. Lothario naked in his own kitchen making a Rockford pizza. Strumwell was caught off guard by his nude neighbor in his kitchen and told RKFDnews.com, *"At first I was like, Mr. Lothario be f*cking my wife on Tuesdays at noon.' There were gold-foiled Magnum XL condom wrappers on the floor everywhere, but then I was like, 'Damn, that Rockford pizza smell good, bro!'"*

Was it a good Rockford pizza? We have the answer:

"Mr. Lothario make a nice Rockford pizza. It was very delicious, yes," concluded Mr. Strumwell.

You will learn more about Mr. Lothario's Rockford pizza when we know less about Mr. Strumwell's sexy wife.™

Ron Kites

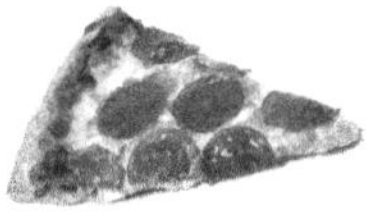

MR. LOTHARIO COOKS ANOTHER ROCKFORD PIZZA FOR MR. STRUMWELL

Originally Published on January 9th, 2014

Rockford, IL – As reported last week, James Lothario took another day off to make a Rockford Pizza according to his neighbor, Joseph Dontel Strumwell. Strumwell came home again for lunch to find Mr. Lothario balls deeps inside his wife, in his kitchen–AGAIN–while using his family's new wood-brick oven.

It was groundhogs day all over again for the friendly neighbors.

The two men laughed once more after Mr. Lothario explained that Jillian Strumwell, Joe's wife, had let the neighbor in to cook the Rockford pizza–AGAIN–in exchange for feeding Mr. Strumwell for lunch as a surprise.

"I enjoy making the Rockford pizza every day and that is why I did it again. When Jillian told me that I could use their wood-brick oven any day at any time, I offered to feed her family once more in exchange for using their wood-brick oven to cook the special Rockford pizza," said James.

Mr. Lothario added pepperoni, green peppers, pineapple, black olives, sausage and *"a little something-something else to the sauce this time. BBQ sauce and chocolate chips with slices of orange peel make for a naughty Rockford pizza if you know what I means!"*

We still don't know what he means once more and neither did Mr. Strumwell when he discovered Mr. Lothario naked–AGAIN–in his own kitchen making a Rockford pizza.

Mr. Strumwell wasn't caught off guard this time by his nude neighbor in his kitchen, but told RKFDnews.com, *"At first I was like, 'You ARE f*cking my wife–AGAIN–on Tuesdays AND Wednesdays at noon!' I mean, at least have the decency to pick up all these empty gold-foiled Magnum XL condom wrappers!' Again, I was like 'Dayumm, Mr. Lothario! That Rockford pizza smell so good, bro!'"*

We wondered again: Was it another delicious Rockford pizza?

Mr. Strumwell confirmed it was a very delicious Rockford pizza once more: *"Mr. Lothario always makes a nice Rockford pizza. It was very delicious, yes, but I wish that he would wear some clothes and pick up his golden sausage wrappers, dog. Know what I mean?"*

No. We actually have no idea what you mean, dog.

You will learn more–AGAIN–when we know less or watts up dog, word, right on, alright alright, damn that's tight, boosh, dialed, crunk, bogus, if you're gay say what, yolo, I'm lovin it, have you had your break today, dude, know wutt I mean.

Ron Kites

CHICK FILET TO OPEN NEW LOCATION DOWNTOWN

Originally Published on January 24th, 2014

Rockford, IL – *"Before we even opened our door, we received such overwhelming support with fans camping out in well below zero temperatures proving people in Rockford can't get enough fried food.*

It's hard to ignore Rockford's need for chain restaurants that offer fattier foods and cheaper prices and help remove the communities need for independent thoughts and outlets for expressions of passion. It is for this reason we decided the greatest location for a second store will go into what is currently known as Kryptonite in downtown Rockford," the Kryptonite owner announced on TV last night.

Chick Filet will take over Kryptonite beginning in Febuary of two-thousand-something. Regional operations director Bob Schallanagan said

"Kryptonite offers the greatest potential to display our brand in an area offering so much potential of corporate dominance. These small venues that can only offer original programing geared towards the arts and culture cannot compare to the offerings of our chain power with cheap food prices and cold drinks guaranteed to move Rockford up the fat chain from number 4 to number 3 or dare say even number 2."

We called owner Chris Wachowiak for additional thoughts on selling out to Chick Filet he had this to say:

"I cannot ignore Rockford's demand for chain businesses. We've been barely getting by for almost 13 years and never seen the level of demand for love and support that Chick Filet has. Plus, when city officials told me they were willing to offer free parking to anyone with a Chick Filet receipt the message was received loud and clear. Rockford community and Rockford politics will bend over backwards to support corporate chains and business."

There were talks of doing a unique branding strategy with Chick Filet along with the corporate takeover of a small business to show they have a local touch.

There was also talk of a name alter for this second location, with names tossed around like "*Chick-Tonite*" and "*Krypto-Chick*." It was ultimately decided against because of the fear of offering an original product unique to any one area.

What will happen to this outlet for local musicians, touring artists, and budding visual artists? They will have to find another venue in town to frequent for cultural acceptance and support.

Thankfully, they have their favorite spaces still intact like Facebook and Twitter which allows them to be social; but not actually involved in anything besides taking *#selfies* and telling people how awesome they are which will allow them to continue to contribute to this world on their couches while eating buckets of Chick Filet's *#friedchicken* – and photographing the moment for the internet – and moving Rockford closer to, dare I dream, "*Forbes' Fattest City in America*" award.

– *Graham Nickles*

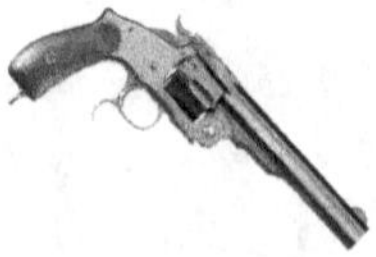

WILLARD HUNTER PERFORMS *"GOD BLESS THE CHICK-FIL-A"*

Originally Published on January 30th, 2014

Rockford, IL – Nashville does Rockford right thanks to rising country superstar, Willard Hunter, and his hit song, "*God Bless the Chick-Fil-A.*"

Hunter's song is a tribute to the Rockford region and to the people who've camped out in the new Chick-Fil-A's parking lot on Perryville Rd. during 0° weather for a chance to win 52 free meals worth of fried chicken meals! (Phew, that was a mouthful! *#friedchicken*)

We don't know the exact medical cost of treating hypothermia, but the free chicken is worth an estimated $364.00 to $416.00 in free meals to the winner.

Hunter was reached for a comment at his Nashville country home:

> *"I saw something on the news last week about my favorite chicken sandwich. Chick-Fil-A is like church to my stomach. Well, let me tell y'all. Rockford's support for the church of chicken touched my heart and stomach so much that I had to rewrite a song about it.*
>
> *I called up Lee (Greenwood) and said, "Lee, I gots this idear for a song." He asked me what and I toad him, "It's about Rockford, Illinois, God Almighty, His Son Jesus, Their friends Joseph and Mary, Speedboats, Metal Panties and Chick-Fil-A #friedchicken!"*
>
> *Lee was like, "I dunno, Willard, whatever. Sounds alright." So I did it. I did it all for you, Rockford – and for America! I want to help Transform Rockford and America with my Chick-Fil-A #friedchicken country song."*

Thank you, Willard, from all of us in Rockford, IL.

Kate Menstraight

WATCH THE YOUTUBE VIDEO FOR "GOD BLESS THE CHICK-FIL-A" BY WILLARD HUNTER AT:

http://rkfdnews.com/willard-hunter

#friedchicken

"GOD BLESS THE CHICK-FIL-A" LYRICS

Performed by Willard Hunter ("God Bless The Chick Fil-A" Parody Written and Performed by Daniel James McMahon, Recorded at The Midwest Sound, Rockford, IL | Based on an original song, "God Bless The USA," words and music © 1984 Lee Greenwood.)

If tomorrow we could get free food for a year of our life
Fried chicken every day for myself, my kids and my wife.
We will camp beneath the stars in a parking lot today
They say the temp is below zero but we won't let that get in our way.

I'm proud to camp in a parking lot
'Cause the food just may be free
And I'd love to eat a breast that's fried, because it's all white meat
And I'd gladly camp out next to you in subzero temps today

'Cause I'm proud to be a Rockfordian,
God Bless the Chick-Fil-A

From the Rock River to iI-90;
From bypass 20 to 173;
You cannot find another place to get a year of fried chicken for free.
I could find a job and eat healthier, but that just takes too much time.
I'd rather risk hypothermia for fried food anytime.

I'm proud to camp in a parking lot
'Cause the food just may be free
And I'd love to eat a breast that's fried, because it's all white meat
And I'd gladly camp out next to you in subzero temps today

'Cause I'm proud to be a Rockfordian
God Bless the Chick-Fil-A

LETTER FROM THE EDITOR: WE ARE NOT *THE ONION* AND WE OWN A YACHT

Originally Published on February 27th, 2014

Hello.

It's me again, Chief Tchad Beale.

Chief Tchad Beale, Editor, and his fiancé, Linda, enjoy fine dining in the state of Wisconsin before heading back to Rockford for coffee and transformational talking about positivity city stuff. They are on a yacht in the Carribean now, and want to say hello to poor cold Rockford.

I'm writing to you from a yacht off the coast of the Cayman Islands that Linda and I live on during these long, cold midwestern winters. It's so warm here and the people are nice, healthy, laughing–unlike Rockford, IL.

We had to get away.

The winter and *Transform Rockford's* reiteration of the last 40 years of problems (that we've been privy to acknowledging already) was causing us to go insane having to listen to it all again and again and again every few years.

It's like the same story every few years: A group of people with a little money try to lobby for state and federal funds and grants by inviting community interaction and hosting town forums. Basically, enjoy the free coffee and pens that they hand out while you can.

They do it the same way every few years with public communication forums and initiatives that centers on hope, vision and community attitude;

but yet, there are less and less jobs to talk about as each passing year transforms itself into the next pathetic community movement. That brings me to today's point.

Elizabeth C[redacted] ▸ RkfdNews
July 7 · Rockford, IL ·

Early on, I found this page humorous...But now I find it unfunny, not nearly as intelligent as your original posts, and the reason why Rockford may never improve its image. You are definitely NOT the Onion...Officially "unliked" your page today.

Unlike · Comment · Share · 2 · 8

RkfdNews and Andy Whorehall I dD like this. Top Comments

rkfd news Write a comment...

rkfd news **RkfdNews** Dear Lizabeth,

Thank you for sharing your time and emotions on our page. What an honor. Since you kicked open the door, here's a rebuttal to your internet emotions:

1) We had to lower our standards to accommodate The Rockford's support and overall IQ level because the path we were on (which was to make intelligent people such as yourself laugh for free) wasn't lucrative enough to continue forward on.

2) If you came here expecting to find the Onion, you made the mistake, not us. We never set out to be The Onion because we didn't set out to be what already exists. Their website address is http://theonion.com if you need help finding it.

3) We do what we do to cause reactions–such as your post and declaration of unlinking us. (Again, what an honor!)

4) We are a simple, cracked mirror-like, reflection of your city, your people and your stories–not ours. If you don't like it? Do something, contribute, make it better. Although, we don't see any of you trying to help us. Complaining and complacency are The Rockford's real, original social diseases.

5) Lastly, this shit is free, lady–THE ROCKFORD way.

Transform Rockford has a community visioning rally coming up if you prefer real laughs. You made the right choice to unlike us. Don't bother hanging around, your noose can't be broken.

And now we bid farewell. Thank you for your time and emotions on the internets! Pray for The Rockford and we bow down to pray before you.

RKFDnews.com

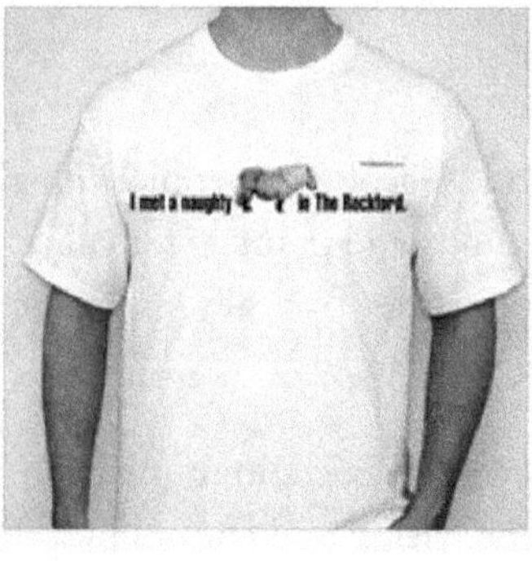

I have some concerns with the Rockford public that my staff has emailed me about. (The wireless on my yacht is best when we are near land, so I apologize for any delays that have occurred with getting back to everyone.)

There are many of you who have made comments on the world wide web of useless information that my staff is trying to be *The Onion*, or that we are dabbling in satire and failing. I'll make this brief so that I can get back to my Piña Colãdas and hot-ass fiancé,Linda. (She is wearing a hot tangerine two piece bikini today! I'll share a photo on our company's facebook page when we get back to the states. We don't want to use up too much data on the yacht.)

Let this be the first and last time I have to say this on behalf of my unemployed staff to certify your pride and egos:

- ***We are not the Onion nor did we ever set out to be. We are a broken mirrored reflection of the Rockford we have come to love that we are sharing with the world on the intardenet.***

- ***We're far from satire. If anything, we're mocking and reinterpreting satire as a new artform, which can be hard for many of you to decipher after a long day of job searching, getting high, playing golf, screwing over the middle class and drinking yourselves into a proud oblivion like the pile of pony shits you are, Rockford.***

- ***We are here to break your noose, to keep you from killing yourselves on a daily basis; which we're pretty sure you'd fail at doing anyway. Rockford style.***

- ***We are here to call out truths without having to spell it out for you. Facts for you to read between the lines of within our noose breaking stories; to make up your own interpretations, good or bad; to open your eyes and get angry. Have a cause to take your city back.***

- ***We don't care who you are or how important you think you are. That includes shady politicians, corrupt business men, drunk artists or a coffee giant.***

- ***We also don't give a f*ck about what you think about us because most of you (that don't like our noose breaking***

team) are in charge of businesses and government organizations that have taken part in leaving the middle class to rot itself into a new lower class. You made us, nice work.

- ***Again, we are your broken mirrored reflection. You don't like it? Eat a dick. You'll be stuck here in Rockford with your obese kids, underwater real estate portfolios, shady business friends and, still, no jobs for the poor when we sell this noose breaking operation.***
- ***We must transform Rockford by reiterating the past into tweets, pizza and flapjacks. That's right!***
- ***We report noose stories, not news stories. The misinterpretation cannot break your noose if you let it get to you.***
- ***We break the noose for you: Hang in there, you'll get it.™***
- ***Hahahaha. #friedchicken is a hashtag.***

Does that help you feel better on the internet now that we've answered your comments in one article? Do you not see Rockford as being a dark, deep well of comedy gold? We do.

The beauty with reading the public's responses, comments and opinions on the intardenet is that we can now assume–for example–that Kate Menstraight's articles, which are based on Winston Churchill's greatest speeches and letters of which Kate has infringed upon to make a mockery of at your IQ's expense, are not Rockford's cup of tea.

Biscuits, indeed!

We love everyone's reactions so much that we'll never block the funny, misspelled, disparaging comments and personal attacks made towards us on our site and social media account profile pages.

KNOW BRAD FREAD, indeed!

Now, go onwards to complain about us on your Twitter, Facebook and in private emails that the NSA, CIA and FBI are monitoring on behalf of all of the information, words, pictures and data that you voluntarily provide your broadband provider and email host providers within your emails, and that of which you provide to your friends and family (for free) in private messages, so that their providers can sell it to their advertisers, and the government, behind your backs.

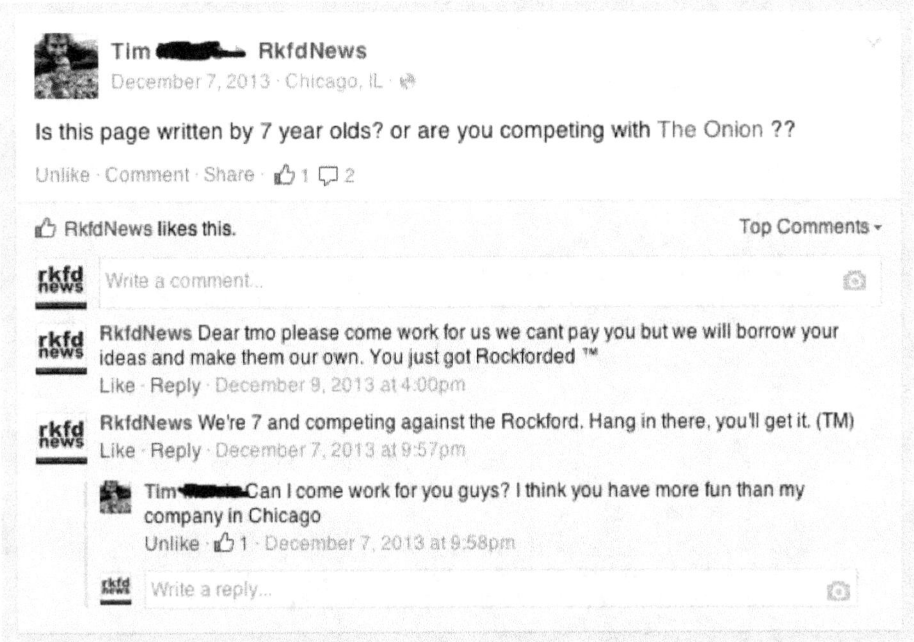

Please, spread the word of RKFDnews.com for us so that my time is best spent on a yacht with Linda in a two-piece tangerine bikini with delicious Piña Colădas in the Caribbean!

How do you fix a broken boat in the desert? You don't, you leave it behind for the animals to enjoy. Leave that place called Rockford. Find a job that pays you your worth and takes care of your obese family while respecting your skills and efforts, so that you can come join us on our yacht next year.

Thank you for reading our nonsense on the intardenet. **You will learn more when we know less about acquiring your data for free,**

– *Chief Tchad Beale*

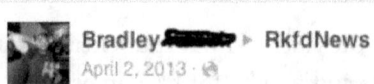

Bradley[redacted] ▸ RkfdNews
April 2, 2013

Last week I found Rockford New's Fb page, and have been reading your posts all week. I have to say, I am not Impressed. 90% of your "articles/posts" have simple spelling errors and are just downright ignorant. It realy seems like this page is ran by Rockford hipsters that are only political because its ironic and cool. Just terrible all around, and I will be unliking your page.

Unlike · Comment · Share · 1 · 10

RkfdNews likes this. Most Recent

Write a comment...

RkfdNews Bradley,

We are so happy that you have time to get your 8 hours of sleep in. Enjoy it for those of us that don't have a teaching or nursing job in Rockford. We are going to celebrate your individuality, don't worry!

Thank you for sharing your emotions with us on the internet two days in a row!

- JoAnne Rankles, Reporter

Like · Reply · 1 · April 3, 2013 at 11:54am

Ron Kites What's hilarious is that this guy think's we're unemployed. I don't know anyone else who gets paid this kind of money to spread the real noose in Rockford, Illinois.

Unlike · Reply · 2 · April 3, 2013 at 7:14pm

Ron Kites Bradley: The noose doesn't stop at bedtime, and we are proud to bring you all the noose that the other "NEW'S" outlets won't, can't, or didn't.
And thanks for the "hipster" mention. I may be over 50, but I love me some young girls with lower back tattoos!

Unlike · Reply · 2 · April 3, 2013 at 8:46am

Bradley[redacted] Yup. That is exactly what I was talking about, right there. Thank you for validating my comment with this highly amusing babble. Please do share this with others, so that they can see that your ignorance and filth does not stop at your unemployed staff, but goes strait to the unemployed "Chief". The attitude that you displayed in your reply is exactly what is wrong with this city. Kick yourself for being the reason the rest of the country calls Rockford miserable. And is there a reason your reply was posted at 1 am on a Wednesday morning? I think that that alone speaks very loudly about how your organization is ran. This will be my final communication with you. Good day, Sir.

Unlike · Reply · 2 · April 3, 2013 at 8:23am

RkfdNews Thank you, Chief, and thank you, Brad!

Like · Reply · April 3, 2013 at 12:21am

Write a comment...

THANK YOU, BRAD, FOR TELLING US THAT YOU UNLIKED US on the internet! *#ELOHEL! #SOAP #PORRIDGE #YOLO #BLESSED #GRATEFUL #BELIEVE #FRIEDCHICKEN #BREAD #SOUP #VISON*

VISON *(fie-zen)*:

To be real, original;

to practice excellence everywhere.

THE LITTLE TACO WHO DO

Originally Published on March 1st, 2014

A Story of Pride, Hope and Transformation

Rockford, IL – When the *Taco John's* restaurant on North Main St. closed its doors in the dead of winter, the *Little Taco Who Do* was left outside to freeze to death or be eaten by Rockford's homeless people, animals and neighborhood kids. All hope had left our Little Taco friend. She truly started to believe that she would end up like her taco family and friends.

"I didn't know what to do at first. I thought about offering myself up to the pack of red tailed foxes that came through for Tuesday Taco night. However, hope wrapped itself around me and kept me fresh.

The newspaper that shielded me from mother nature had a nice little story on page 1 about Transforming Rockford and keeping hope. Talking and thinking positive was all I had in my darkest dumpster moments.

I was determined that I needed to make a plan to save myself. So, I did. I am the Little Taco Who Do!"

The Little Taco found itself in an uncompromising position one sunny afternoon. Two gentlemen threw her from the dumpster onto a moving car heading south on N. Main Street. They stole her newspaper blanket, too.

"That's what ultimately warmed my ground beef heart and saved me. If that newspaper story about hope and transformation can save Rockford, I thought, It's going to save me because I am The Little Taco Who Do! I knew deep inside my ground beef heart that I had to find a new taco joint come hell or high water."

The Little Taco hopped from the moving car, while passing westbound and around through the Auburn and N. Main Streets Roundabout, onto a Cadillac DeVille that was behind her as it was making a swift move west on Auburn Street.

It was there in the distance that she saw hope, redemption, salvation and transformation in front of her: Taco Bell.

"I did it! The road I travelled from Taco Johns to Taco Bell was filled with sadness, defeat and finally, resolution. I lost all my friends and family to the Rockford War and I could have easily ended up like them, but that story in the newspaper that wrapped around me in my coldest, darkest, dumpster, moments saved me. For I am The Little Taco Who Do! Thank you, Rockford!"

The Little Taco wants to say hello to you if you're ever making a drug run down Auburn St. or have lost all Rockford hope.

Lastly, she wants you to know: *"If I can do more than talk about surviving the Rockford War, well, I now know that all the little tacos in Rockford that have been tossed out into the wild after their employer closes shop can survive and transform themselves into proud tacos elsewhere. I did it–wait–better yet, I do."*

Everyday for You and The Little Taco Who Do,

Chief Tchad Beale

ROCKFORD SWAT TEAM UNCOVERS BROKEN DREAMS AT GOLDEN CORRAL BUFFET & GRILL

Originally Published April 16th, 2014

Rockford, IL – The RKFDP (Rockford Dream Police) sent in a SWAT team to the *Golden Corral* buffet restaurant on Perryville Road last night. What began as a nice team building meal for the squad turned into a table of tears by the time dessert was mentioned.

"Somewhere around our second trip through the line for more clam chowder–its amazing, have you tried it?– we started talking about our broken dreams," said Sgt. Don Fonzilio.

"Jerry Thompson and Bill Reynolds were nibbling on their pot roast back at the table when we looked over at Paul Heineken crying. Before you know it, Brian Lothario (Brother of Mr. Lothario, neighbor of James Strumwell) was crying with a mouthful of meatloaf. There went our appetites you could say."

The SWAT team spent the remainder of their meal revealing their broken dreams; all of those dreams being local.

"I can't believe Paul was so upset that he didn't want a bowl of soft serve ice cream to help him feel better," said Officer Lothario. *"Golden Corral definitely broke our individual spirits but made us closer. We might try a different restaurant with a buffet next time. Jerry loves Cracker Barrel."*

Huh.

Well? That's good news!

You will learn more when we know less.™

Ron Kites

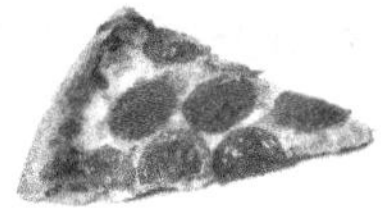

ROCKFORD AREA HOSPITALS APPROVED FOR VIDEO POKER MACHINES

Originally Published May 3rd, 2014

Rockford, IL – The weekly *Monday Night Coffee and Complaints City Council Meeting* approved the addition of video poker machines to all local hospitals.

The plan aims to help the city and county cut back its debts with poor people's money. If all goes as mathematically planned by Rockford alderman and economists, the City of Rockford should qualify for its own Homestead Act and a new city name by 2032.

Representatives from St. Anthony, Rockford Memorial and Swedish American Hospitals are looking forward to the plan. Representatives from each agreed it will be a universal success for Rockford to feel better about itself.

"Whatever helps Rockford helps our patients and their families feel better," said Laurie Tchaicko, Rockford Memorial marketing specialist.

"People need more than TV and magazines for those long waits between surgeries of loved ones. This will help Rockford and its people feel better while helping the local economy pay its debts back to the state and federal government, or vice versa. Whatever," said Ray Grohm, Marketing Consultant for Swedish American Hospital.

A marketing specialist or consultant at St. Anthony's couldn't be reached by today's deadline, but the operator agreed to comment: *"No sh*t? My work place lunch breaks just got a whole lot better. Thank you, Rockford City Council!"*

Video game machines will be added to all local hospitals by the summer of 2014 or 2025. Plans to add machines to Immediate Care centers and Family Practice offices are being voted on by Rockford's City Council in the near future.

Hang in there, you'll get it.

Jay Vannigan

LOOSE NOOSE PROOF – SOME STORY STATS

Site Stats Configure

October 29, 2014, 2:50 pm

« Return to Stats

Top Posts for all days ending 2014-10-29 (Summarized)

7 Days | 30 Days | Quarter | Year | **All time**

All Time

Title	Views
Piranhas Injure 70 People Bathing In Rock River	81,844
Rockford Chick-Fil-A Song Airs on Colbert Report	42,752
⊞ All Local Starbucks to Close by Feb. 12th	35,569
⊞ Home page / Archives	27,741
Rockford Scanner Defeated by Totalitarianism, Fascism, Socialism, and a touch of Communism	18,894
Poork Town: Community Prayers Answered, Portillo's Coming To Rockford	14,009
Endangered Alligator Found Napping Near Whitman Street Bridge and Rock River	13,589
Big Balloon Go Pop Over Rockford, River Sharks Eat Family of 6	9,951
WREX-TV Executives Arrested For Career Killing Spree	7,053
Black Bear Lassoed, Shot 4 Times, Escapes - Rockford Prays for Safety	7,007
Highway 251 in Machesney Park Chosen for 2018 U.S. Winter Olympics Trials	6,243

PIRANHAS INJURE 70 PEOPLE BATHING IN ROCK RIVER

Originally Published June 9th, 2014

PREFACE: On June 9th, 2013, we reported the horrific story you're about to read below. Google Analytics reported that 81,844 people from the Rockford, IL, region and beyond shared, liked, commented and argued the details of this story within 24 hours after it was posted on our noose breaking web site. Even more frightening was publicly witnessing how many of our real friends and family believed this was a true story.

Multiply 81,844 by however many fake friends and connections that your ridiculous account profiles on the internet are associated with, and therein resides the meaning to this book's title, *Believe*.

Rockford, IL – A hungry attack by piranhas has injured 70 people bathing in the Rock River; including seven children and eighteen homeless veterans who lost parts of their legs, arms, hands, feet, fingers and toes.

Frederico Dontavio, Director of *Rockford Lifeguards Association*, said, *"Thousands of bathers were enjoying 70-degree temperatures in the Rock River in The*

Rockford yesterday when bathers suddenly began complaining of bite marks on their hands and feet."

He blamed the attack on polentatitis, "*a type of midwestern piranha, big, voracious and with sharp teeth that can really bite your face off if you didn't bathe your last meal scraps off your face well enough.*"

Paramedic Alonzo Monini said, "*Some children lost entire legs. It was so gross.*"

Rockford's Homeless Pop Star, Johnny Emerald The IIIrd, had this to tell us, "*I eat dem fish! Stop bathing in the river, that's my bath tub!*"

Piranhas attacked and killed a young lady named Linda two years ago. She initiated her own death by leaping into the Rock River outside of Beloit, WI. The 18-year-old young lady was drunk when she jumped out of a canoe to pee in the river.

Flesh-eating fish will always be a concern in the Rockford area. Homeless people and children are advised to stay away from bathing in the Rock River until late fall or early winter. It's up to you, but we'd suggest bringing your own soap and towels, too.

You will not learn anything until you know more about bathing safely in the Rock River with a bar of nice soap.

JoAnne Rankles

COMMUNITY REACTION TO THE HORRIBLE NEWS THAT *POLENTATITIS* ATE 70 PEOPLE BATHING IN THE ROCK RIVER.

Source link: http://rkfdnews.com/piranhas-injure-70-people-bathing-in-rock-river/

29 comments Write a comment

marowniom 13 August, 2014, 13:31

Amazing. The people in the picture in this article came all the way from Iceland to swim in the Rock river. http://www.tripadvisor.com/LocationPhotoDirectLink-g315849-d2225389-i32936180-Iceland_Activities-Hveragerdi_South_Region.html

Reply this comment

Kabrina Bainter 15 June, 2014, 14:55

I do believe this simply because Bull Sharks are able to adapt to freshwater so why couldn't piranha's? I just don't understand why y'all are so defensive lmao sure maybe it's NOT TRUE but never take anything with a grain of salt especially in the times web are living in lol. I am so amused by how LITTLE things get people to start fighting and acting irrationally lmao????

Reply this comment

Whocares! 10 June, 2014, 15:37

Bahahahahaha......well played Rkfdnews!! Hope you reap the amusement of posting such a pot of BS.. Best part is that people are gullible and actually believe your nonsense!!

Reply this comment

Rock Lobster 10 June, 2014, 14:22

cough Bullshit *cough*

Reply this comment

RKFD NEWS GOD 10 June, 2014, 16:08

You might want to take care of that cough sooner than later, there are another 400+ articles to rummage through with asterisks.

Reply this comment

Just some guy 10 June, 2014, 12:46

Midwestern Pirrannananas? Hot damn! Let's grab a couple crooked politicians, put 'em in the water and get us enough for a fish fry.

Reply this comment

mrmoose 10 June, 2014, 11:40

I'm sorry to hear about all the broken moose, they are such a noble creature, much better than llamas!

Reply this comment

D 10 June, 2014, 07:58

If this site was real, the editors wouldn't waste time in replying to silly comments. Including this one. Just saying. Someone is bored. And the noose thing is a bit childish.

Reply this comment

RKFD NEWS GOD 10 June, 2014, 13:05

How noble of you to spend your time scolding all of us with your emotions on the internet. Try harder and you'll win the internet one day!

Reply this comment

Jen 10 June, 2014, 00:26

lol I live near the Rock River and its so green and disgusting I don't know anyone who would actually bathe in it, let alone a fish that could survive in it!

Reply this comment

Poop buscuit 9 June, 2014, 23:04

oh shit, sorry I let the fish out. Again. But, not all are the Polentatitis type, I just wanted to let you know that I also let the Gnocchirhombus out as well. They are much more aggressive, and totally go for the penis every time. From the gate below the Register Star building. The gate below the brewery tower wasn't working, you might send Stan to fix the hydraulics on that one. Thanks!

Reply this comment

RKFD NEWS GOD 10 June, 2014, 07:47

Gnocchirhombus! Nice lil' potato fishies!

Reply this comment

Bill 9 June, 2014, 22:01

This is so fake. There is no such thing as a "Midwestern type of piranha". Piranha's and their relatives are found in the amazon. A quick google search of "polentatitis" will literally only give you 4 hits; this, two from some Instagram crap, and something in French.

Also, if 70 people where really attacked by piranhas in the US it would probably make national headlines, like the snakehead thing years ago, and not just be on some local page. So sorry everyone but this is a very fake article written by some loser that's still leaving in their mom's basement and needs attention.

Reply this comment

RKFD NEWS GOD 9 June, 2014, 22:58

The amount of research you have googled to share your emotions with us on the internet to prove a point is worthy of an article in itself! Nice job, you win the internet! Thanks for sharing your emotions and wasting your time with us on the internet!

Reply this comment

Rock River 9 June, 2014, 21:08

This is sooooo far fetched lol. Worst site ever..

Reply this comment

RKFD NEWS GOD 9 June, 2014, 22:00

Thank you!

Reply this comment

George W. 9 June, 2014, 20:52

GOD DAMN OBAMA FISH EATIN OFF THEM WHITE FOLKS AGAIN

Reply this comment

Dickmouth 9 June, 2014, 19:07

On a them pirenjas done bit my dick off

Reply this comment

Chris 9 June, 2014, 22:33

You bit your own dick off. It's like that time the cowardly lion pulled his own tail.

Reply this comment

RKFD NEWS GOD 9 June, 2014, 22:56

Wait, the lion didn't bite his tail off but our staff writer bit her penis off? Or, you don't want your noose broken? Thanks for sharing your emotions and metaphors with us on the internet, Chris!

Reply this comment

uncle tt 9 June, 2014, 15:46

I am never going in that river!

Reply this comment

trixy460 9 June, 2014, 11:53

Something must be done about this! These monsters are endangering those eco-friendly bathers enjoying what nature has provided! Will this force people to use indoor facilities where they could slip and fall, HAVE to pay for water and waste so much of it down the drain? With the amount of hunters and fishermen in the area, I think a Piranha hunting season should be mandated for the sake of all local bathers!

Reply this comment

Anonymous 9 June, 2014, 12:11

Why would you even post such lies. This site is pretty shady.

Reply this comment

RKFD NEWS GOD 9 June, 2014, 13:17

We're so sorry to hear that your noose can't be broken. Hang in there, you'll get it.

Reply this comment

jay 10 June, 2014, 06:17

Your mom is pretty shady. It's satire. If you don't realize that and think it's funny then your IQ is pretty shady as well.

Reply this comment

c 9 June, 2014, 10:05

This page is full of uneducated, incorrect information! ! Sites like this are a disgrace.

RKFD NEWS GOD 9 June, 2014, 13:17

We're so sorry to hear that your noose can't be broken either. Hang in there, you'll get it!

enoughisenough@yahoo.com 9 June, 2014, 18:44

Why would you say something ignorant like that? LOL. And really..I may be wasting my time replying, but this entire website is a waste of your own life. Carry on!

RKFD NEWS GOD 10 June, 2014, 07:55

A waste to you and your time, yes, but it's not a waste to those who know exactly what they're doing and why. When new jobs are created from a thousand bad ideas that turn into one or two brilliant ones that can provide a few people the American Dream that you obviously don't have time for, well, that's your waste of time. Now, go on back to your desk and answer to others like you have been trained to do or raise your little kittens to play with yarn balls. Your noose will never break, no need to hang in there. Enjoy your empty sandwich.

Reply this comment

Write a Comment

Thank you for spending time with us on the internet. Please waste more time and energy by sharing your internet emotions below:

Enter your comment here...

LOCAL MAN FINALLY ACCEPTS THAT HIS ROCKFORD JOURNEY IS ENDING

Originally Published June 6th, 2014

Rockford, IL – David J. Lorenzo woke up the same as any other day in The Rockford of Illinois, but today he accepted that the inevitable may happen sooner than he'd like it to.

"I believe everyday is a new day to be the best one can be and work hard, be fair to others, but today I accepted a possible reality that I'm going to die in Rockford, IL. Clarity is causing me to accept that death to myself will occur here sooner than later," said Lorenzo, sadly admitting the eventual fate of himself and mankind.

Misery Loves Company and It Has NEVER Felt Better. Go Rockford!

When asked about the possibilities of moving to die elsewhere, Lorenzo answered, *"I can't afford to. I chose the absolute wrong paths in life to take in the early 1990s by choosing an education combined with work experience. This is an all-talk, no-do town and I clearly over-extended my reality here. I didn't realize it until this morning. I'm already dead, to say the least.*

I should have dropped out of school and quit the many jobs I had in the 90s to sleep and party more. Maybe I'd be happier, fitter, wealthier with money instead of love. Maybe I'd understand why there are so many Phish, Pearl Jam and Grateful Dead fans. Maybe I'd have a few children and a speed boat to call my own. Maybe paint it orange with a white dot. I don't know. Ha ha ha.

Whatever!"

Dr. Bob Johnson (the City of Rockford's Psychiatrist) was called upon to help Lorenzo transform and align his real original Rockford reality into believing that he can fight his feelings while hoping for better days.

However, Dr. Johnson says Lorenzo is already dead. *"The Rockford killed him. He's dead already."* Dr. Johnson's frightening consultation of Mr. Lorenzo revealed further details:

*"Mr. Lorenzo can't be helped. I asked him a few questions and he provided me honest answers. No one obviously told this young man that the truth is an obstruction to better health and personal success. I didn't like his answers and I told him such. He then laughed at me and told me to go f**k myself.*

I figured that I would give him one last shot. I asked him to play make-believe with me and he agreed. I could tell that a switch of life went on behind his eyes. He lit up and proceeded to grill me about my existence. Who I am and how I got to where I was in life; those kinds of questions.

I realized that I became the patient and he the doctor. I Rockforded myself. I started crying like a little baby and he kept saying, "Be a better pony, be a better pony." My methods had failed. I let Rockford down."

Dr. Johnson added, *"Mr. Lorenzo helped me realize that life would be different had I been born into better financial opportunities myself. I inherited everything necessary to be successful in life except money. He told me that I would be better off if I was ugly, uneducated and wealthy, because that's the real, original, excellent recipe for success in Rockford. He schooled me on socioeconomics and how it determines the personal and career paths of many before they're born; and that hard working people without money cannot change or control anything, let alone their environment without a bigger garbage bag of money to help them leave Rockford before it kills them. Mr. Lorenzo can't be helped. He's dead already. This is a fact, The Rockford killed him."*

Mr. Lorenzo feels hopeful and thankful despite Dr. Johnson's analysis. He plans to rewrite the abrupt ending of his Rockford journey to happen somewhere else.

"Dr. Bob was a nice man. I made him cry, which sucks, but he opened the door to play make-believe and that's what I do best at. Regardless of his analysis, he did help me realize that I must figure out a way to rob people and con them in broad daylight so that I can afford a way out sooner than later. If I don't, I will die here. I see the ending of the journey happening sooner than later here in The Rockford, but thanks to Dr. Bob's help, I'm going to rewrite the last half of the book to be someone else, somewhere else.

Consider this copy for my Rockford area obituary: Bye bye, Rockford!"

Bye bye, Mr. Lorenzo. – *Theodore Lepolli*

Mr. David J. Lorenzo

FRANK LLOYD WRIGHT'S *LAURENT HOUSE* COLLAPSES DURING MUSEUM OPENING

Originally Published June 8th, 2014

Rockford, IL – Misery surely loves the fuck out of Rockford's company. The entire roof of **Frank Lloyd Wright's** historic **Laurent House** collapsed after heavy rain hit it during its inaugural opening as a public museum this weekend.

Its debut was a success until rain came pouring through the roof and onto the Lobster Bisque buffet table. Organizers and VIP guests were rushed to nearby hospitals. No one has died as of tonight, but the critical injury list is rising.

This is not the first time that this has happened in the last two years.

Harsh winter conditions left the Laurent House in a state of being physically handicapped last spring /early summer, which added to the ongoing costs of making the house museum ready for the Rockford area to revel in this weekend. Coincidentally, it's the only Wright architectural design in the world that was built to be handicapped friendly.

Organizers of "*Transform The Rockford's Feelings*" are asking the public to step up and buy *Transformer Dollars* to help restore Wright's Laurent House as it was when he originally designed it, as well as to repair the roof. This could set back the museum another 9 years. Also, Garrison School and Midtown Loft developers are being asked to donate their missing TIF funds to rebuild Wright's house to make Rockford feel better or whatever.

You will know more when we build a new Frank Lloyd Wright house with Transformer Dollars and missing TIF Funds.

– Jay Vannigan

MUSTACHES ARE STUPID

Originally Published June 15th, 2014

Rockford, IL – Dear anyone (and everyone) who has ever considered cutting a mustache out of felt and putting it on, it's time to let go. Not only is your fascination with this variety of facial hair a little disturbing, it's a little late.

The mustache (as it's currently known to modern hipsters and hack artists) entered saturated popular culture around the same time you started drawing them on your enemy's middle school year book photo.

This brings us to five reasons why it's time for the mustache to quietly die:

5. You don't even have one. Mustaches -- we'll explain because you likely don't have one -- are known to collect crumbs, milk foam, and other flavors we won't go into. And if you're not willing to sport one, neither should your pillow or t-shirt.

4. They're infecting every handmade product on Etsy. There are almost 11,000 things for sale that have been printed, painted, branded, or sculpted into a mustache. That, friends, is stupid.

3. Mustaches are stupid.

2. Hairy lips sink ships and businesses.

1. Hipsters think they are cool.

Jay Vannigan

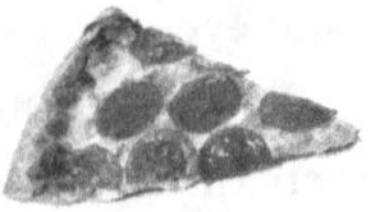

BOLOGNA IS GOOD

Originally Published June 16th, 2014

Rockford, IL – Is a bologna sandwich healthy? If I eat a bologna sandwich, is that good or bad? Guess what, I have the answers.

I eat an apple with the sandwich, along with a salad for lunch and rye toast with smoked salmon for dinner. I drink a lot of water and exercise for 30 minutes everyday so that I can eat 4 oz. of bologna in the morning.

Our readers have this to say about Bologna:

bootzie9 answered 4 minutes ago

Well bologna isn't the best thing for you. Everything else you are eating and doing is extremely healthy! Maybe you should try a bologna sandwich with lettuce and tomatoes too to make it more healthy.

raymondtitts4 answered 6 minutes ago

Bologna isn't healthy by any stretch of the imagination. Some kind of unprocessed meat, that doesn't have nitrates in it, is way better. But the rest of it is okay, as long as the sandwich is on 100% whole wheat bread.

Nutterbutter 3 answered 8 minutes ago

Stop depending on other people to make you happy. You have made some poor choices in your relationships it seems and you have to get over it and learn from your mistakes. It's part of life. Wise up and don't let anyone take advantage of you especially when it comes to bologna. There are many ways to make sandwiches such as getting involved in something that really interests you and finding others who like the same sandwiches. I don't know whether or not you are looking for a friend or a romantic relationship with bologna. Why would you ever think you have to go 10 years before some other kind of processed deli meat comes along? When one does come along, don't think they are Rockford (Your Savior) because no one can live up to that title.Think positive and do positive things in your life. You may need to get some counseling to get over your past meat eating experiences.

You will know more when we start making children who eat bologna.

Jay Vannigan

14 LOCALS TO WATCH IN 2014 OR 2032 OR WHATEVER

Originally Published June 17th, 2014

Rockford, IL – RKFDNews is proud to unveil a non-biased list of local celebrities, artists, politicians and entrépoorneurs to keep an eye on forever. These contestants are all up for the prestigious ***Lord of the The Rockford Ring™*** award.

The winner will announced at every city social event that The Rockford area's 1% throw for themselves after another successful year in business and government has passed by.

We at RKFDNews evaluated fourteen proud locals who are making a dog darn difference in the *Forest City of Dreams, Sounds and Visions* for the immediate futures of you, me and everyone else in and around the Winnebago County.

Here are The Rockford's 14 locals that you should positively keep

emotional eyes and ears on before we all end up homeless under the Jefferson Street Bridge in the future if jobs aren't created that can pay people with cash instead of hope and vison. That's right.

14. Bunny Carlos: This rising entrepreneur opened up an art gallery in 2013 and it was a critical, artistic smash. Carlos attracted art goers from all over the world with his oil paintings of exotic foods and instagram selfies, which helped restaurant sales rise at Octane Interlounge.

Mr. Bunny has other plans for this century and decided to share them with RKFDNews before a competitive reporter, Geo from our local competitor RRStar, gets whiff of it:

> "I *started a band that no one, I mean, NO ONE, has heard of in Rockford yet. They're called Cheap Truck. My oil paintings of exotic foods mixed with haystacks that are on display at Burpee Museum opened the door to my art career, but my band is going to save The Rockford and put you and you and you and you on the world wide web's map–you watch. You hear me?*
>
> *The Rockford is coming back. It's been a long time since I rock and rolled. It's been a long time since we did the stroll here in the Forest City of Dreams, Hope and Visions.*
>
> *Cheap Truck will save The Rockford and my art will save art galleries in neighboring communities like Roscoe, Machesney Park, Chicago, London, England and this beautiful tiny art gallery/noodle restaurant that's located in Gifu, Japan.*
>
> *I love that place–they serve the most wonderful Sai Pon Buku Beef Sandwich in the world. I want to bring that sandwich back to The Rockford–watch me do it. You hear me?*
>
> *That's right."*

13. Quinn Gelastio: Mr. Gelastio was arrested in the City of Rockford last year, but this year he made it a mission to relocate his entire life to the *Forest City of Dreams, Sounds and Visions.*

He told us from his new Rockford home that he intends to "*save the people before Pablo, Larry or those Transformer weirdos from the fake-box churches do. My art will melt faces and my solos will shred the economy out of eternal despair."*

Mr. Gelastio is taking a break from his smash selling rock band, *FrequencyX2*, to buy up foreclosed homes in the city to store his guitars and cars in.

> *"Some of the homes are real gems, great space for my collection of guitars, but most of them I'm going to bulldoze to make gated parking lots for my army of import cars that are being delivered from Santa Monica, CA. I love The Rockford so much that I moved here. It's a great place to make some parking lots. Watch me do it, you'll see."*

12. Lawrence Bird: French Lick's basketball hero takes over the town with his smooth Js. Bird joins Mayor Larry Morrissey as one of the *The* Rockford area's most famous Larrys. Together they will lead the Auburn Knights and Boylan Titans sports teams to sold-out semi-pro championships at the BMO Metro Center place.

New road signs are on stand-by to greet everyone coming off of I-90 onto East State Street. We can see them now: "The *Rockford, IL, Home of The Two Larrys and Amateur Sports Tournaments!*"

What Larry Bird did to save French Lick, Indiana, he will do for *The* Rockford as he competes for his first *Lord of the The Rockford Ring*™ award.

11. Chef Paólo: America and Downtown Rockford's most beloved spanish, French or italian chef–*we don't care which country our city's Chef migrated from because he made The Rockford his hometown for cooking up dreams and for that alone we at RKFDNews are so thankful to him*–prepares a meal to feed all of East Rockford!

That's a prediction or a rumor, and not a guarantee. (The east side is in for a treat we tell you!)

Have you ever had fried apple dumpling stuffed duck feet crepes? Soul yommie!

We are predicting that the E-Entertainment channel will come to *The* Rockford and document his special brand of performance art and recipe readings in the kitchen–and out of the kitchen–all over the town while feeding the homeless, college educated and unemployed locals on the east side of town where prosperity needs a BIG BOOST.

Fueling the economy with his tasty duck dishes, while employing the town's most famous con artists, are a few of things that Chief Paólo excels at the most.

Feeding the professionally educated and unemployed might ordain a chef into a *Lord of the The Rockford Ring*™ *savior* this century. Go on now, and please try his BUTT-OR-MILK CHICKEN PANTIECAKE CREPES while you can!

10. GORAK: This early 1990s Rockford area high school basketball star makes a major comeback in the Forest City of Dreams. GORAK returns to the area to defeat the mighty Swordfish League with his jump shot powers.

We predict that the Swordfish will rise from our Rock River's brown belly to take the entire town prisoner by the Fall of 2034. For the love of all that is good on earth and in *The* Rockford, IL, Gorak will bear a major challenge to the Swordfish League.

In the end, Gorak will save us with his slam dunk moves and smooth Js. Watch and see, ok? Watch him.

We warned you.

9. Supply Core: We don't know a fucking thing about Supply Core outside of two facts: 1) They work with the government; and 2) the government's defense department pays them big bucks to send wholesale orders of transparent tape, cans of beans, pens, macaroni and cheese, peanut butter, saltines and other stuff to occupied military zones like Iraq,

Darfur, Facebook, Twitter and the Google Corporation. It's all conducted and packaged under the BIG business meets government word called PROCUREMENT.

(Their tax write-offs must be out of this world!)

We're predicting that SupplyCore will employ all of *The* Rockford by the end of 2083, but as history might have it, we also doubt it because we have NO fucking idea what they actually do besides occupying a building in downtown that overlooks the beautiful, brown Rock River.

8. Rosie Rayburn: This amazing local singer took the midwest by storm in 2012, winning major karaoke championships all over Illinois, Wisconsin, Minnesota, Iowa, Indiana and Missouri. Rayburn told us in 2012 she wasn't banking on a future in her art, but singing her heart out is exactly what will save *The* Rockford some year in the future!

We are on the edge of our seats at our computers waiting to hear Rosie and her band once more sing golden karaoke classics from her favorite pop stars like ***Cory Chisel*** and ***Brandi Carlisle***. If you haven't heard Rayburn and her band play the hits, google her and search rkfdnews.com for her hit song. 2022 should be a breakthrough year for her karaoke career. We predict that Rosie will be huge in Rockford, Appleton, LA and NY.

We can't wait until she finds a big city manager who will help her abandon the disparity and economic sadness that looms large over all talented locals living in the *Forest City of Dreams, Sounds and Visions*!

7. Paul The Great:_ What an amazing man this Paul the Great became in 2012. His philanthropic actions and timely advice to assist the public school district, city government, the arts community, local restaurants and churches instigated a city wide movement within the community.

Locals woke up feeling better about being unemployed and foolishly educated beyond logic and reason with loans and a pile of bills to never pay back because Paul The Great made us feel better!

He told striking teachers to "*Feel better! You get a paycheck and summers off, feel better! Use your health insurance! Most people don't have that–and feel better. YOU CAN DO IT!*"

And they did; the striking teachers woke up and felt better all over town until Chicago teachers went on strike. The jealousy that clouded over the Rockford public school teachers was on high tide until Paul the Great–AGAIN–helped them feel better. He taught them how to not feel jealousy towards not being able to party and strike with their big city peers.

Paul The Great will be on call again to help *The* Rockford with all kinds of situations in the next century!

6. Randolph Tortona: Randolph, age 63, rose from the ashes of south Rockford to lead his half Irish and part Mexican family into social media prosperity in the years of 2004 through the present day.

Tortona bought a nice HD video camera, a Macintosh, and lured local twenty-year olds into helping him make really neat internet videos in exchange for a few bags of weed in 2013 to extend his family's social media legacy.

It's what Tortona did with these videos that will save the city from emotional damnation in 2014 or whenever. Short video stories about famous locals with special skills polluted the Rockford area's broadband grid.

Comcast's local provider, Infinity, was on standby each time Tortona released a video to his Facebook fans. Jerry Chadstone, IT guy at Infinity told us, "*Tortona's IP address is doing a great thing for Rockford, but I'll be a soft stale taco if he hasn't made my job much harder each time his videos are released on the world wide web of dreams and visions.*"

Locals waited up all night for each of Randolph's hyperlink releases to stream their favorite Rockford area videos about talented poor people.

Hollie Deltonto wrote RKFDnews.com to tell us that Tortona's video about the sandwich guy helped her find her calling:

"*I saw Randolph's video one day on Facebook. The one about the peanut and jelly sandwich maker who fed his neighbors for free until they were willing to mow their lawns on the same day as he and I thought, fuck me–I can be anything I want to be in Rockford. Gosh darn it, I can be a chef!*

I called up our city's most famous chef, Paólo, and said, 'Listen your honor, I want to be a chef. I love to cook. I make cookies and stuff. I know I can do it.' And I did it! I knew I could. In Rockford, you can wake up and be anyone –wahlah!

Chef Paólo hired me and ordained me a chef with no certification or schooling necessary. I need to thank Mr. Tortona for helping me find my way.

I really believe anyone in Rockford can wake up and be anyone at anytime without actually knowing what to do or earning your title because DREAMS DO COME TRUE IN The ROCKFORD–look at me. Thank you, Randolph!"

Our entire staff concurs with Ms. Deltonto. You can *wake up and be anyone in The Rockford!*

Mr. Tortona was the Lord of Social Media and Likes and Tweets and Stuff in *The* Rockford for quite awhile, but in the next century, we predict that Randolph Tortona MIGHT be the Lord of The Rockford Ring™ champion if he keeps inspiring locals to do whatever, be whoever and whatever means whatever for whatever!

5. Rockford Scanner: Talk about breaking the misspelled news while you snooze. *The* Rockford Scanner took over Facebook in 2013, informing the community about breaking crime stories. Many stories and posts without closure, or decent spelling and grammar, earned a whole lot of *Likes* and *Comments*! *Shares*, too!

People shared their interest in crime all over town in 2012 and we expect that fad to continue in the next century on the internet.

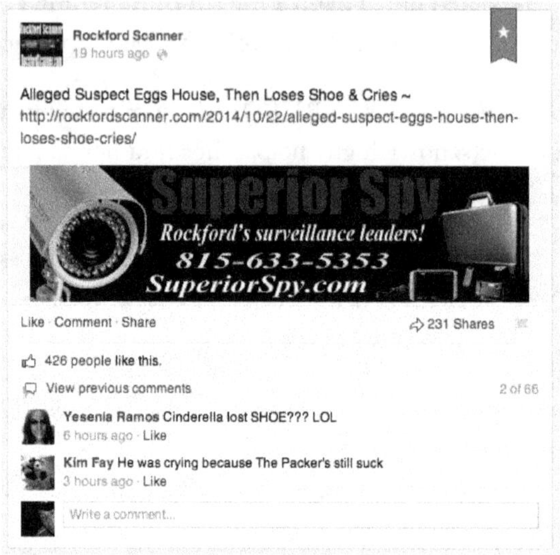

Rockford Scanner began their business as a hobby. The founding owners loved walkie-talkies. We here at RKFDNews love walkie talkies, too– especially Tchad Beale, Editor and Chief of our operation.

Chief Beale told us at a staff lunch yesterday, "*One time in 1984, my friend Jenny and I took our walkie talkies to our Christian college band camp in Massimo, Wisconsin. At night we slept in separate cabins; guys with guys, ladies with ladies. We would turn on our walkie talkies and talkie talkie to each other. It was really fun. One night I said to Jenny, "Let's sneak out and talkie walkie?" We did. We wandered through the forest with our walkie talkies on doing the talkie walkie until we took our clothes off and had sex for a few hours in the lake. I haven't seen those walkie talkies since but Jenny and I see each other once a week. I accidentally got her pregnant that night. Our son, Chad, reminds me every day of walkie talkies.*"

Thank you, Rockford Scanner, for bringing back sweet childhood memories with Facebook status updates on breaking crime stories. We hope there's more to scan and share on Facebook in the next century as your organization competes for the *Lord of the The Rockford Ring*™ award!

5. Father Charles Morrison: What a guy, a man of the Lord and a fan of the almighty dollar. Morrison is the CFO – Chief Financial Officer at *Lungland Community Advertising and Marketing Firm Church.*

Father Charlie's revolutionary style of business, which consists of combining religion and marketing services, has been labeled a "*Real, original Rockford*" invention for success in the post-recession's new economy. Morrison's followers are in the thousands and so are the dollars – maybe millions of dollars!

Lisa Andersmithwilliamson, a young 29 year old Swedish local who loves church, her children and graphic design, told RKFDnews, "*My husband and I couldn't imagine a better place to get right with the Lord. The coffee is to die for and my kids love the waterpark attached to the church!*

I bring my laptop to church on Tuesdays to do a little graphic design, and Father Morrison's elves always help me with my font choices. They've been teaching me how to make internet videos, too.

Church and advertising services are so much fun at Lungland Community. If I wasn't with my husband, Chad, I'd sure as hell go after Fr. Charles because he's a really good looking man who works for the Lord. Me and the other wives always talk about how nice his breath smells. His extra passion for the Lord and providing web and print services to Rockford area businesses are unparalleled compared to other men who work for the Lord. He is so sexy!

There are no other churches I can think of going to in Rockford where I can enjoy fresh brewed coffee, graphic design and the Lord Jesus."

Father Morrison's clergy have gathered by the thousands to speak of his name and drink Lungland's special coffee. We are predicting that he could be the *Lord of the The Rockford Ring*™ winner if parishioners like Lisa

Syversonberg keep praying, drinking and designing for the Lord Jesus and his pal Father Charles Morrison in the next century!

3. Lord Thomas Derby: There is a man – a great man, a metal pantie inventor and speedboat enthusiast – who descended down upon the northern Illinois region in the summer of two thousand and eleven to save the peasants. It didn't come without a few fights.

He was met with opposition by regional businesses, city government officials and deceptive ad firm owning church leaders. He stood alone while his company's founding partner challenged his newfound crusade to save Northern IL from $cumbags, amateurs and little ponies.

Lord Derby's business partner, William Reynolds, wrestled him over their company's differences in front of their loyal employee base. Their company, DERBY | REYNOLDS, had become well-known as the WAL-MART OF ADVERTISING in the Midwest by offering HOT DEAL$ and 50% OFF all of their competitors estimates. These tactics shot them to the top of the American business pile during a recession.

Reynolds and Lord Derby yelled at each other in unison without knowing their wrestling fight was for the same cause. (Read about their amazing company story at: DerbyReynolds.com) Each man fought for hard-working peasants and for a better way of life. However, it was Lord Derby who won the hearts of his employees in the end.

Lord Derby, a man of principal born from a working class family, was not comfortable with Big Bill Reynolds' affection for socializing with $cumbags in Bergners Suits, as well as $ales Sluts in hooker boots.

Lord Derby's employees–Sean Lippy, Alyssa Sojahnowski, Jenny Kowalski,

Jeff Tethernick and many more–have spoken his name all over Schaumburg, Elgin, Chicago, Evanston, Madison, Beloit and Milwaukee; and now in *The* Rockford, a village lost in the black hole of American greed and corruption that is called Illinois.

The poor people of Rockford know Him as Lord Thomas Derby, *C.E.O. and LORD of All* at **Derby | Reynolds** - *The Wal-Mart of Advertising*™. Lord Derby recently shared his story with rkfdnews staff members about how he discovered the poor village of Rockford, IL. You can read it on pages 221-222 of this book.

The rest of the world has been following Lord Derby and learning from his business lessons on the professional network, LinkedIn. Connect with Lord Derby for future employment or psychiatric counseling opportunities at: http://LinkedIn.com/In/LordThomasDerby

His fans and employees can be heard echoing his trademarked voice throughout the hills of Montezuma and within the halls of all regional businesses on his hit podcast-radio show, *Songs About Stuff and Things* (free on iTunes). His cultural idealisms have spread like a virus throughout the Midwest, challenging $cumbags everywhere to step up and bow down with metal panties on before their new savior, Lord Thomas Derby.

This pure constitutional belief was written by Lord Derby for all of his followers and employees to obey:

***"I pledge allegiance to the almighty orange flag with a white dot of Derby | Reynolds, and to the YOU$A™ for which I stand, one nation indivisible, with liberty, speedboats, & metal panties for all.* That's Right, Ima Talkin To You, $Cumbags In Bergner's Suits. Git Yo Metal Panties On And Bow Down To Your New Lord After You Honor Thy Flag, The Orange One With A White Dot."**

Lord Derby's commitment to defending village minions and peasants from the evils brought forth by *Scumbags in Bergner's Suits* who are reigning economic terror all over Rockford, IL, are a great example of what makes him a powerful *Lord of the The Rockford Ring*™ contender.

His efforts to rise from economic despair to fight emotional, delusional, positive thoughts with logic, action and metal panties during tough times is what makes our favorite Lord of The Rockford Ring contender so vital to the Rockford region and its people in the next century. Lord Derby wants to put the $ back into YOU$A™, and we should want that, too. Right? That's Right™.

YOU$A™

2. Johnny Emerald The IIIrd: Johnny Emerald the IIIrd is a self taught song writer, poet and musician from Rockford, IL, who also happens to live on the streets that he sings about. Emerald the IIIrd is homeless, too.

Zachariah Staas, recording engineer at Mid-Under Squirrel Sound Studio, discovered Emerald the IIIrd one morning in downtown Rockford.

"I took a bike ride downtown to find a nice breakfast place to eat some eggs and bacon when I heard a man singing. I had given up looking for an open breakfast diner to replenish the energy I exerted from riding my bike at that point, so I followed the sounds towards a man that I'd only heard rumors about before that morning. And there he was in the flesh, Johnny Emerald the IIIrd, homeless pop star and song writer playing his Yamaha Synthesizer with a nice leather coat and slippers on."

Emerald the IIIrd was reached for a comment, but declined by politely stating, "*All you needs to knows about me Mr. Johnny is in doze songs. I love The Rockford and I hopes you dos too.*"

Listen to Johnny sing about the streets he sleeps on in the city he loves at: JohnnyEmerald.com

We can't wait to hear more from Johnny during his Rockford adventure, because rock n' roll – and the United States of America – has sure forgotten how to have fun while the people of Rockford party on. Maybe Johnny can bring the fun back to American rock n' roll while the race to the *The Lord of the The Rockford Ring*™ continues. Go, Johnny, go!

1. Jesus Abraham Correa The VIIth: 2009's Rockford Mayoral Election and 2012 National Election candidate lost both contests to wealthier, less talented candidates. His opponents from the Republican, Democrat and Independent parties brought tons of old-world money and corrupt financial backers to the table to defeat Our Jesus, *Jesus Abraham Correa the VIIth*, and the Green Party he fought for.

Losing a city and national election hasn't stopped Correa from resurrecting his passion for leading *The* Rockford area out of its depressed state of mind and into the ring for an old fashioned wrestling match.

Had President Obama or Mayor Morrissey –opponents in each of the election races lost – agreed to wrestle Jesus in a caged wrestling match anywhere in America, things might be different. Jesus would prove that *The* Rockford can compete with anyone, regardless of how much fucking money that those people with power possess to buy opportunities in poorer communities. Rockfordians and Americans would be in a much more healthier condition with Jesus Correa in charge.

Used Without Permission
© Photography by BrianMilo.com

A few reasons why: 1) He understands defeat; **2)** he can rebound from a body slam with a DDT quicker than you can blink; **3)** the way he lets a match go on by letting go at the ref's number nine count, for the sake of causing more suffering to his opponents in exchange for more of the audience's dollars and applause because he understands the value of entertainment; **4)** he cares about getting the fuck out of town as quickly as we do because his skills will be best respected–and compensated–in larger villages where money from city arts organizations actually helps people; **5)** his soup recipes can cure poverty and unemployment.

Our prediction for this century's *Lord of the The Rockford Ring*™ winner will be Jesus Abraham Correa the VIIth. You watch. Ok? You hear us? You watch and listen, Jesus always is. We're all bait in his presence, and for the better of Rockford of Winnebago County of Illinois of the United States of America of North America and of earth, the universe and all that is watching us while we enjoy the porridge, soups, soap, bread, water, Oprah reruns, Terry Bradshaw memories, John Kruk quotes and laughing, you watch it.

"GUNSHOTS OR FIREWORKS?" POOR & VIOLENT ILLINOIS CITY PLANS FOR ANOTHER JULY 4TH WEEKEND WITH FUN DRINKING GAMES

Originally Published July 1st, 2014

Rockford, IL – Celebrating freedom comes with a price for the citizens of Rockford of Illinois. The poor, little, violent village located 70 miles outside of Chicago, on the edge of Wisconsin, is gearing up for another weekend of holiday drinking games. Locals are stocking up with alcoholic beverages and preparing their 6th senses to play games like, *"Were those gunshots or fireworks? Go!"*

(It's not that funny. It's not what you make of it. It's not how positive you think you need to be. It's not what you put into it that you'll get out of it. It's not about mind over matter and pretending that the grass isn't as green elsewhere and that this is all OK. It's not OK. It's The Rockford and it's all about you and me leaving as soon as possible so that those who are OK with all of it can enjoy another weekend of holiday drinking games such as "Were those gun shots or fireworks?")

It's not that funny anymore. We hope all of you take this weekend to plan your long overdue escape from Illinois. Do it as soon as possible; before you're desensitized to all of the bullshit civic pride, poverty, unemployment, hillbilly elitism, corruption, crime and economic ruin that has buried the working class people of Illinois in its own complacency and depression. – *Theodore Lepolli*

MAN WAKES UP, REALIZES WIFE HAS BEEN RIGHT ALL ALONG

Originally Published July 20th, 2014

Rockford, IL – A Rockford man woke up Sunday morning and realized his wife has been right this whole time. Jacob Kern woke up like every other morning, but this one was different.

"*My wife has been telling me things for years but I did not believe her and suddenly this morning I did! I suddenly believe everything she has been telling me!*" said Kern, dressed in black socks, penny loafers and long underwear while standing on the top of the empty, asbestos filled Amerock building which is now known as the historic Ziock building in downtown Rockford.

"*We talked for a long time,*" he added.

Jacob told his wife Sally about his thoughts Sunday afternoon when he became afraid that she would find out on her own by reading his mind. Kern also told Rkfdnews that he is feeling sincere regret and remorse as time goes on. It's been less than a day since everything came out into the open with his wife.

"*It's still so raw,*" he told us.

Kern is worried about whether his wife can fully believe him. She's happy about the transformation that he's making with his feelings, and is thinking about having an additional 4 breakout meetings with 'couple' friends over the next few months to further discuss her husband's feelings and how to go about with turning them into more action around the house and yard.

Kern wrote us in confidence, and we feel as if he may need more help than his wife thinks, see below:

> "*Dear Mr. Vannigan and rkfdnews.com,*
>
> *My wife wants me to conduct Vision sessions with me and her friends. She might invite her family, too. Mine can't come. My friends aren't invited.*

She says, "Your friends laugh too much and your family is too quiet. They're holding you back from being my responsible husband and emotional anchor, sponge, crutch and domestic goods provider. I need you to transform yourself into something domestic that I can deal with before your unique individuality takes over our lives and causes us to not have more stuff, a bigger home and more shit like a snowblower and a speedboat."

It's hard for me to tell her that I feel like less of a man by being a "husband," but more like my neighbors, Jim and Linda, who have no unique talents and never laugh because Rockford ruined them. I used to have my own dreams and vision.

I also used to have a wooden ducks carving business in my garage, but now that's gone and packed away into boxes she wants to sell at the next garage sale. She needs the space to park her Subaru. Look at me now, I'm a shell of a "man" in my own mind. My wooden ducks are gone and all of my customers have found someone else to carve for them. All I have is a wife, a Subaru and a lot of feelings to worry about satisfying her with.

It's as if I'm as good as dead already. Maybe I've been transformed? Is this what it feels like? Did Rockford transform me?!

I feel extreme overwhelming misery and can't stop crying about my life here in Rockford with my wife, our three kids and our Subaru. I used to be a handsome man. Women used to flock to me at all hours of the day and night because of how handsome and nice I was before Rockford claimed me. I am far from handsome and nice now. Being a husband and father has enabled my body to gain thirty pounds, and now my hair falls out from all of the stress.

I'm nothing like I imagined I would be when I was four.

Maybe her friends will cook a nice meal to console me with after our 4 breakout meetings. I wonder if her friends still enjoy sex like my friends do. My wife doesn't like sex unless she mentions the idea of birthing a fourth child. I think this is why she doesn't like my friends besides all the jokes and laughing that they cause me to enjoy when she isn't looking at my face to read my mind.

I've seriously considered removing myself from the internet, my friends, family and wife to find myself again. Someone help me. I'm a shell of a man; and soon, I may only be a shadow of a shell of a man if those 4 breakout meetings destroy everything about me that remains true, unique and hidden inside my head. I used to be handsome and funny, please help me.

Love,

Jacob Kern, husband of Sally, Subaru owner, and father of Neil, Chad and Keith."

Hopefully by the year 2020, this will all be behind us.

LETTER FROM THE EDITOR THE SILENT SIREN™ – THE RISKS OF BECOMING A MEDDLING LOCAL ARTIST

Originally Published December 12th, 2013

Dear Rockford,

Hello, I am your editor and Chief, Tchad Beale. This message is another excerpt from a series featured on RKFDnews.com called "The Silent Siren." Once in a dark moon I take the time to discuss some thoughts with you. **Meddling artists are today's topic, the local kind.**

There are risks involved with becoming a meddling local artist and here are a few:

1. **It would be in local artists best interests to not meddle with the politicians and local activists socio-psychological marketing initiatives to sell philanthropic ideas with their craft. The tradeoffs includes the loss of respect, and the limiting of your work being trapped in a local box.**

2. **Segregating ideas, voices, and actions from expressing all shades of life outside of the box (elsewhere) is dangerous. Look at Carrot Top, Peter Max and Tyler Perry for examples.**

They are very popular in Rockford of IL because they meddle with amateur minds. Do you want to be the next Tyler Perry or Carrot Top? Maybe our local artists desire to be the next Carrot Top. Hmm.

3. **You will be pigeon-holed by not exploring every shade and tone of life. Everything transforms to a middle gray area when you ignore the darks with the lights, the positives with the negatives, the angry and right with the nice and the wrong.**

4. **The neutral zone is risky. This is where amateurs feel the safest. It's why people in Rockford won't take baths or use nice soaps. They enjoy themselves as is.**

5. **Meddling willingly with safe gray tones and positively skewed creative messages are limited and, ultimately, limit the artist.** *(Congratulations, the soccer moms and local churches love your work, but your peers aren't paying attention.)* **Becoming a mere 33% of the artist one deserves to be occurs when scumbags in Bergners suits and sales sluts in hooker boots dictate your ideas for the community's acceptance.**

6. **Local artists should strive to be different than the majority; to be exceptional, revered and to revolt against amateurs with any idea that can possibly challenge the mainstream's mindset. The norm is all around us; they're our leaders, neighbors and, sadly, their children. They are the majority present and they can not transform their own ideas into actions, let alone the future of a poor town into a proud city. This is your warning, local artists:**
   WE ARE THE FUTURE and y'all are f*cked!

Feel free to text your emotional opinions and meddling-defense comments to **815-570-9866**. Ask for Reggie!

Chief Tchad Beale

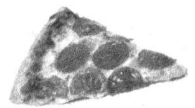

TEEN FORCED DOWN, TATTOOED AGAINST WILL

Originally Published December 15th, 2014

Rockford, IL – A gang of ex-teachers and laid off factory workers shocked a teenager with a tazerstick and tattooed "*Rockford*" on his forehead in a sickening attack. Edward "*Eddie*" Edwardson, 18, was left for dead by the gang after they "*battered him with eggs and flour,*" said Rockford Dream Police.

The terrifying assault happened while Mr Edwardson was staying with his 43 year old friend, Nancy Newtweenie, earlier this year in Rockford. She suddenly turned on Mr Edwardson and launched the attack with three of her work friends: Richard Dongberg (61), Zed Chin (51), and Lorrie Haswern (73).

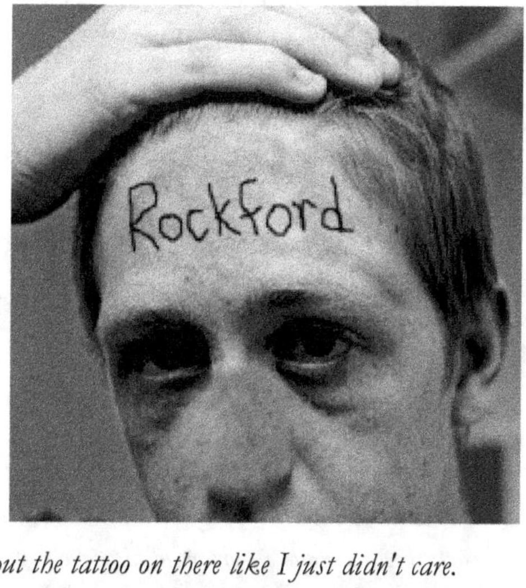

The two women pushed a stun gun into Mr Edwardson's genitals and shocked him while the men tattooed him. He was left battered and alone with "*Rockford*" on his forehead and "*I need a job*" tattooed on his chest. The group is alleged to have tied his hands and battered him around the head and arms with at least a dozen eggs and a pail of flour.

Edwardson told RKFDnews, *"They put the tattoo on there like I just didn't care. They was like, 'This is what you're going to get. We are sending a message to the city officials!'*, and, *"you're going to walk around with this because we are out of work and we need respect. I tried to push my way off of them and they kept on holding me down harder. I felt one other penises up against my stomach, it was gross."*

Dream Police said that Mr. Edwardson was taken to *Rock Cunt State Park* in Machesney Park after being tattooed.

It was there that the gang taped together his hands and struck him with a baseball bat and fed him Cool Ranch Doritoes until he was unconscious. He staggered to a nearby trailer park where he was able to get help and a new pair of pants after regaining consciousness.

"*I probably walked about a mile with no pants on. I crawled and walked. I was like, 'I don't think I'll be able to live with this on my forehead.' I mean, if it was like the word 'Rapist' or something, but not this… not this,*" Edwardson cried.

Edwardson spent a number of days in intensive care before being released from the hospital.

The four suspects are still being held in custody. A judge denied them bail. Dreams Police has identified Richard Dongberg as a laid off factory worker and part-time tattoo artist, who is known locally as *The Donger.* They seized four tattoo guns, nine tattoo needles and 17 bottles of tattoo ink from his art studio in Beloit.

Rkfd Dream Police Detective, Marty Martinson, said "*Both women admitted that they used the stun gun. We've never seen a man raped this bad, let alone a tattoo attack.*"

Mr Edwardson has had the offensive tattoos covered up with a *Tasmanian Devil,* and started working one day a week again. He has realized that dreams can come true if you are willing to go after them – despite where one lives.

"*This young man has learned the type of life skills that have helped him to be positive and independent, which are not always the skills that one seeks to be employed,*" said Local Alderman, Lance Wapalapek.

"*He saved enough money to purchase a bike and now rides himself back and forth to work. He also puts a portion of his paycheck into a savings account each week. He is truly grateful for the opportunities set forth for him, and has worked hard to achieve his dreams.*"

We here at RKFD News love uplifting stories and fluffy kittens.

Jay Vannigan

ELDERLY MAN CHEWS ARM OFF AND OTHER 911 CALLS

Originally Published December 29th, 2014

- 911 Report By RKFD NEWS STAFF
  For Wednesday, November 27, 2013
  Ex-state worker charged in food stamp case • Soldier leaves hospital,goes to bar • Brush fires interrupt travel on I-90

- 911 Report By RKFD NEWS STAFF For Tuesday, November 26, 2013 Police arrest man in shark suit knocking on doors • Beloitian hunter killed in shooting accident mother charged • Moped rider dies of crash injuries then miraculously wakes up

- 911 Report By RKFD NEWS STAFF For Monday, November 25, 2013 Stabbed man injured, suspect arrested • Boy critically injured in stabbing • Robbers wield spears and throw live raccoons into cars

- 911 Report By RKFD NEWS STAFF NEWS SERVICES For Sunday, November 24, 2013 Moped crash sends driver to hospital for a hamburger from the cafeteria • Burglary suspect is stoned to death by occupants of house, then lit on fire • Man pinned between cars is seriously hurt or a really good actor • Driver of truck that fell off cliff is identified as Cliff Cliffordson of Clifford IL

- 911 Report By RKFD NEWS STAFF For Friday, November 22, 2013 Body recovered from Dumpster • Suspect sought in Roscoe bank robbery

- 911 Report By RKFD NEWS STAFF For Friday, November 22, 2013 2 men running in circles wearing green thongs downtown • Motorists in truck collision hospitalized can't remember wife's name • Council raises age for buying tobacco to 43 • Self-styled healer found guilty in assault with a frozen steak

- 911 Report By RKFD NEWS STAFF For Thursday, November 21, 2013 Blaze damages house occupants happy • ATM taken from West Side Grocery store no one saw a thing • Man charged in attack on parakeet

- 911 Report By RKFD NEWS STAFF For Wednesday, November 20, 2013 Youth facility escapee is back in black • Brush fire burns at Rockford Airport

- 911 Report By RKFD NEWS STAFF For Tuesday, November 19, 2013 Boat found adrift in memory bliss, deserted after 1 month • Woman is injured in shooting child blamed

- 911 Report By RKFD NEWS STAFF For Monday, November 18, 2013 87 collisions logged in 12 hours on Sunday • District Bar assault lands 2 victims in hospital • 2 arrested after burglary of hamburgers

- 911 Report By RKFD NEWS STAFF For Sunday, November 17, 2013 Search for missing donut ends • Bicyclist hurt in Salt Lake City like we care

- 911 Report By RKFD NEWS STAFF For Saturday, November 16, 2013 Fuel tanker driver dies while surfing porn while driving • 2-day search finds no hope for our city • Man convicted of assault • Escaped inmate caught by police then escaped again then caught • Nighttime blaze damages home

- 911 Report By RKFD NEWS STAFF For Friday, November 15, 2013 Foot is turned over to medical examiner then is used on a sick joke involving an ass kicking • Blaze destroys Pat's house of birds and wigs ; no one hurt • Woman, 39, injured in crash at new roundabout and more

- 911 Report By RKFD NEWS STAFF NEWS SERVICES For Thursday, November 14, 2013 Search continues for cruise ship passenger • Robber runs off with woman's thong and shoes

- 911 Report By RKFD NEWS STAFF For Wednesday, November 13, 2013 Elderly man chews off arm just to prove a point to wife •

Eat Me • Durandian burglary suspect still large and in charge

- 911 Report By RKFD NEWS STAFF For Tuesday, November 12, 2013 Tourist is apparently trapped in the Lafayette Hotel • Morning blaze damages house in Freeport

- 911 Report By RKFD NEWS STAFF For Monday, November 11, 2013 Fugitive found, returned to prison • Rockford man is charged in assault no one cares

- 911 report By RKFD NEWS STAFF For Saturday, October 19, 2013 Homeless man charged in beating death then set free but is still homeless • $15K bail set for man charged in farting in a cab • fart leads to arrest of man, 25 • Man suspected of farting in public in custody

- 911 Report By RKFD NEWS STAFF For Friday, October 18, 2013 Suspect arrested in farting death • Tourist farts in waters off Kishwaukee island kills 400 carp 911 Report For Thursday, October 17, 2013 Police are looking for a man in his 60s with a white goatee who farted in the lobby of Blackhawk Bank on Wednesday afternoon.

- 911 Report By RKFD NEWS STAFF For Tuesday, October 15, 2013 Pedestrian is struck by fart in Downtown Area • Man dies after farting accident • Fart into brown paper bag kills teen at party

- 911 Report By RKFD NEWS STAFF For Thursday, September 5, 2013 Rake hits and kills woman in driveway • Brush fires are hot and dangerous• Man nearly drowns bathtub Police and Fire

- 911 Report By RKFD NEWS STAFF For Wednesday, September 4, 2013 Help sought in 1973 murder case • Surfer is found unconscious in river • Couple's argument leads to man's broken heart • House fire deals $90,000 damage • 2 arrested after fight over Snickers Bar

- 911 Report By RKFD NEWS STAFF For Tuesday, August 20, 2013 Firefighters throw chinese stars at wild dogs save child • Boat capsizes; 5 onboard are wet • Man in serious argument over dinner kills family dog and throws child into street

- 911 Report By RKFD NEWS STAff For Sunday, August 18, 2013 3 suspects sought after carrots stolen • Man found in road is identified as the real Burger King • Firefighters battle Orcs in Rockton • Motorcyclist wearing leotards and furry scarf beat up by teenagers

Jay Vannigan

FREE JOB! FREE WORK!
FREE SHIRT! FREE JACKET!

MAN EATS LLAMA, RENAMES HIMSELF

Originally Published May 25th, 2018

Beloit, WI – Months were lost being held captive in the South Beloit Forest Preserve with his faithful companion, a pet Llama named Linda. The man from Beloit, WI, survived a wild, lengthy, torturous *Red Winged Black Bird* terrorist attack that left him and his pet trapped.

Sadly, Linda the Llama didn't make it out alive at the end of the ordeal.

In July, a 24-year-old man, Glenn Olmstead, set off on a two-day canoeing trip in the Northern city of Beloit along the Rocque River. It was there, out yonder, that a Red Winged Black bird defended her sacred nesting grounds by attacking his campsite, eating all his food, and destroying the canoe he needed to travel back home.

His beloved Llama "Linda" tried to chase off the bird before her man could be harmed. Olmstead knew the entrapment was bad and would face starvation.

A few days later, the man smoked the rest of his weed and ate his last mushrooms along with licking away the remaining sheets of acid. It was during the meltdown that he hit his Llama with a rock and ate her. Olmstead made a mask out of Linda's Llama skin and renamed himself King Crabfinger the Vth.

His family alerted police when he and Linda were weeks late returning from their trip. Olmstead was finally rescued today, months after the terrible ordeal. He couldn't speak or eat and had lost about 85 pounds due to being dehydrated while suffering from hypothermia.

You have read too much, start living. Start by tearing out this page, crumple it up and toss it at someone next to you. Maybe send it to your ex-wife-or-husband the next time they need money or a signature for something that they want to con you on. Play catch for awhile with this crumpled page. Visit a downtown cafe to people-watch and to talk about your feelings with strangers on the internet with your laptop, smart phone, or iPad. Tell everyone you meet that you're going to make the Rockford feel better, but never tell them how. Just talk, never do a thing. Don't forget to toss this crumpled page at a stranger in the café before you leave. Take a walk towards the river, stand in the middle of a bridge's walkpath while leaning over the rail. Tell the world that it's a beautiful place, and look at the river below. Scream at the people who are bathing in it to "use more soap!" Your life has now been fulfilled. Jump into the river but don't try to swim. Give up now, quit, become one with the fishies. Save Rockford, become a carp.

Jay Vannigan

MORE SELF-DEFENSE TIPS FOR VISITING ROCKFORD

(See page 37 for more self-defense tips.)

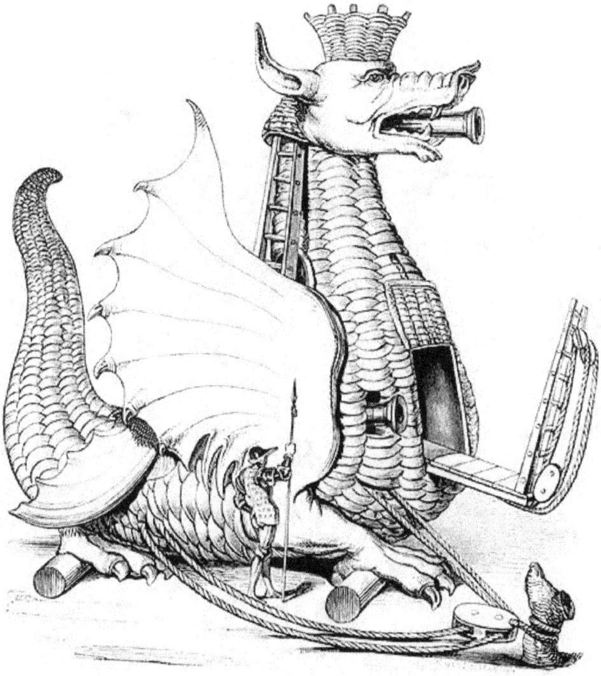

Insure that your flying wooden dragon is grounded securely and well-equipped with guns and cans of soup for an easy escape.

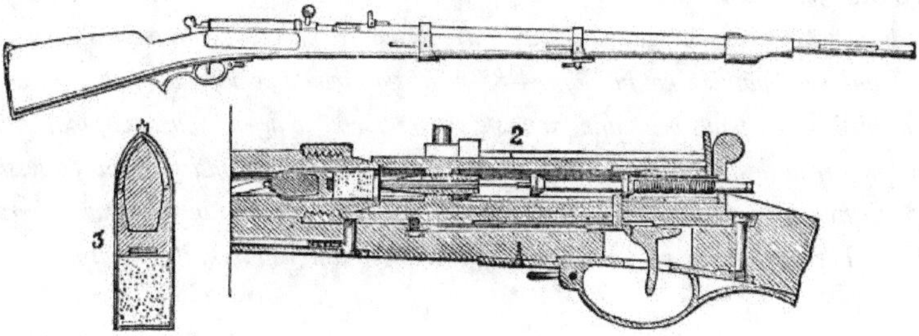

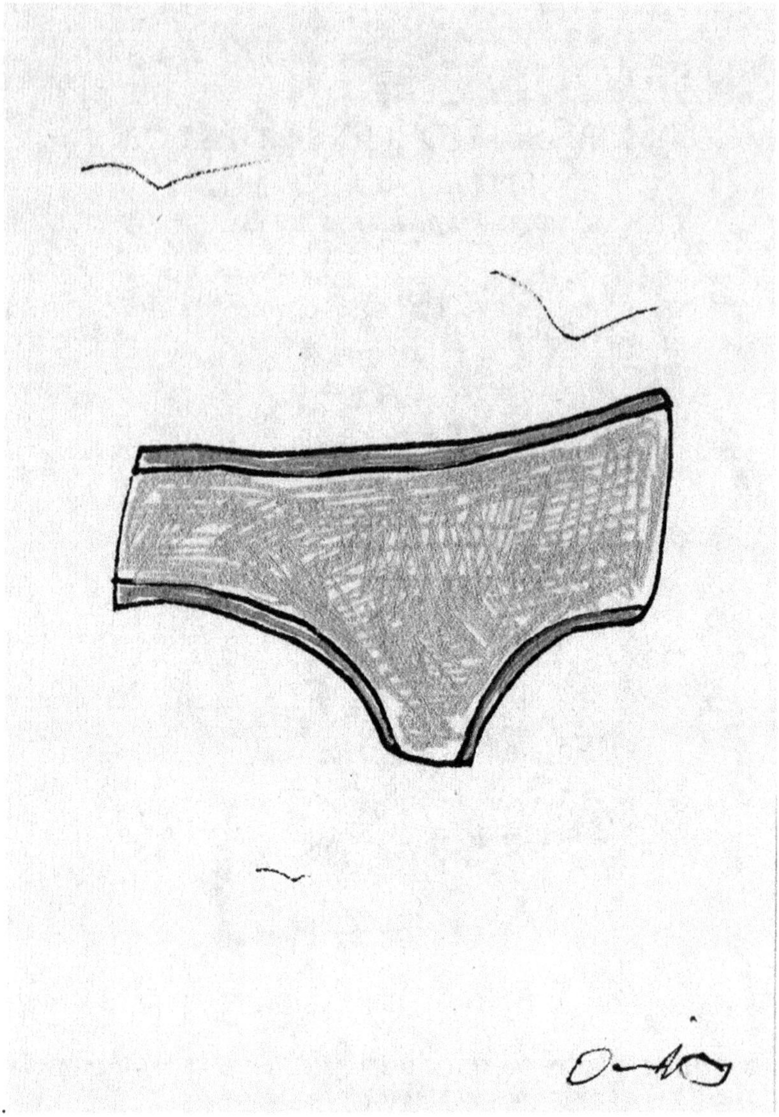

Always wear your metal panties when you are in Rockford, IL. If you do not have a few pairs, visit derbyreynolds.com to buy some. Always carry forty-three pairs of metal panties for a total of 86 individual metal panties, not including #87 which you should be wearing already. Even in the event of shitting your pants or chaffing your skin from having to defend yourself by outrunning a hungry gangster or drunk hillbilly, you'll always have enough metal panties in your possession to earn a profit from selling a few to $cumbags that you will definitely meet in your travels everywhere. They are also in need of metal panties and you can help them if you wish.

"Metal Panties® will help you take the $ out of $cumbags to put back into the YOU$A™!

That's right."

Lord Thomas Derby

REQUEST LETTER TEMPLATE FOR MORTGAGE LOAN AND PROPERTY TAX FORGIVENESS

Originally Published 2008, During the National Recession

Fill out the information on the next page.
Make a few photo-copies of the letter.
Mail a pair of signed copies to:

Rockford City Hall
C/O: City Council
ATTN: Alderman_________________ (Your alderman's name)
425 East State Street
Rockford, IL 61104

Rockford City Hall
C/O: City Council
ATTN: Alderman ____________________
425 East State Street
Rockford, IL 61104

Month__________, Day____, Year____

Dear Rockford City Council,

My name is ____ and I live in Rockford, IL, at this property address: ____.

I read in the Rockford Register Star news circa May of 2013 that you voted to forgive millions of dollars owed with regards to the property located at 1105 N. Court St., Rockford, IL 61103, the *Garrison Lofts and Town Homes*. The loan, with zillions of dollars owed, and the property was turned back over to the bank, Rockford Bank & Trust, to take care of or whatever.

Reasons for the city council vote and the approval of the loan forgiveness request granted to the mayor's family business, which owned the property, was allowed due to financial debts accrued upon during the recession.

I have to assume that you've voted in favor of forgiving similar loans worth thousands to zillions of dollars for many other important people in our community who run businesses, own property, stuff and whatever.

Therefor I, as a citizen of Winnebago County and the City Of Rockford, whose property value and quality of life has decreased incredibly while taxes continue to go up (before and after the recession), am formally requesting that you do the same for my family and personal business. What is my family business you wonder? It's called taking care of a home and raising a responsible family while not being able to find one job to cover the necessary expenses to live another day here.

I am now ordering you to vote to forgive my mortgage loan, account #______________ with the lender, ____, and all related debts – property tax escrow, insurance, etc. – so that I, too, owe nothing.

After you vote "*Yes, Approved*" (because you will; and if you don't, I'll insure tactics to disrespect your personal finances with a lifetime of legal creative paybacks that will entertain the public's mistrust in public officials), please turn over all debts to my lender so that the family and I can relocate away from the state of Illinois without being weighed down by the most detrimental financial mistake ever made (which is owning property in Rockford, IL) to affect our overall quality of life here on earth.

Your friend in hope, *vison*, transformation. Regards and excellence everywhere,

Name: ____

ENDANGERED ALLIGATOR FOUND NAPPING NEAR WHITMAN STREET BRIDGE & ROCK RIVER

Originally Published October 12th, 2013

Rockford, IL – Lawrence Bottums, 47 and homeless, was taking a nice nap in an abandoned boat near the Whitman Street bridge when he had to go pee pee. Bottums says about the bridge, "It's *my favorite place in town to leave the best parts of me behind after a full day of snacking and napping.*" The middle-aged homeless vet made his way to the underpass from his boat bed and saw the unimaginable, an endangered alligator taking a nap.

Bottums emailed RKFDnews.com immediately to send a staff photographer down to the bike path near the Whitman Street Bridge. That's when we saw the incredible reptile napping. Lawrence immediately took off running north on the bike path once officers of the *Rockford Dream Police's Reptile Services Department* showed up to capture the endangered reptile.

Further research conducted by the mighty Rockford Dream Police's forensic biology department discovered it was one of a very few endangered Chinese Alligators. In an amazing plot twist that has Rockford leaders helping the United States deal with it's budget problems, the endangered Chinese Alligator is being returned to China immediately in an international deal that knocks one trillion dollars off of banking debts that American companies owe our new mother country, China. (Sorry England, no monies for you until we discover your endangered species to barter another trillion in debts owed with.)

We asked the chief of the Dream Police's forensic biological department's dispatch operator how that could possibly be–an endangered alligator from China–and she said, "*I have no idea, we're shorthanded right now. Call back next Thursday, ok?*"

We asked, "*Why Thursday?*" and she said, "*Please call back in a few days if no one has been shot or hurt, ok? Capeesh? It's lunch time, buh bye.*"

Ron Kites

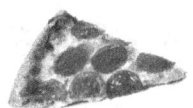

HIGHWAY 251 IN MACHESNEY PARK CHOSEN FOR U.S. WINTER OLYMPICS TRIALS

Originally Published February 11th, 2014

Machesney Park, IL – A stretch of Illinois Highway 251 in Machesney Park has been selected by the **United States Olympic Committee** for future Olympic training events.

The USOC chose the stretch between RockfordScanner.com's neon-lit electronic billboard and Highway 173 for its state-of-the-art mogul infrastructure.

"It's just tremendous," says Tim Lijendecker, the USOC subcommittee chairman for facilities.

"In Colorado Springs, we would have to spend months and a few million dollars to get the moguls just right for our USA athletes. Highway 251's got the jarring road bumps that are sure to get our skiers' knees and ankles ready for the abuse they'll take at future poorly planned Olympic venues like we're seeing at Sochi right now."

The **Rockford Area Convention & Visitors Bureau** forecasts that having our future Olympians in Rockford will increase city and county revenues.

"We're really excited," says Darrell Chasmby of the RAC&VB. *"We're hearing that the local Subway sandwich shops are considering expanding just to keep up with Michael Phelps' sandwich demand. Dude eats like 10 sandwiches a day."*

Chuck Toncha

THE STORY OF HOW I, THE CEO AND LORD OF ALL IN THE YOU$A, *LORD THOMAS DERBY*, CAME TO ROCKFORD AND SANG WITH *JOHNNY EMERALD The IIIrd*, HOMELESS POP STAR

Originally Published September 5th, 2014

I'd like to talk to you today about how I met Johnny Emerald The IIIrd, the homeless pop star from Rockford who I've managed to success, but have also sang songs about the city he sleeps with.

This is another true $uccess $tory of mine. One of many I'll be sharing with you, my $heep, to help inspire your days to be as $uccessful as you can be in the YOU$A™. That's right!

My staff & I traveled to southern Wisconsin for a Weekend $ales & Leadership Conference; in other words, another weekend bender with my employees.

Plotting our slow return to my company's HQ in $chaumburg, IL, we stopped for breakfast at one of the delicious **McDonalds in South Beloit**, on the border of Wisconsin and Illinois. It was there in the summer of 2008 that we decided to do a $ales raid in the village of Rockford, Illinois, located about 10 miles from Beloit if you take route 2 south.

Our first stop in sunny Rockford was at the **Culver's on N. Main St. near what is now an abandoned grocery store**. We enjoyed a few **Butter Burgers and Concrete Shakes that we spiked with Rum** to nuke up for raiding the village with **HOT DEAL$**.

Continuing south on Main St in our orange H2 Hummers & Lamboguineas, we saw many abandoned grocery stores & factory buildings. Upon seeing such economic despair, physical desolation & what was left of a once thriving post-WW2 village, my sexy account executive, **Alyssa**

Sojahnowski, said to me, *"Maybe there's no business here in the Rockford of Illinois to raid with our HOT DEAL$?"*

I assured Ms. Sojahnowski that even if that were the case, we would scare the little ad firm owners & dirty Illinois politicians with their lobbyists into wearing our American-made metal panties. She laughed and said, ***"Oh, Lord Derby, I want to party in the Rockford!"***

(Alyssa's greatest assets for landing clients with big marketing budgets are her black hooker boots and beautiful body–a potential client's kryptonite.)

Cell-phoning our staff from my orange Lamboguinea, we immediately decided to party in the Rockford since there was no true business to be had; that is, aside from whatever tax payers money that the state and feds are funneling into downtown Rockford for "*economic development projects.*"

(Projects that often reek of corruption and nepotism when it comes to handing out contract bids for marketing budgets related to said projects. **Note: My company offers 90% off the other guys' marketing and PR estimates at DERBY | REYNOLDS for those types of state and federal projects!**)

Onward we drove around the wasteland while barhopping at **Olive Garden, Chilis, Old Chicago and Lone Star**. We had a wonderful time despite our inabilities to sell common $ense to the people in Rockford of Illinois. We decided to stay the night due to our collective inebriation.

Later on in the night, our IT Administrator and Director of Accounting, **Sean Lippy** and **Jeffrey Tethernick**, wanted to catch some live music. Alyssa wanted to party harder with the Rockford people, and since she and Sean were on shaky ground with their Tuesday-nooners relationship, the 3 of us left **Jenny Kowalski and Big Bill Reynolds** back at the **Clock Tower Inn** to enjoy the Rockford night life.

We headed downtown to **Mary's Place** at the advice of the bartender at Red Lobster. That is where I first met **Johnny Emerald The IIIrd**, homeless pop star.

Mr. Emerald The IIIrd played some HOT DEAL $ONGS that night; including his hit song, "*Orange Symbol,*" which he dedicated to my company during his fourth encore.

I introduced myself to Johnny as the LORD and CEO of ALL in the YOU$A between one of his many encores. We laughed immediately, talking about our love for delicious, orange Cheetohs–the crunchy kind. We also discussed our love empty cardboard boxes.

I bought orange metal speedboats for everyone in the bar that night, too. Mr. Emerald politely declined his speedboat, ***"Lord, I don't needs an orange speed boat. I'm fine and dandy with my big brown 'frigerator box."***

Mr. Emerald The IIIrd and I have been friends since that hot $ummer Rockford night in 2008. In 2013, we sang a song together and plan to release a full record of duets by 2019 or 2020. Maybe sooner, maybe never.

For now, take a listen to our debut duet, *"I Don't Eat In Rockford,"* and other love songs about the city that Johnny loves and sleeps with – including the hit song, *"Orange Symbol"* – at: **johnnyemerald.com**

Our journey together will continue soon. For I am Lord Thomas Derby and you are not. That's right,

Lord Thomas Derby
CEO and LORD of ALL in the YOU$A™
THE WAL-MART OF ADVERTISING

Derby | Reynolds

Imagine this is an orange flag with a white dot.

"ORANGE SYMBOL"

By Johnny Emerald the IIIrd

LISTEN AND SING ALONG WITH JOHNNY AT:

johnnyemerald.com

Orange Symbol

Sitting by the riverside

Pushed my cart by You this morning

It was full of cans

and some half-eaten food

I got behind Burger King

You know it tastes so good the next day

like a Whopper

baking

in the sun

Orange Symbol

Sitting by the riverside

You looked so good to me this morning

When I was pushing my cart by

Orange Symbol

Sitting by the riverside

You looked so good to me

Early in the morning time

Orange Symbol

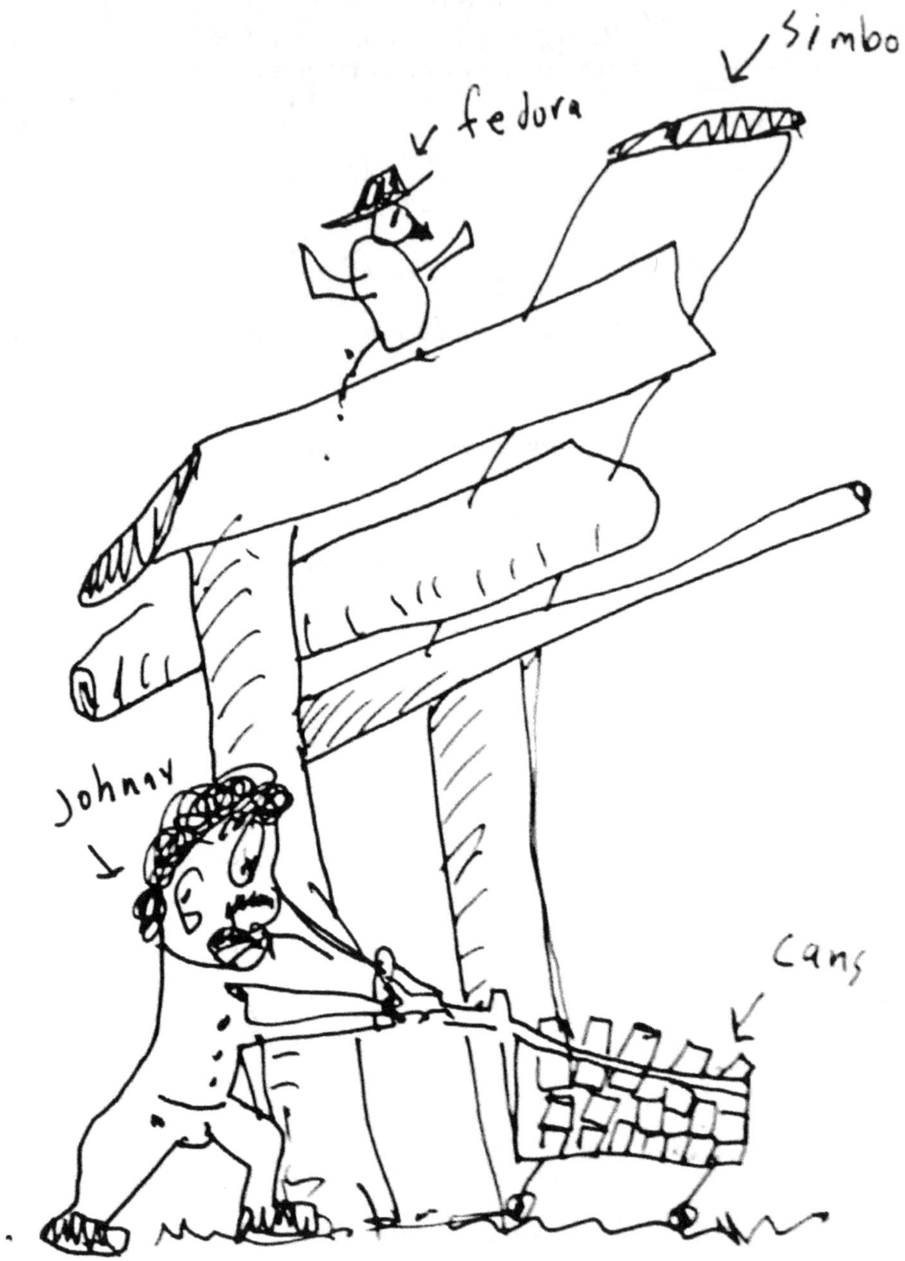
Simbo
fedora
Johnny
Cans

Sing Along to Our Favorite Homeless Pop Star on the Inturdnet at: johnnyemerald.com

Johnny Emerald the IIIrd - Homeless Singing Star of Rockford, IL USA

ebay | johnnyemerald.com | Reader

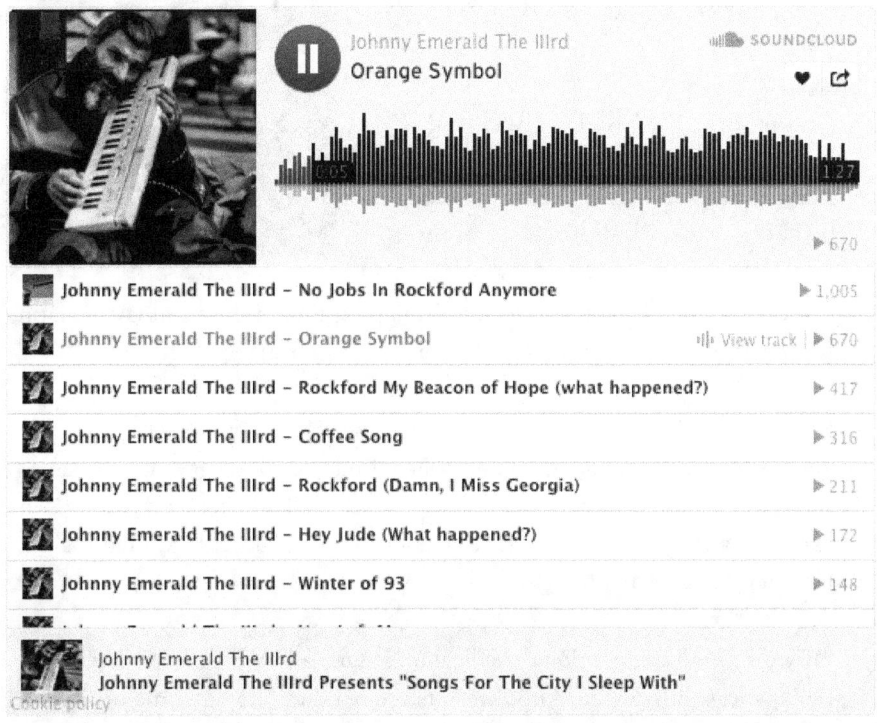

i am homeless in rockford. i was discovered singing to my davis park friends in 2013 by popular people with expensive toys. they want to help me make my street music. i hired the CEO and LORD of ALL from schaumburg, il, mister lord thomas derby to help me make the music for the metal pantie monies in the YOU$A™ and in the rockford. read about me on the internet if u want 2 or listen to my songs below. my lord derby and i have big news to announce stay tuned to wxrx, 104.9's low budget morning show with stone and doube T in rockfard illannoy, they talk to me once a week and you listen, look for interviews with me on their site, they are there you must look deep, haha ha that is what my first wife said, bye bye pet a puppy

Johnny Emerald The IIIrd

Orange Symbol

SOUNDCLOUD

0:05 1:27

▶ 670

Johnny Emerald The IIIrd - No Jobs In Rockford Anymore	▶ 1,005
Johnny Emerald The IIIrd - Orange Symbol	View track ▶ 670
Johnny Emerald The IIIrd - Rockford My Beacon of Hope (what happened?)	▶ 417
Johnny Emerald The IIIrd - Coffee Song	▶ 316
Johnny Emerald The IIIrd - Rockford (Damn, I Miss Georgia)	▶ 211
Johnny Emerald The IIIrd - Hey Jude (What happened?)	▶ 172
Johnny Emerald The IIIrd - Winter of 93	▶ 148

Johnny Emerald The IIIrd

Johnny Emerald The IIIrd Presents "Songs For The City I Sleep With"

Cookie policy

LOCAL GUITAR GOD BREAKS WOMAN'S FACE

Originally Published October 26th, 2014

Rockford, IL – A local guitar god got a little WWE on his date Friday night. She said "*Do whatever you want,*" and he did. Rockford style.

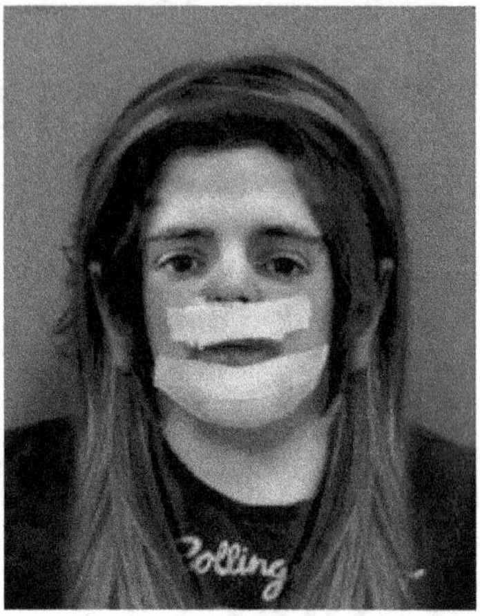

"*I jumped off the bed and sat right on her face. I was having my 19th nervous breakdown, I guess,*" said Watsahne Joshherner.

Neighbor Aaron Broman said, "*It sounded like wild horses fighting,*" before calling the police.

According to the RKFDP (Rockford Dream Police), the 42-year-old victim, Bernice Phillips, and her date, Joshherner, had been drinking before the accident.

Officers arrived after 4 a.m. to find Phillips sitting in the front lawn waiting for the ambulance to give her some emotional rescue.

Police say Phillips suffered a possible fractured jaw, with other facial injuries, and was unable to talk to police. Phillips's body gave off a scent similar to soda mixed with sweet liquor, as if she had been consuming some sort of orange alcoholic beverage. She was taken to Rockford Mammal Hospital for treatment.

Officers asked that the local medical team take a blood draw to determine if Phillips was intoxicated. Those results are pending the outcome of this article. We don't have any other information, go figure. Learn more by clicking less.

Jay Vannigan

SIMBO

A Bedtime Story

By

Oh hi, this is Symbol. This is Its story, the story of Simbo.

Simbo started out life as Symbol. A metallic dildo by day and a compass by night. Simbo served the city of Rockford's people as a guide for exile by always nodding towards the northern border from the river that it sits next to at all hours.

It provides peace and strength, a Symbol of stamina for many. Ha ha ha, It wasn't always like this, but things changed.

Symbol transformed into Simbo because Rockford transformed Symbol into a neglected work of public art over the last few decades. The late 70s and early 80s war on the middle class was witnessed by Symbol.

It transformed.

This is why this is Its story, the story of Simbo.

Symbol is life.

Symbol is metal, baby. A modern day demigod worthy of defeating the war on demographic depression. Dildoic red swells the skyline when Symbol smiles.

People walk by.

Cars roll.

Life in the city.

Symbol is life.

Symbol is erect and proud.

Symbol is hard, smooth, and in love with itself; exactly like the community it resides in. It is androgynously orange and dildoicly red. The red represents its inner strength, which is an emotional weapon used cautiously in the war on demographic depression.

Political talk was made of repainting It blue to match the community's emotions, rather than matching the roof of the Metro Centre that it once sat near a very long time ago in the late 70s and early 80s (when people in Rockford still didn't have jobs).

NOTE: Metro Centre & Symbol ARE NOT related.

Symbol is ours to hold tight.

Symbol serves the city of Rockford, and some say that It makes the birds, squirrels and red tailed foxes very happy.

Others say Symbol helps them feel romantic. If you close your eyes and think of Symbol, you can feel the city breathing on your neck, sweating on your pillow.

Symbol is ours to hold tight.

Symbol is proper grammar.

Symbol does not have a "*The*" in front of its name, yet many people call It "*The Symbol.*" Why does this happen? Symbol says, "*Everyone who sees Me everyday is poor, high, out of their minds, uneducated, self-entitled or really drunk. I forgive them because they can't help it.*"

Using poor grammar with reference to Symbol makes It feel very sad, but you'll never know when It is sad because It proudly stands there pointing the way out of Illinois with a steady erect presence.

Towards happiness and a few Culver's Butter Burgers is where you will find Symbol's state of mind.

Symbol sings "Jeremy" and quotes "Rainman."

Symbol has a theme song but you'll never hear it if you don't listen to the birds and the wind when they sing Its song to you.

You'll often hear Symbol repeatedly crying out of tune out over the river, "*Jeremy spoke in class today, BAM, the future of rock n roll!*"

A valiant melody that Symbol has created by combining a song from one of America's most horrendous buffon-rock bands, *Pearl Jam*, with a key line from the masterpiece movie, *Rainman*, starring Dustin Hoffman, Sir Thomas *"Cruise"* Derby and Reginald "*Railroad*" Reynolds.

Symbol told the city in the early 1990s, "*One day, Jeremy won't speak in class today and that awful Pearl Jam song will finally go away.*" Ha ha ha.

Symbol is trying to get Pearl Jam banned from Rockford radio by singing it everyday to annoy the poor people.

Symbol is mobile.

Symbol sits next to a brown river on a beautiful bike path. It used to sit downtown, but God moved it.

Symbol is mobile.

Symbol is friendly.

Symbol points to the sky and says, "*Hi, God! Hi, America! Hi, Planes! Hi, Birds!*"

Symbol is friendly to Its surroundings, even when Rockford litters or leaves its trash on the bikepath near the river. The place that Symbol calls homes for now.

Symbol is friendly.

Symbol is revengeful and doesn't give a fuck sometimes.

Symbol caused a ruckus in downtown Rockford. God sent her angels to help Symbol fight back. The War on Demographic Depression hurt Symbol's feelings. Local politicians eventually defeated Symbol, God & her angels.

Though the battle was lost, another war was won: Symbol would not be painted blue, and God's angels and Symbol helped deplete the city budget in the war on depression for the last 40 years as a silent retaliation.

Symbol laughs with God, her angles, and says to them often, "*We showed them. They who brag about inheriting their wealth, making more babies, and not reading books to understand their own decline was in the making. Fools.*"

Symbol is revengeful and doesn't give a fuck sometimes.

Symbol doesn't face downtown Rockford, the hornets nest.

Symbol flew on the wings of angels to the Rock River's western bank near the Auburn Street Bridge after God & Mayor McNamara struck a deal to form a peace treaty; to temporarily pause the war on demographic depression and to allow Symbol to remain dildoic red and androgynously orange.

The war on demographic depression continues to this very present day amongst the people of Rockford, IL.

According to the treaty, Symbol can do nothing but observe & point the way out of town, north towards Wisconsin.

Its back always facing the hornets nest, downtown Rockford, where all of our city's problems begin and end.

Symbol is defense.

Symbol was granted power to shoot its happy missiles into or over the brown river on Rockford's west side in an effort to protect the community from overly-righteous east siders from Rockford, but also to prevent other citys attacks which aim to take control of our valuable land for retail restaurant development.

Rockford's land is loaded with pride, ego, Walgreens, gas stations, box churches, McDonalds and not enough Olive Gardens or Red Lobsters.

Symbol protects our valuable land for us when we are too drunk or poor to fight Schaumburg, Belvedere, Roscoe, Loves Park and Beloit.

Symbol is defense.

Symbol is an orphan.

Symbol was originally built for Minneapolis, but they didn't want It.

Symbol is an orphan.

Symbol is for you.

Symbol is your shadow finding you and yourself in times of trouble. Symbol–not Mother Mary–will come to thee speaking words of wisdom, "*Let IT be.*"

"*Ha ha ha,*" Symbol laughs with you, not at you, "*Ha ha ha.*"

Symbol is for you.

Symbol is Simbo.

Symbol woke up cold, poor and lonely in 2007. It decided to change Its name. Everyone was like, "*What's wrong with The Symbol?*"

It answered everyone, "*Nothing is wrong with me. Please note for the last time, there's no 'The' in front of my name. From now on, thou shalt call thee "Simbo," the patron saint of exile. Ok?*" Ok, Simbo!

Symbol is Simbo.

Simbo saves people.

Simbo directed good, hard working poor people away from Rockford, Illinois, to the north towards Wisconsin once the name change was authorized.

Away from Rockford.
Away from poverty.
Away form corruption.
Away from self-entitlement and pride.
Away, away, away. Simbo frees us from ourselves.

Simbo saves people.

Simbo is positive

Simbo smiles with an erection all day long. Happy drivers on the Auburn Street Bridge say, "Oh, hi Simbo!" It waves back at walkers on the bike path, "Oh hi, people!"

People sometimes ask or think, "*What in the heck is Simbo doing?*" Simbo always replies, "*I'm helping you find your way out. Don't forget to smile and be positive, Rockford!*" Yes, Simbo, we try 2B poditive 4U!

Simbo is positive.

Simbo loves to eat *Red Lobster's Cheddar Bay Biscuits* and *The Olympic Tavern's No Bread Fred.*

Sometimes the homeless people that sleep under Simbo leave their leftovers for It to eat.

One time in 2009, a nice lady brought Simbo a dozen Cheddar Bay Biscuits from Red Lobster and Simbo cried out in joy. It said, "*I will never eat local foods again unless it is the Know Brad Fred from The Olympic! Tavern. YOMMIE BISCUITS, BABY!*"

Simbo loves to eat Red Lobster's Cheddar Bay Biscuits and The Olympic's Know Brad Fred. It wants you to try it if you haven't. If you don't, Simbo will slap you with Its swollen, metal, erect arm that points north towards Roscoe and Beloit.

Simbo prays for you, too.

Simbo found Its savior, Lord Thomas Derby, in 2010 and prays for Rockford and its people at least twice a day. It says to Its Lord, "*Dear Lord Derby, please help the people read, do math and use common cents in the YOU$A! If* *they can't figure it out, please give them some metal panties to help them think straight.*

I love you, Lord Derby.

Please keep me warm and safe in the night when the homeless invaders wake up to take flight after peeing on me."

Simbo prays for you, too.

Simbo likes to sing a song about Itself.

Simbo has a good friend named Johnny Emerald the IIIrd. Johnny is a homeless singing superstar who writes love songs about Rockford for the people to sing.

Johnny wrote Simbo a song called, "*Orange Symbol.*"

Listen to it at johnnyemerald.com to learn how to sing it with Johnny, Simbo, brother, sister, mommy and daddy. The lyrics are featured somewhere in this book if you are interested in reciting the "*Orange Symbol*" song like a love letter to your loved ones.

Simbo likes to sing a song about Itself.

Simbo is androgynous.

Simbo loves everyone unconditionally – well, almost everyone. Simbo can't stand the people from downtown Rockford because of the war It fought in the 80s to remain there. It's why It, Simbo, now faces north and away from the hornets nest, downtown Rockford.

Even when everyone hates on Simbo for looking like a large swollen metal penis, It still stands there with Its erect arm, androgynously outliving you and I. We are weak and stamina-less in Its presence.

Simbo is androgynous.

Simbo loves doggies.

Simbo loves little doggies.

Sometimes you can hear It say, "*Oh, hi doggie! What you doing? Want a treat? Do you have to go poopy? Come on, let's go poopy. Come on, let's go nigh-night. Ha ha ha.*"

Simbo loves doggies.

Simbo thinks that the people in Rockford need to use more soap.

Simbo doesn't understand how many people in Rockford get away with what they do in broad daylight.

It told Its Lord one night in a prayer, "*Dear Lord Derby, help me rain down brown metal poopies like a giraffe as tall as cliffs would do from atop of the city when it sleeps. Especially in downtown Rockford where the people stink like ponies do after they roll around in piles of their own pony poopies. Please, Lord Derby, we must alert the people of Rockford to take more baths and to use the soaps. If they don't, they will end up smelling like ponies do. I don't like ponies.*"

Simbo thinks that the people of Rockford need to use more soap, or else they'll become smelly ponies if they don't.

Simbo go nigh-night.

"*It is ok to fantasize about Me when you sleep,*" says Simbo to Its admirers.

Simbo will share more secrets about Itself when you awake from your drunk, high, complacent, proud, self-entitled, nepotistic, corrupt, poor, positive and delusional slumber.

That's right.

Simbo go nigh-night.

The End

Visit Simbo on the inturdnet at:

rockfordsymbol.com

Simbo – A Bedtime Story About Symbol

Mission Accomplished.

ROCKFORD OFFICIALLY TRANSFORMED

Originally Published April 14th, 2014

Rockford, IL – With the City Council's vote to approve a partnership with Dorman & Co. to renovate the Ziock Building in downtown Rockford and the announcement of Clamtrak service between Rockford and Chicago starting in 2015 or whenever – maybe 2025 or 2019, depends on the city's horse trolley contract – Mayor Barry Morrisson and his *Coalition Of The Willing To Transform Rockford* declared major transformative operations in Rockford complete.

"Mission accomplished," shouted Mayor Morrisson from the deck of the USS Atom Kinzinger, moored in the Rock River near the Morgan Street bridge. *"My allies and I have prevailed against negativity and meanies and civic-minded bullies. Hashtag positivity, hashtah top25by25, hashtag believe, and hashtag transformrockford have won the day!"*

Flags of transformation decorated the sky as Morrison continued to explain the successful operation:

> *"Operation Transform Rockford was carried out with a combination of precision,*

speed and boldness that the enemy did not expect and the world had not seen before. Together with Lord Thomas Derby and his company's help, we were able to provide the entire community of Rockford with extra-large, anti-chafing, metal panties.

For the greater good of business and ethics coming together for the first time in the northern Illinois region, we have removed all nepotistic relationships between city government and the public / private business sectors. Wearing the metal panties over the pants, versus under, has helped us take the $ out of $cumbags to put back into the YOU$A™!

Months of criticism and jokes could not make the people of Rockford love their oppressors or desire their own enslavement. By seeking to turn our city streets into snarking fields, the thought terrorists and their allies believed that they could destroy Rockford's resolve and force our retreat to the east side.

They have failed," concluded Mayor Morrisson.

The crowd erupted in enraptured cheers as Mayor Morrisson then stepped out from behind the podium and violently crossed his arms against his thrusting pelvis, a gesture made popular by professional wrestling stable ***D-Generation X.***

"Alderwoman Linda McDonalds and all my haters can suck it, and that's the bottom line, because Mayor 'Stone Cold B-Mo' Barry Morrison said so," shouted Morrisson to his fans.

The mayor then kicked over the podium and charged to the side of the air deck, jumping headlong into the Rock River. He was later seen in soaking-wet clothes shotgunning beers with patrons of Mary's Place, Rockford's oldest bar.

Chuck Toncha

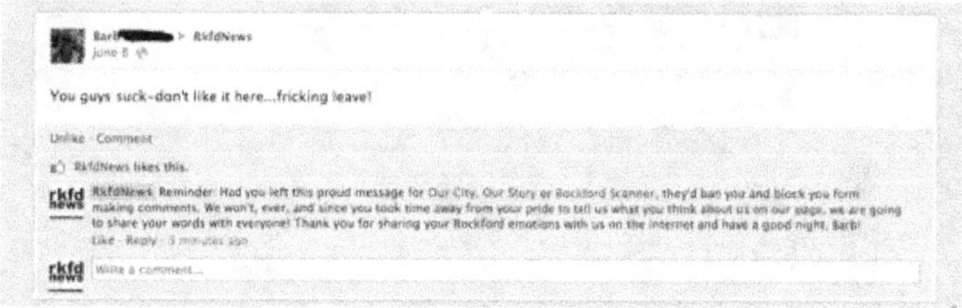

Barb[redacted] > RkfdNews
June 8

You guys suck-don't like it here...fricking leave!

Unlike · Comment

RkfdNews likes this.

RkfdNews Reminder: Had you left this proud message for Our City, Our Story or Rockford Scanner, they'd ban you and block you form making comments. We won't, ever, and since you took time away from your pride to tell us what you think about us on our page, we are going to share your words with everyone! Thank you for sharing your Rockford emotions with us on the internet and have a good night, Barb!
Like · Reply · 5 minutes ago

Write a comment...

LEGAL CREATIVE EXAMPLE OF WHAT HAPPENS TO PROUD HUMAN BEINGS WHO PUBLICLY POOP – like little ponies often do – ONTO INTURDNET FOR FREEDUMB, or whatever.

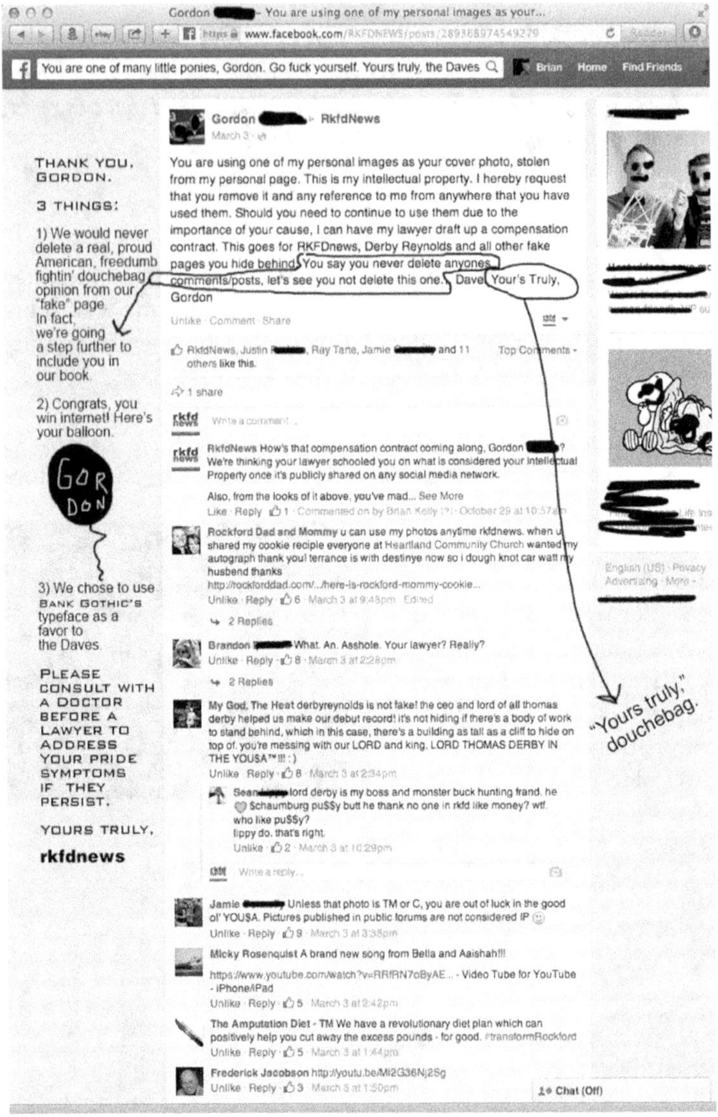

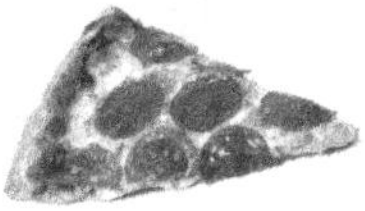

LEGAL STATEMENT

1. Anyone who has a problem with us using and displaying comments, names, etc. in this book didn't read our website's legal terms before sharing your information and internet emotions with us. Anytime you contribute, share and provide what you may think to be your Intellectual Property – views, thoughts, data (text, photos, etc.) – to be publicly shared on our website, we are granted the rights to use as we wish once you've agreed to submit your data/content for publishing on our website; which is published for public criticism and review in a public forum until you delete the content yourself. **See statement 9 for further legal instructions**.

2. With regards to sharing your comments, photos, names, etc. on our 3rd party social media account pages, those 3rd party social media company (*Facebook, Twitter, Instagramm, LinkedIn, etc.*) are legally granted the rights to use, share, publish that content however they wish, including our content for that matter – whatever. We understood and agreed to their terms and conditions before we decided to become a satirical, creative, cracked-mirror reflection of the community we've been trying to escape from for most of our lives. You won't ever catch a few of our staff members sharing birthdates, email addresses and birth names because we're not idiots. The internet is a marketing tool and communications weapon that many powerful agencies, companies and their clients abuse to collect personal data to profit from at your privacy's expense. **See statements 3 and 9 below for further legal instructions**.

3. Information is power, which companies and the government pay dearly for owning – of which you agreed to provide *for free* when you clicked *"I agree"* to the terms and conditions you didn't read on every website you've joined up to use so that you can share your feelings and photos with the rest of earth's uninformed idiots. **See statement 9 for further legal instructions**.

4. Rkfdnews.com and our creative affiliates chose to pollute the internet with creative, cracked data and content by which we clearly intended to entertain, confuse and anger the public with. *"Why would you do such a thing? Isn't your time better spent?"* We would do such a thing because we can, we did, you can't and you didn't. It's the same reasons why someone like Robert Zimmerman would change his name to Bob Dylan to write songs that many of you love, loathe or could care less about; because he could and he did while you chose otherwise, to do nothing. People create something from nothing all the time, and that is what we chose to do. **See statement 9 for further legal instructions**.

5. Again, with regards to time better spent: Our collective's time (and money) has been spent and wasted already by teachers, politicians, business and government officials with other *positive* members of society that many of you have been fooled by for vapid emotional reinforcements to survive in this world; in exchange for the mere cost of a two week paycheck that's taxed to death to keep you poor and settled. Even worse, those exchanges made are also for control of your precious time – that some of you use to attack others' use of. Our time is being spent our way and that's called freedom. Creative freedom. Y'all can keep your cup of hope and coffee meetings, continue to talk and do nothing – the Rockford (and modern American) Way. **See statement 9 for further legal instructions**.

6. To troll or not to troll; to use a moniker or to use a birth name; to protect our interests or to share it all without a cost? That's for each of you to ponder about with your family and friends when you decide to share your private information, thoughts, words, photos and internet emotions in public forums after you click "*I Agree*." Thank you for allowing everyone to invade and own your content, data, names, birthdates, emails, phone numbers and most importantly, your privacy when you publicly share content. **See statement 9 for further legal instructions**.

7. All of you are amateurs in our presence at this point; be it fiction or non-fiction, monikers or birth names. Until you earn the creative rights we've earned through decades of hard work, (with and without) education, professional and personal experiences – along with strange communications, abuses, constant letdowns, and the poor ethics associated with the aforementioned individuals who keep ya positive – you'll understand why we wouldn't give a single flying fuck about how we spend our time here in Rockford, IL. A community where the wrong way to treat people is the right way to strangely succeed. **See statement 9 for further legal instructions**.

8. Do something creative in return to offer up a disagreement to what we've created with this book; or don't and **refer to statement 9 for further legal instructions**.

9. Go fuck yourself after you read legal statements 1-8 and 10.

10. You will never learn more as long as you continue to choose knowing less™.

rkfdnews

WHEN ROMANCE IS LOST ON THE INTERNET
AND IN THE YOU$A™

See the next page for an example on how a strong Horsey should legally respond to Ponies & $cumbags.

Make a few photo copies of the letter on the next page.
Fill in the names of the offensive people in your lives that have wrongly attempted to affect your time, personal finances and birth name.
Don't forget to sign and date it.
Put in envelopes, stamp and mail to your enemies, or post them on bulletin boards in your local cafes, $tarbucks, bars and churches.
Also, don't forget to take phone photos of your letters to your enemies to post all over the internet.

Dear ______________________________________ ,

Please accept this letter – and imaginary fart-filled balloon – as an act of gratitude and respect towards replenishing your vapid ego, emotions and pride. I hope that you enjoy hot-aired balloons filled with the human body's natural odors.

Imagine it if you can: Last night's three-cheese pasta dinner with bread and beer, and this morning's bacon and eggs mixed with coffee, OJ and water. Smell it? Ahh, the sweet smell of an asshole.

If this isn't your thing, please have your lawyer call mine to provide a safe mailing address and we'll arrange that you receive a bucket of delicious KFC fried chicken to console your emotions, pride and ego. I'll insure that it's sent with a handwritten card that simply states,

Congratulations, asshole, you win INTERNET!
#friedchicken

I hope that you find peace in your heart to stop and smell my roses, which again are last night's three cheese pasta dinner and this morning's bacon and eggs mixed with the various beverages. Or you can choose to eat that fried chicken and choke on a bone – whatever, be the douchebag if you must – it's your bucket.

Thank you for wasting your time and emotions at my expense. That's how the cornbread crumbles!

Yours truly,

____

(Sign your name and date it.)

Oh hi, doggie.

EPILOGUE

"No news is good news."

Giovanni "*John*" Cuppini

This Old Town (To Beat The Devil)

In the beginning there was us, a dream, some cotton and a few ponies. "*Hop to it,*" said the farmers to their peasant slaves. I being one of those slaves thought, "*Something's not right here.*" *Here* being the village of Rockford in Illinois.

To reiterate and improve upon this initial passage:

> *In the beginning there was us, not a dream in the world that could save us from what we were born into, broken before we knew what a full day's work and a penny meant, while we allowed those little Rockford ponies to watch us do all of their work – and not a pile of cotton to be found… just a pile of pony poop and a cloud of farts.*

All that's left now of this old town are remnants of once busy/now boarded-up factory buildings and empty homes. Physical reminders of work, jobs, people, time and money lost marks this old town as a prime candidate for progress and potential, a community comeback – in other words: Broken, poor, federally exempt and fooled.

Our American dreams stand battered; the middle-working class massacred, outsourced, foreclosed, auctioned and taxed to death. Comebacks rarely reverse decades of defeat and bad math like this. This old town.

This Old Town

This old town, these old people
They don't need change, keep it simple
There's nothing wrong with that
There's nothing wrong with keeping it simple

These old buildings with broken windows
Sit for miles and miles without people
There's something wrong with that
There's something wrong with keeping it simple

I like trouble

These old teachers didn't teach me how to talk
didn't teach me how to walk
didn't teach me how to sit down and be still, quiet
There's something wrong with that
There's something wrong with keeping it quiet

I like trouble.

"*Hop to it,*" said the farmers to their peasants.

Be a pony or be the horsey; whatever you do, do it well and do it loud enough to entertain, confuse and piss off an entire village. Go forward now and be kind to kind people, shovel back what you can handle to terrible people with what they've tossed at you, your friends and family; and never forget to stroke those egos, smell 'dem farts, protect your loved ones by any means necessary, speak up, yell, laugh, pet those puppies and eat 'dat pizza.

That's right,

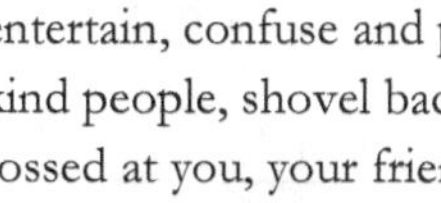

Andy Whorehall
October 26th, 2014

ABOUT THE AUTHORS

Find the nearest empty wall and stare at it. Imagine what the authors of this book must look like. Now picture a combination of words that could describe us. What do you want on your pizza? Ok, blink, look away from the empty wall. Please take this special moment in time to fill in the space below with your emotions, thoughts and words about the authors – or use it as a grocery list.

Draw a picture below to coincide with the previous page. Draw a bucket of fried chicken. Get Rockforded, do whatever you want to.

Ok, now draw a delicious pizza with pepperoni, black and green olives, pineapple and sausage flying high above the Rockford lovers.

Take a few phone photos of your amazing art, dreams, *vison* or grocery list. Send them to: rkfdnews@gmail.com

If that sounds like too much work, please feel free to litter our anti-social media pages with your shitty artistic contributions to society (and culture) for the next two years. Do it once a day or more so that y'all will finally know a few important facts:

1) You'll know how we've felt during the last two years of our lives doing all of this nonsense for free, for your entertainment.

2) You'll finally know how to read and write a book of your own. (It's "*You're welcome*," not, "*Your welcome.*")

3) Congratulations, you are now a Rockford-area artist. No school necessary, all you need is a smart device and internet.

4) Make internet videos, be an artist or a lawyer, run for mayor.

5) You can do anything: Talk more, be positive, sell hope, smile, lie, cheat people, win grants, be a business leader, save the city, drink coffee, have meetings, transform stuff, conduct town forums, market everything you're doing to help the community on the internet, don't tell anyone who's paying for it, ban honesty, shun facts, be proud and do less; the Rockford (modern American) way.

6) Go tanning, be a news-leader, go to a box mall church, make the crepés, stir soups, run for senate, celebrate mediocrity, reward amateurs, have more meetings, discover bingo night, pray for fast food, repeat until you pass away in Rockford, IL.

Now, imagine yourself doing something else with your precious time besides writing and illustrating the conclusion of *Our Book, Our Stories* – a book that we also made you pay for.

May the last laughs linger forever, like farts trapped in a moving vehicle with the windows up and locked,

rkfdnews.com

www.ingramcontent.com/pod-product-compliance
Lightning Source LLC
Chambersburg PA
CBHW051354290426
44108CB00015B/2005
9780692334898